The
BOOK LOVERS'
Anthology

The
BOOK LOVERS'
Anthology

*A Compendium of Writing
about Books, Readers & Libraries*

Bodleian Library
UNIVERSITY OF OXFORD

This edition published in 2014 by
the Bodleian Library
Broad Street
Oxford OX1 3BG

www.bodleianbookshop.co.uk

ISBN 978 1 85124 418 8

This edition © Bodleian Library, University of Oxford, 2014

Originally published in 1911 by Oxford University Press,
as *The Book-Lovers' Anthology*, edited by R.M. Leonard

Every effort has been made to obtain permission to use material
that is in copyright. The publishers apologise for any omissions
and would welcome these being brought to their attention.

Cover design by Dot Little
Designed and typeset in 12 on 14 Perpetua
by illuminati, Grosmont
Printed and bound on 70 gsm Holman book cream
by TJ International Ltd., Padstow, Cornwall

British Library Catalogue in Publishing Data
A CIP record of this publication is available from the British Library

CONTENTS

Grace before Books

I own that I am disposed to say grace upon twenty other
occasions in the course of the day besides my dinner. I want
a form for setting out upon a pleasant walk, for a moonlight
ramble, for a friendly meeting, or a solved problem. Why
have we none for books, those spiritual repasts—a grace
before Milton—a grace before Shakespeare—a devotional
exercise proper to be said before reading the *Fairy Queen*?
—but, the received ritual having prescribed these forms to
the solitary ceremony of manducation, I shall confine my
observations to the experience which I have had of the grace,
properly so called; commending my new scheme for extension
to a niche in the grand philosophical, poetical, and perchance
in part heretical liturgy, now compiling by my friend Homo
Humanus, for the use of a certain snug congregation of
Utopian Rabelaesian Christians, no matter where assembled.

Charles Lamb, *Grace before Meat*

The Delightful Society of Books

These friends of mine regard the pleasures of the world as
the supreme good; they do not comprehend that it is possible to renounce these pleasures. They are ignorant of my
resources. I have friends whose society is delightful to me;
they are persons of all countries and of all ages: distinguished
in war, in council, and in letters; easy to live with, always
at my command. They come at my call, and return when I
desire them: they are never out of humour, and they answer
all my questions with readiness. Some present in review
before me the events of past ages; others reveal to me the
secrets of Nature: these teach me how to live, and those
how to die: these dispel my melancholy by their mirth, and
amuse me by their sallies of wit: and some there are who
prepare my soul to suffer everything, to desire nothing, and

to become thoroughly acquainted with itself. In a word, they open a door to all the arts and sciences. As a reward for such great services, they require only a corner of my little house, where they may be safely sheltered from the depredations of their enemies. In fine, I carry them with me into the fields, the silence of which suits them better than the business and tumults of cities.

Petrarch, *Life* by S. Dodson

He that Loveth a Book Will Never Want

The calling of a scholar ... fitteth a man for all conditions and fortunes; so that he can enjoy prosperity with moderation, and sustain adversity with comfort: he that loveth a book will never want a faithful friend, a wholesome counsellor, a cheerful companion, an effectual comforter.... The reading of books, what is it but conversing with the wisest men of all ages and all countries, who thereby communicate to us their most deliberate thoughts, choicest notions, and best inventions, couched in good expression, and digested in exact method? The perusal of history, how pleasant illumination of mind, how useful direction of life, how spritely incentives to virtue doth it afford! how doth it supply the room of experience, and furnish us with prudence at the expense of others, informing us about the ways of action, and the consequences thereof by examples, without our own danger or trouble!

Isaac Barrow, *Of Industry in Our Particular Calling as Scholars*

The Company of Mutes

I often derive a peculiar satisfaction in conversing with
the ancient and modern dead,—who yet live and speak
excellently in their works.—My neighbours think me *often
alone*,—and yet at such times I am in company with more
than five hundred mutes—each of whom, at my pleasure,
communicates his ideas to me by dumb signs—quite as intel-
ligibly as any person living can do by uttering of words.—
They always keep the distance from me which I direct,—and,
with a motion of my hand, I can bring them as near to me
as I please.—I lay hands on fifty of them sometimes in an
evening, and handle them as I like;—they never complain of
ill-usage,—and, when dismissed from my presence—though
ever so abruptly—take no offence. Such convenience is not to
be enjoyed—nor such liberty to be taken—with the living.

Lawrence Sterne, *Letters*

A Consolation for the Deaf

I read with more pleasure than ever; perhaps, because it is
the only pleasure I have left. For, since I am struck out of
living company by my deafness, I have recourse to the dead,
whom alone I can hear; and I have assigned them their stated
hours of audience. Solid *folios* are the people of business,
with whom I converse in the morning. *Quartos* are the easier
mixed company, with whom I sit after dinner; and I pass my
evenings in the light, and often frivolous, *chit-chat* of small
octavos and *duodecimos*.

Lord Chesterfield

Sweet Unreproaching Companions

I armed her [Olivia] against the censure of the world, showed her that books were sweet unreproaching companions to the miserable, and that if they could not bring us to enjoy life, they would at least teach us to endure it.

Oliver Goldsmith, *The Vicar of Wakefield*

A Heavenly Delight

Talk of the happiness of getting a great prize in the lottery! What is that to the opening a box of books! The joy upon lifting up the cover must be something like what we shall feel when Peter the Porter opens the door upstairs, and says, Please to walk in, sir. That I shall never be paid for my labour according to the current value of time and labour, is tolerably certain; but if any one should offer me £10,000 to forgo that labour, I should bid him and his money go to the devil, for twice the sum could not purchase me half the enjoyment. It will be a great delight to me in the next world, to take a fly and visit these old worthies, who are my only society here, and to tell them what excellent company I found them here at the lakes of Cumberland, two centuries after they had been dead and turned to dust. In plain truth, I exist more among the dead than the living, and think more about them, and, perhaps, feel more about them.

Robert Southey, letter to S.T. Coleridge

The Best of All Possible Company

Coleridge is gone to Devonshire, and I was going to say I am alone, but that the sight of Shakespeare, and Spenser, and Milton, and the Bible, on my table, and Castanheda, and Barros, and Osorio at my elbow, tell me I am in the best of all possible company.

Robert Southey, letter to G.C. Bedford

Worthy books
Are not companions—they are solitudes;
We lose ourselves in them and all our cares.

P.J. Bailey, *Festus*

The Fellowship of Books

What were days without such fellowship? We were alone in the world without it. Nor does our faith falter though the secret we search for and do not find in them will not commit itself to literature, still we take up the new issue with the old expectation, and again and again, as we try our friends after many failures at conversation, believing this visit will be the favoured hour and all will be told us....

One must be rich in thought and character to owe nothing to books, though preparation is necessary to profitable reading; and the less reading is better than more;—book-struck men are of all readers least wise, however knowing or learned.

Amos Bronson Alcott, *Tablets*

A Company of the Wisest and the Wittiest

There are books which are of that importance in a man's
private experience, as to verify for him the fables of Cor-
nelius Agrippa, of Michael Scott, or of the old Orpheus of
Thrace,—books which take rank in our life with parents and
lovers and passionate experiences, so medicinal, so stringent,
so revolutionary, so authoritative,—books which are the work
and the proof of faculties so comprehensive, so nearly equal to
the world which they paint, that, though one shuts them with
meaner ones, he feels his exclusion from them to accuse his
way of living.

Consider what you have in the smallest chosen library. A
company of the wisest and wittiest men that could be picked
out of all civil countries, in a thousand years, have set in best
order the results of their learning and wisdom. The men
themselves were hid and inaccessible, solitary, impatient of
interruption, fenced by etiquette; but the thought which they
did not uncover to their bosom friend is here written out in
transparent words to us, the strangers of another age.

Ralph Waldo Emerson, *Books*

We should choose our books as we would our companions,
for their sterling and intrinsic merit.

C.C. Colton, *Lacon*

A Magnate in the Realm of Books

One, with his beard scarce silvered, bore
   A ready credence in his looks,
A lettered magnate, lording o'er
   An ever-widening realm of books.
In him brain-currents, near and far,
Converged as in a Leyden jar;

The old, dead authors thronged him round about,
And Elzevir's grey ghosts from leathern graves looked out.

He knew each living pundit well,
   Could weigh the gifts of him or her,
And well the market value tell
   Of poet and philosopher.
But if he lost, the scenes behind,
Somewhat of reverence vague and blind,
   Finding the actors human at the best,
   No readier lips than his the good he saw confessed.

His boyhood fancies not outgrown,
   He loved himself the singer's art;
Tenderly, gently, by his own
   He knew and judged an author's heart.
No Rhadamanthine brow of doom
Bowed the dazed pedant from his room;
   And bards, whose name is legion, if denied,
   Bore off alike intact their verses and their pride.

Pleasant it was to roam about
   The lettered world as he had done,
And see the lords of song without
   Their singing robes and garlands on,
With Wordsworth paddle Rydal mere,
Taste rugged Elliott's home-brewed beer,
   And with the ears of Rogers, at fourscore,
   Hear Garrick's buskined tread and Walpole's wit
     once more.

J.G. Whittier, *The Tent on the Beach*

Choose an author as you choose a friend.

Wentworth Dillon, Earl of Roscommon, *Essay on Translated Verse*

To My Books

Silent companions of the lonely hour,
    Friends who can never alter or forsake,
Who for inconstant roving have no power,
    And all neglect, perforce, must calmly take,—
Let me return to *you*, this turmoil ending,
    Which worldly cares have in my spirit wrought,
And, o'er your old familiar pages bending,
    Refresh my mind with many a tranquil thought;
Till, haply meeting there, from time to time,
    Fancies, the audible echo of my own.
'Twill be like hearing in a foreign clime
    My native language spoke in friendly tone,
And with a sort of welcome I shall dwell
On these, my unripe musings, told so well.

Caroline Norton

On Parting with My Books

Ye dear companions of my silent hours,
Whose pages oft before my eyes would strew
So many sweet and variegated flowers—
Dear Books, a while, perhaps for ay, adieu!
The dark cloud of misfortune o'er me lours:
No more by winter's fire—in summer's bowers,
My toil-worn mind shall be refreshed by you:
We part! sad thought! and while the damp devours
Your leaves, and the worm slowly eats them through,
Dull Poverty and its attendant ills,
Wasting of health, vain toil, corroding care,
And the world's cold neglect, which surest kills,
Must be my bitter doom; yet I shall bear
Unmurmuring, for my good perchance these evils are.

J.H. Leigh Hunt

True Friends that Cheer

It is a beautiful incident in the story of Mr. Roscoe's misfortunes, and one which cannot fail to interest the studious mind, that the parting with his books seems to have touched upon his tenderest feelings, and to have been the only circumstance that could provoke the notice of his Muse. The scholar only knows how dear these silent, yet eloquent, companions of pure thoughts and innocent hours become in the season of adversity. When all that is worldly turns to dross around us, these only retain their steady value. When friends grow cold, and the converse of intimates languishes into vapid civility and commonplace, these only continue the unaltered countenance of happier days, and cheer us with that true friendship which never deceived hope nor deserted sorrow.

Washington Irving, *The Sketch Book*

My Books

Sadly as some old mediaeval knight
   Gazed at the arms he could no longer wield,
   The sword two-handed and the shining shield
   Suspended in the hall, and full in sight,
While secret longings for the lost delight
   Of tourney or adventure in the field
   Came over him, and tears but half concealed
   Trembled and fell upon his beard of white,
So I behold these books upon their shelf,
   My ornaments and arms of other days;
   Not wholly useless, though no longer used,
For they remind me of my other self,
   Younger and stronger, and the pleasant ways,
   In which I walked, now clouded and confused.

Henry Wadsworth Longfellow

To Sir Henry Goodyer

When I would know thee, Goodyer, my thought looks
Upon thy well-made choice of friends, and books;
Then do I love thee, and behold thy ends
In making thy friends books, and thy books friends:
Now must I give thy life and deed the voice
Attending such a study, such a choice;
Where, though it be love that to thy praise doth move,
It was a knowledge that begat that love.

Ben Jonson

Our Best Acquaintance

While you converse with lords and dukes,
I have their betters here—my books;
Fixed in an elbow chair at ease
I choose my companions as I please.
I'd rather have one single shelf
Than all my friends, except yourself;
For after all that can be said
Our best acquaintance are the dead.

Thomas Sheridan

The True Elysian Fields

In my garden I spend my days; in my library I spend my nights.
My interests are divided between my geraniums and my books.
With the flower I am in the present; with the book I am in the
past. I go into my library, and all history unrolls before me.
I breathe morning air of the world while the scent of Eden's
roses yet lingered in it, while it vibrated only to the world's
first brood of nightingales, and to the laugh of Eve. I see the
pyramids building; I hear the shoutings of the armies of Alexander; I feel the ground shake beneath the march of Cambyses.
I sit as in a theatre,—the stage is time, the play is the play of

the world. What a spectacle it is! What kingly pomp, what processions file past, what cities burn to heaven, what crowds of captives are dragged at the chariot-wheels of conquerors! I hiss or cry 'Bravo' when the great actors come on shaking the stage. I am a Roman Emperor when I look at a Roman coin. I lift Homer, and I shout with Achilles in the trenches. The silence of the unpeopled Syrian plains, the out-comings and in-goings of the patriarchs, Abraham and Ishmael, Isaac in the fields at eventide, Rebekah at the well, Jacob's guile, Esau's face reddened by desert sun-heat, Joseph's splendid funeral procession—all these things I find within the boards of my Old Testament. What a silence in those old books as of a half-peopled world—what bleating of flocks—what green pastoral rest—what indubitable human existence! Across brawling centuries of blood and war, I hear the bleating of Abraham's flocks, the tinkling of the bells of Rebekah's camels. O men and women, so far separated, yet so near, so strange, yet so well-known, by what miraculous power do I know ye all! Books are the true Elysian fields where the spirits of the dead converse, and into these fields a mortal may venture unappalled. What king's court can boast such company? What school of philosophy such wisdom? The wit of the ancient world is glancing and flashing there. There is Pan's pipe, there are the songs of Apollo. Seated in my library at night, and looking on the silent faces of my books, I am occasionally visited by a strange sense of the supernatural. They are not collections of printed pages, they are ghosts. I take one down and it speaks with me in a tongue not now heard on earth, and of men and things of which it alone possesses knowledge. I call myself a solitary, but sometimes I think I misapply the term. No man sees more company than I do. I travel with mightier cohorts around me than ever did Timour or Genghis Khan on their fiery marches. I am a sovereign in my library, but it is the dead, not the living, that attend my levees.

Alexander Smith, Dreamthorp

A blessed companion is a book,—a book that, fitly chosen, is a life-long friend.

Douglas Jerrold, *Books*

May I a small house and large garden have!
And a few friends, and many books, both true.

Abraham Cowley, *The Wish*

The Desirable Tabernacle

O celestial gift of divine liberality, descending from the Father of light to raise up the rational soul even to heaven! ... Undoubtedly, indeed, thou hast placed thy desirable tabernacle in books, where the Most High, the Light of light, the Book of Life, hath established thee. Here then all who ask receive, all who seek find thee, to those who knock thou openest quickly. In books cherubim expand their wings, that the soul of the student may ascend and look around from pole to pole, from the rising to the setting sun, from the north and from the sea. In them the most high incomprehensible God Himself is contained and worshipped....

Let us consider how great a commodity of doctrine exists in books, how easily, how secretly, how safely they expose the nakedness of human ignorance without putting it to shame. These are the masters who instruct us without rods and ferules, without hard words and anger, without clothes or money. If you approach them, they are not asleep; if investigating you interrogate them, they conceal nothing; if you mistake them, they never grumble; if you are ignorant, they cannot laugh at you.

Richard de Bury, *Philobiblon*

To His Books

Bright books: the perspectives to our weak sights,
The clear projections of discerning lights,
Burning and shining thoughts, man's posthume day,
The track of fled souls and their Milky Way,
The dead alive and busy, the still voice
Of enlarged spirits, kind Heaven's white decoys!
Who lives with you, lives like those knowing flowers,
Which in commerce with light spend all their hours;
Which shut to clouds, and shadows nicely shun,
But with glad haste unveil to kiss the Sun.
Beneath you, all is dark, and a dead night,
Which whoso lives in, wants both health and sight.
   By sucking you the wise, like bees, do grow
Healing and rich, though this they do most slow,
Because most choicely; for as great a store
Have we of books as bees of herbs, or more;
And the great task to try, then know, the good.
To discern weeds, and judge of wholesome food,
Is a rare scant performance: for man dies
Oft ere 'tis done, while the bee feeds and flies.
But you were all choice flowers; all set and dressed
By old sage florists, who well knew the best;
And I amidst you all am turned a weed!
Not wanting knowledge, but for want of heed.
Then thank thyself, wild fool, that wouldst not be
Content to know—what was too much for thee.

Henry Vaughan

The Legacies of Genius

Quod nec Iovis ira, nec ignis,
Nec poterit ferrum, nec edax abolere vetustas. —OVID

Aristotle tells us, that the world is a copy or transcript of
those ideas which are in the mind of the first Being, and that
those ideas which are in the mind of man are a transcript of
the world. To this we may add, that words are the transcript
of those ideas which are in the mind of man, and that writing
or printing is the transcript of words. As the Supreme Being
has expressed, and as it were printed, his ideas in the creation, men express their ideas in books, which, by this great
invention of these latter ages, may last as long as the sun and
moon, and perish only in the general wreck of nature. Thus
Cowley, in his poem on the Resurrection, mentioning the
destruction of the universe, has these admirable lines:

> Now all the wide extended sky,
> And all the harmonious worlds on high
> And Virgil's sacred work shall die.

There is no other method of fixing those thoughts which
arise and disappear in the mind of man, and transmitting
them to the last periods of time; no other method of giving
a permanency to our ideas, and preserving the knowledge
of any particular person, when his body is mixed with the
common mass of matter, and his soul retired into the world
of spirits. Books are the legacies that a great genius leaves
to mankind, which are delivered down from generation to
generation, as presents to the posterity of those who are yet
unborn.

Joseph Addison, *Spectator,* 166

In Prison

O happy be the day which gave that mind
Learning's first tincture—blest thy fostering care.
Thou most beloved of parents, worthiest sire!
Which, taste-inspiring, made the lettered page
My favourite companion: most esteemed,
And most improving! Almost from the day
Of earliest childhood to the present hour
Of gloomy, black misfortune, books, dear books,
Have been, and are, my comforts. Morn and night,
Adversity, prosperity, at home,
Abroad, health, sickness,—good or ill report,
The same firm friends; the same refreshment rich
And source of consolation. Nay, e'en here
Their magic power they lose not; still the same,
Of matchless influence in this prison-house,
Unutterably horrid; in an hour
Of woe, beyond all fancy's fictions drear.

William Dodd, *Thoughts in Prison*

Love that is Large

There is a period of modern times, at which the love of
books appears to have been of a more decided nature than
at either of these—I mean the age just before and after the
Reformation, or rather all that period when book-writing
was confined to the learned languages. Erasmus is the god of
it. Bacon, a mighty book-man, saw, among his other sights,
the great advantage of loosening the vernacular tongue, and
wrote both Latin and English. I allow this is the greatest
closeted age of books; of old scholars sitting in dusty studies;
of heaps of 'illustrious obscure', rendering themselves more
illustrious and more obscure by retreating from the 'thorny
queaches' of Dutch and German names into the 'vacant

interlunar caves' of appellations latinized or translated. I think
I see all their volumes now, filling the shelves of a dozen
German convents. The authors are bearded men, sitting in
old woodcuts, in caps and gowns, and their books are dedicated to princes and statesmen, as illustrious as themselves.
My old friend Wierus, who wrote a thick book, *De Praestigiis
Daemonum*, was one of them, and had a fancy worthy of his
sedentary stomach. I will confess, once for all, that I have
a liking for them all. It is my link with the bibliomaniacs,
whom I admit into our relationship, because my love is large
and my family pride nothing. But still I take my idea of books
read with a gusto, of companions for bed and board, from the
two ages beforementioned. The other is of too book-worm a
description. There must be both a judgement and a fervour;
a discrimination and a boyish eagerness; and (with all due
humility) something of a point of contact between authors
worth reading and the reader. How can I take Juvenal into
the fields, or Valcarenghius *De Aortae Aneurismate* to bed with
me? How could I expect to walk before the face of nature
with the one; to tire my elbow properly with the other,
before I put out my candle and turn round deliciously on the
right side? Or how could I stick up *Coke upon Littleton* against
something on the dinner-table, and be divided between a
fresh paragraph and a mouthful of salad?

J.H. Leigh Hunt, My Books

A Catholic Taste in Books

> To mind the inside of a book is to entertain one's self with the
> forced product of another man's brain. Now I think a man of
> quality and breeding may be much amused with the natural
> sprouts of his own.—Lord Foppington in *The Relapse*

An ingenious acquaintance of my own was so much struck
with this bright sally of his Lordship, that he has left
off reading altogether, to the great improvement of his

originality. At the hazard of losing some credit on this head, I must confess that I dedicate no inconsiderable portion of my time to other people's thoughts. I dream away my life in others' speculations. I love to lose myself in other men's minds. When I am not walking, I am reading; I cannot sit and think. Books think for me.

I have no repugnances. Shaftesbury is not too genteel for me, nor Jonathan Wild too low. I can read any thing which I call a *book*. There are things in that shape which I cannot allow for such.

In this catalogue of *books which are no books—biblia a-biblia—* I reckon Court Calendars, Directories, Pocket Books, Draught Boards bound and lettered at the back, Scientific Treatises, Almanacks, Statutes at Large; the works of Hume, Gibbon, Robertson, Beattie, Soame Jenyns, and, generally, all those volumes which 'no gentleman's library should be without'; the Histories of Flavius Josephus (that learned Jew), and Paley's *Moral Philosophy*. With these exceptions, I can read almost any thing. I bless my stars for a taste so catholic, so unexcluding.

I confess that it moves my spleen to see these *things in books' clothing* perched upon shelves, like false saints, usurpers of true shrines, intruders into the sanctuary, thrusting out the legitimate occupants. To reach down a well-bound semblance of a volume, and hope it is some kind-hearted play-book, then, opening what 'seem its leaves', to come bolt upon a withering Population Essay. To expect a Steele, or a Farquhar, and find—Adam Smith. To view a well-arranged assortment of blockheaded Encyclopaedias (Anglicanas or Metropolitanas) set out in an array of Russia, or Morocco, when a tithe of that good leather would comfortably re-clothe my shivering folios; would renovate Paracelsus himself, and enable old Raymund Lully to look like himself again in the world. I never see these impostors but I long to strip them, to warm my ragged veterans in their spoils.

Charles Lamb, *Detached Thoughts on Books and Reading*

A Sense of Humour

I am not prepared to back Charles Lamb's Index Expurgatorius. It is difficult, almost impossible, to find the book
from which something either valuable or amusing may not be
found, if the proper alembic be applied. I know books that are
curious, and really amusing, from their excessive badness. If
you want to find precisely how a thing ought not to be said,
you take one of them down and make it perform the service
of the intoxicated Spartan slave. There are some volumes in
which, at a chance opening, you are certain to find a mere
platitude delivered in the most superb and amazing climax of
big words, and others in which you have a like happy facility
in finding every proposition stated with its stern forward,
as sailors say, or in some other grotesque mismanagement of
composition. There are no better farces on or off the stage
than when two or three congenial spirits ransack books of
this kind, and compete with each other in taking fun out of
them.

J.H. Burton, *The Book-Hunter*

Books the True Levellers

It is chiefly through books that we enjoy intercourse with
superior minds, and these invaluable means of communication
are in the reach of all. In the best books great men talk to us,
give us their most precious thoughts, and pour their souls into
ours. God be thanked for books! They are the voices of the
distant and the dead, and make us heirs of the spiritual life of
past ages. Books are the true levellers. They give to all, who
will faithfully use them, the society, the spiritual presence, of
the best and greatest of our race. No matter how poor I am.
No matter though the prosperous of my own time will not
enter my obscure dwelling. If the Sacred Writers will enter
and take up their abode under my roof, if Milton will cross

my threshold to sing to me of Paradise, and Shakespeare to open to me the worlds of imagination and the workings of the human heart, and Franklin to enrich me with his practical wisdom. I shall not pine for want of intellectual companionship, and I may become a cultivated man, though excluded from what is called the best society in the place where I live.

To make this means of culture effectual a man must select good books, such as have been written by right-minded and strong-minded men, real thinkers, who instead of diluting by repetition what others say, have something to say for themselves, and write to give relief to full, earnest souls; and these works must not be skimmed over for amusement, but read with fixed attention and a reverential love of truth. In selecting books we may be aided much by those who have studied more than ourselves. But, after all, it is best to be determined in this particular a good deal by our own tastes.

William Ellery Channing, *Self-Culture*

Authors as Lovers of Books

I love an author the more for having been himself a lover of books.... We conceive of Plato as a lover of books; of Aristotle certainly; of Plutarch, Pliny, Horace, Julian, and Marcus Aurelius. Virgil, too, must have been one; and, after a fashion, Martial. May I confess that the passage which I recollect with the greatest pleasure in Cicero, is where he says that books delight us at home, *and are no impediment abroad*; travel with us, ruralize with us. His period is rounded off to some purpose: 'Delectant domi, non impediunt foris; peregrinantur, rusticantur.' I am so much of this opinion, that I do not care to be anywhere without having a book or books at hand, and like Dr. Orkborne, in the novel of *Camilla*, stuff the coach or post-chaise with them whenever I travel. As books, however, become ancient, the love of them becomes more unequivocal and conspicuous. The ancients had little of what we call learning. They made it. They were also no very eminent buyers of books—they made books for posterity. It is true, that it is not at all necessary to love many books, in order to love them much. The scholar, in Chaucer, who would rather have

> At his beddes head
> A twenty bokes, clothed, in black and red,
> Of Aristotle and his philosophy,
> Than robès rich, or fiddle, or psaltry—

doubtless beat all our modern collectors in his passion for reading. . . . Dante puts Homer, the great ancient, in his Elysium, upon trust; but a few years afterwards. *Homer*, the book, made its appearance in Italy, and Petrarch, in a transport, put it upon his bookshelves, where he adored it, like 'the unknown God'. Petrarch ought to be the god of the Bibliomaniacs, for he was a collector and a man of genius, which is an union that does not often happen. He copied out, with his own precious hand, the manuscripts he rescued from time, and then produced others for time to reverence. With his head upon a book he died.

J.H. Leigh Hunt, My Books

The sweet serenity of books.

Henry Wadsworth Longfellow

The Theory of Books

Books are the best type of the influence of the past. . . . The theory of books is noble. The scholar of the first age received into him the world around; brooded thereon; gave it the new arrangement of his own mind, and uttered it again. It came into him, life; it went out from him, truth. It came to him, short-lived actions; it went out from him, immortal thoughts.

It came to him, business; it went from him, poetry. It was dead fact; now, it is quick thought. It can stand, and it can go. It now endures, it now flies, it now inspires. Precisely in proportion to the depth of mind from which it issued, so high does it soar, so long does it sing.

Ralph Waldo Emerson, *The American Scholar*

Books a Substantial World

Dreams, books, are each a world; and books, we know,
Are a substantial world, both pure and good:
Round these, with tendrils strong as flesh and blood,
Our pastime and our happiness will grow,
There find I personal themes, a plenteous store,
Matter wherein right voluble I am,
To which I listen with a ready ear;
Two shall be named, pre-eminently dear,—
The gentle Lady married to the Moor;
And heavenly Una with her milk-white Lamb....
Blessings be with them—and eternal praise,
Who gave us nobler loves, and nobler cares—
The Poets, who on earth have made us heirs
Of truth and pure delight by heavenly lays!
Oh! might my name be numbered among theirs,
Then gladly would I end my mortal days.

William Wordsworth, *Personal Talk*

To Wordsworth

We both have run o'er half the space
Listed for mortal's earthly race;
We both have crossed life's fervid line,
And other stars before us shine:
May they be bright and prosperous

As those that have been stars for us!
Our course by Milton's light was sped,
And Shakespeare shining overhead:
Chatting on deck was Dryden too,
The Bacon of the rhyming crew;
None ever crossed our mystic sea
More richly stored with thought than he;
Though never tender nor sublime,
He wrestles with and conquers Time.
To learn my lore on Chaucer's knee,
I left much prouder company;
Thee gentle Spenser fondly led,
But me he mostly sent to bed.

Walter Savage Landor, Miscellaneous Poems

Useful and Mighty Things

Except a living man, there is nothing more wonderful than a book!—a message to us from the dead—from human souls whom we never saw, who lived, perhaps, thousands of miles away; and yet these, on those little sheets of paper, speak to us, amuse us, vivify us, teach us, comfort us, open their hearts to us as brothers.... I say we ought to reverence books, to look at them as useful and mighty things. If they are good and true, whether they are about religion or politics, farming, trade, or medicine, they are the message of Christ, the maker of all things, the teacher of all truth, which He has put into the heart of some man to speak, that he may tell us what is good for our spirits, for our bodies, and for our country.

Charles Kingsley, Village Sermons: On Books

An Extraordinary Delight to Study

To most kind of men it is an extraordinary delight to study.
For what a world of books offers itself, in all subjects, arts,
and sciences, to the sweet content and capacity of the reader!
… What vast tomes are extant in law, physic, and divinity,
for profit, pleasure, practice, speculation, in verse or prose,
&c.! their names alone are the subject of whole volumes; we
have thousands of authors of all sorts, many great libraries
full well furnished, like so many dishes of meat, served out
for several palates: and he is a very block that is affected with
none of them.

Robert Burton, The Anatomy of Melancholy

Sweet and Happy Hours

BORNWELL Learning is an addition beyond
    Nobility of birth; honour of blood
    Without the ornament of knowledge is
    A glorious ignorance.
FREDERICK I never knew more sweet and happy hours
    Than I employed upon my books.

James Shirley, The Lady of Pleasure

A Taste to be Prayed For

If I were to pray for a taste which should stand me in stead
under every variety of circumstances, and be a source of
happiness and cheerfulness to me through life, and a shield
against its ills, however things might go amiss, and the world
frown upon me, it would be a taste for reading. I speak of it
of course only as a worldly advantage, and not in the slightest
degree as superseding or derogating from the higher office
and surer and stronger panoply of religious principles—but as

a taste, an instrument and a mode of pleasurable gratification.
Give a man this taste, and the means of gratifying it, and you
can hardly fail of making a happy man, unless, indeed, you
put into his hands a most perverse selection of books. You
place him in contact with the best society in every period of
history—with the wisest, the wittiest—with the tenderest,
the bravest, and the purest characters who have adorned
humanity. You make him a denizen of all nations—a contemporary of all ages. The world has been created for him.

Sir John Herschel, *Address to the Subscribers*
to the Windsor Public Library

More than Meat, Drink, and Clothing

I should like you to see the additional book-room that we have
fitted up, and in which I am now writing.... It would please
you to see such a display of literary wealth, which is at once
the pride of my eye, and the joy of my heart, and the food
of my mind; indeed, more than metaphorically, meat, drink,
and clothing for me and mine. I verily believe that no one in
my station was ever so rich before, and I am very sure that
no one in any station had ever a more thorough enjoyment
of riches of any kind, or in any way. It is more delightful for
me to live with books than with men, even with all the relish
that I have for such society as is worth having.

Robert Southey, Letter to G.C. Bedford

The Book the Highest Delight

In the highest civilization the book is still the highest delight. He who has once known its satisfactions is provided with a resource against calamity. Like Plato's disciple who has perceived a truth, 'he is preserved from harm until another period.' In every man's memory, with the hours when life culminated, are usually associated certain books which met his views. Of a large and powerful class we might ask with confidence, What is the event they most desire? What gift? What but the book that shall come, which they have sought through all libraries, through all languages, that shall be to their mature eyes what many a tinsel-covered toy pamphlet was to their childhood, and shall speak to the imagination? Our high respect for a well-read man is praise enough of literature. If we encountered a man of rare intellect, we should ask him what books he read. We expect a great man to be a good reader; or in proportion to the spontaneous power should be the assimilating power. And though such are a most difficult and exacting class, they are not less eager. 'He that borrows the aid of an equal understanding,' said Burke, 'doubles his own; he that uses that of a superior elevates his own to the stature of that he contemplates.'

We prize books, and they prize them most who are themselves wise. Our debt to tradition through reading and conversation is so massive, our protest or private addition so rare and insignificant,—and this commonly on the ground of other reading or hearing,—that, in a large sense, one would say there is no pure originality. All minds quote.

Ralph Waldo Emerson, *Quotation and Originality*

The Pleasure Derived from Books

It is remarkable, the character of the pleasure we derive from the best books. They impress us with the conviction that one nature wrote, and the same reads. We read the verses of one of the great English poets, of Chaucer, of Marvell, of Dryden, with the most modern joy,—with a pleasure, I mean, which is in great part caused by the abstraction of all *time* from their verses. There is some awe mixed with the joy of our surprise, when this poet, who lived in some past world, two or three hundred years ago, says that which lies close to my own soul, that which I also had wellnigh thought and said.

Ralph Waldo Emerson, *The American Scholar*

Our Debt to a Book

Let us not forget the genial miraculous force we have known to proceed from a book. We go musing into the vault of day and night; no constellation shines, no muse descends, the stars are white points, the roses brick-coloured dust, the frogs pipe, mice peep, and wagons creak along the road. We return to the house and take up Plutarch or Augustine, and read a few sentences or pages, and lo! the air swims with life; the front of heaven is full of fiery shapes; secrets of magnanimity and grandeur invite us on every hand; life is made up of them. Such is our debt to a book.

Ralph Waldo Emerson, *Thoughts on Modern Literature*

Rich Fare

A natural turn for reading and intellectual pursuits probably
preserved me from the moral shipwreck, so apt to befall those
who are deprived in early life of the paternal pilotage. At the
very least, my books kept me aloof from the ring, the dog-pit,
the tavern, and the saloon, with their degrading orgies. For the
closet associate of Pope and Addison—the mind accustomed
to the noble, though silent, discourse of Shakespeare and
Milton—will hardly seek, or put up with, low company and
slang. The reading animal will not be content with the brutish
wallowings that satisfy the unlearned pigs of the world.

Later experience enables me to depose to the comfort and
blessing that literature can prove in seasons of sickness and
sorrow—how powerfully intellectual pursuits can help in
keeping the head from crazing, and the heart from breaking,—nay, not to be too grave, how generous mental food can
even atone for a meagre diet—rich fare on the paper for short
commons on the cloth.

Poisoned by the malaria of the Dutch marshes, my
stomach, for many months, resolutely set itself against
fish, flesh, or fowl; my appetite had no more edge than the
German knife placed before me. But, luckily, the mental
palate and digestion were still sensible and vigorous; and
whilst I passed untasted every dish at the Rhenish *table d'hôte*,
I could yet enjoy my *Peregrine Pickle*, and the feast after the
manner of the ancients. There was no yearning towards calf's
head *à la tortue*, or sheep's heart; but I could still relish Head
à la Brunnen and the *Heart of Midlothian*.

Still more recently, it was my misfortune, with a tolerable
appetite, to be condemned to lenten fare, like Sancho Panza,
by my physician—to a diet, in fact, lower than any prescribed
by the poor-law commissioners; all animal food, from a
bullock to a rabbit, being strictly interdicted; as well as all
fluids stronger than that which lays dust, washes pinafores,
and waters polyanthus. But 'the feast of reason and the flow

of soul' were still mine. Denied beef, I had *Bul*wer and *Cow*per,—forbidden mutton, there was *Lamb*,—and in lieu of pork, the great *Bacon* or *Hogg*.

Then, as to beverage, it was hard, doubtless, for a Christian to set his face like a Turk against the juice of the grape. But, eschewing wine, I had still my *Butler*; and in the absence of liquor, all the *choice spirits* from Tom Browne to Tom Moore.

Thus, though confined, physically, to the drink that drowns kittens, I quaffed mentally, not merely the best of our own home-made, but the rich, racy, sparkling growths of France and Italy, of Germany and Spain—the champagne of Molière, and the Monte Pulciano of Boccaccio, the hock of Schiller, and the sherry of Cervantes. Depressed bodily by the fluid that damps everything, I got intellectually elevated with Milton, a little merry with Swift, or rather jolly with Rabelais, whose Panta-gruel, by the way, is quite equal to the best gruel with rum in it.

So far can literature palliate or compensate for gastronomi-cal privations. But there are other evils, great and small, in this world, which try the stomach less than the head, the heart, and the temper—bowls that will not roll right—well-laid schemes that will 'gang aglee'—and ill winds that blow with the perti-nacity of the monsoon. Of these, Providence has allotted me a full share; but still, paradoxical as it may sound, my *burden* has been greatly lightened by a *load of books*. The manner of this will be best understood by a feline illustration. Everybody has heard of the two Kilkenny cats, who devoured each other; but it is not so generally known that they left behind them an orphan kitten, which, true to the breed, began to eat itself up, till it was diverted from the operation by a mouse. Now, the human mind, under vexation, is like that kitten, for it is apt to *prey upon itself*, unless drawn off by a new object; and none better for the purpose than a book; for example, one of Defoe's; for who, in reading his thrilling *History of the Great Plague*, would not be reconciled to a few little ones?

Many, many a dreary, weary hour have I got over—many a gloomy misgiving postponed—many a mental or bodily

annoyance forgotten, by help of the tragedies and comedies of
our dramatists and novelists! Many a trouble has been soothed
by the still small voice of the moral philosopher—many a
dragon-like care charmed to sleep by the sweet song of the
poet, for all which I cry incessantly, not aloud, but in my
heart, Thanks and honour to the glorious masters of the
pen, and the great inventors of the press! Such has been my
own experience of the blessing and comfort of literature and
intellectual pursuits; and of the same mind, doubtless, was Sir
Humphry Davy, who went for 'consolations in *Travel*', not to
the inn or the posting house, but to his library and his books.

Thomas Hood, letter to the Manchester Athenaeum, 1843

The Commodity Reaped of Book

The commerce of books comforts me in age and solaceth me
in solitariness. It easeth me of the burthen of a wearisome
sloth: and at all times rids me of tedious companies: it abateth
the edge of fretting sorrow, on condition it be not extreme
and over-insolent. To divert me from any importunate imagination or insinuating conceit, there is no better way than to
have recourse unto books; with ease they allure me to them,
and with facility they remove them all. And though they
perceive I neither frequent nor seek them, but wanting other
more essential, lively, and more natural commodities, they
never mutiny or murmur at me; but still entertain me with
one and self-same visage....

The sick man is not to be moaned that hath his health in
his sleeve. In the experience and use of this sentence, which
is most true, consisteth all the commodity I reap of books.
In effect I make no other use of them than those who know
them not. I enjoy them, as a miser doth his gold; to know that
I may enjoy them when I list, my mind is settled and satisfied
with the right of possession. I never travel without books,

nor in peace nor in war: yet do I pass many days and months
without using them. It shall be anon, say I, or to-morrow,
or when I please; in the meanwhile the time runs away, and
passeth without hurting me. For it is wonderful what repose
I take, and how I continue in this consideration, that they
are at my elbow to delight me when time shall serve; and in
acknowledging what assistance they give unto my life. This is
the best munition I have found in this human peregrination,
and I extremely bewail those men of understanding that want
the same. I accept with better will all other kinds of amuse-
ments, how slight soever, forsomuch as this cannot fail me.

Michel de Montaigne

For Wisdom, Piety, Delight, or Use

In vain that husbandman his seed doth sow,
If he his crop not in due season mow,
A general sets his army in array
In vain, unless he fight, and win the day.
'Tis virtuous action that must praise bring forth,
Without which slow advice is little worth.
Yet they who give good counsel, praise deserve,
Though in the active part they cannot serve:
In action, learnéd counsellors their age,
Profession, or disease, forbids to engage.
Nor to philosophers is praise denied,
Whose wise instructions after-ages guide;
Yet vainly most their age in study spend;
No end of writing books, and to no end:
Beating their brains for strange and hidden things,
Whose knowledge nor delight nor profit brings:
Themselves with doubt both day and night perplex,
No gentle reader please, or teach, but vex.
Books should to one of these four ends conduce
For wisdom, piety, delight, or use.

What need we gaze upon the spangled sky
Or into matter's hidden causes pry? ...
If we were wise these things we should not mind
But more delight in easy matters find....
Learn to live well that thou mayst die so too.
To live and die is all we have to do.

Sir John Denham, Translation of Mancini

Instruction or Amusement

Books, we are told, propose to *instruct* or to *amuse*. Indeed!
However, not to spend any words upon it, I suppose you will
admit that this wretched antithesis will be of no service to
us.... For this miserable alternative being once admitted,
observe what follows. In which class of books does the *Paradise Lost* stand? Among those which instruct or those which
amuse? Now, if a man answers, among those which instruct,—he lies: for there is no instruction in it, nor could be
in any great poem, according to the meaning which the word
must bear in this distinction, unless it is meant that it should
involve its own antithesis. But if he says, 'No—amongst those
which amuse,'—then what a beast must he be to degrade,
and in this way, what has done the most of any human work
to raise and dignify human nature. But the truth is, you see,
that the idiot does not wish to degrade it; on the contrary, he
would willingly tell a lie in its favour, if that would be admitted; but such is the miserable state of slavery to which he has
reduced himself by his own puny distinction; for, as soon as
he hops out of one of his little cells he is under a necessity
of hopping into the other. The true antithesis to knowledge
in this case is not *pleasure*, but power. All, that is literature,
seeks to communicate power: all, that is not literature, to
communicate knowledge.

Thomas De Quincey, Letters to a Young Man

Exercise for the Mind

From my own Apartment, March 16, 1709

Reading is to the mind what exercise is to the body. As by
the one health is preserved, strengthened, and invigorated;
by the other, virtue (which is the health of the mind) is kept
alive, cherished, and confirmed. But as exercise becomes
tedious and painful when we make use of it only as the means
of health, so reading is apt to grow uneasy and burdensome
when we apply ourselves to it only for our improvement
in virtue. For this reason the virtue which we gather from
a fable or an allegory is like health we get by hunting; as
we are engaged in an agreeable pursuit that draws us on
with pleasure, and makes us insensible of the fatigues that
accompany it.

Richard Steele, *Tatler*, 147

Why Books Were Invented

Books were invented to take off the odium of immediate
superiority and soften the rigour of duties prescribed by the
teachers and censors of human kind—setting at least those
who are acknowledged wiser than ourselves at a distance.
When we recollect, however, that for this very reason they
are seldom consulted and little obeyed, how much cause shall
his contemporaries have to rejoice that their living Johnson
forced them to feel the reproofs due to vice and folly—while
Seneca and Tillotson were no longer able to make impression
except on our shelves.

Thomas Percy

Why Books Are Read

It is difficult to enumerate the several motives which procure to books the honour of perusal: spite, vanity, and curiosity, hope and fear, love and hatred, every passion which incites to any other action, serves at one time or another to stimulate a reader.

Some are found to take a celebrated volume into their hands, because they hope to distinguish their penetration by finding faults that have escaped the public; others eagerly buy it in the first bloom of reputation, that they may join the chorus of praise, and not lag, as Falstaff terms it, in 'the rearward of the fashion'.

Some read for style, and some for argument: one has little care about the sentiment, he observes only how it is expressed; another regards not the conclusion, but is diligent to mark how it is inferred; they read for other purposes than the attainment of practical knowledge, and are no more likely to grow wise by an examination of a treatise of moral prudence than an architect to inflame his devotion by considering attentively the proportions of a temple.

Some read that they may embellish their conversation, or shine in dispute; some that they may not be detected in ignorance, or want the reputation of literary accomplishments: but the most general and prevalent reason of study is the impossibility of finding another amusement equally cheap or constant, equally independent of the hour or the weather. He that wants money to follow the chase of pleasure through her yearly circuit, and is left at home when the gay world rolls to Bath or Tunbridge; he whose gout compels him to hear from his chamber the rattle of chariots transporting happier beings to plays and assemblies, will be forced to seek in books a refuge from himself.

Samuel Johnson, *Adventurer*, 137

The Influence of Books

Every person of tolerable education has been considerably
influenced by the books he has read, and remembers with a
kind of gratitude several of those that made without injury
the earliest and the strongest impression. It is pleasing at a
more advanced period to look again into the early favourites,
though the mature person may wonder how some of them
had once power to absorb his passions, make him retire into a
lonely wood in order to read unmolested, repel the approach-
es of sleep, or, when it came, infect it with visions. A capital
part of the proposed task would be to recollect the books that
have been read with the greatest interest, the periods when
they were read, the partiality which any of them inspired to
a particular mode of life, to a study, to a system of opinions,
or to a class of human characters; to note the counteraction
of later ones (where we have been sensible of it) to the effect
produced by the former; and then to endeavour to estimate
the whole and ultimate influence.

Considering the multitude of facts, sentiments, and characters, which have been contemplated by a person who has
read much, the effect, one would think, must have been very
great. Still, however, it is probable that a very small number
of books will have the pre-eminence in our mental history.
Perhaps your memory will promptly recur to six or ten that
have contributed more to your present habits of feeling and
thought than all the rest together.

John Foster, *On a Man's Writing Memoirs of Himself*

Remunerative Reading

Cultivate above all things a taste for reading. There is no
pleasure so cheap, so innocent, and so remunerative as the
real, hearty pleasure and taste for reading. It does not come
to every one naturally. Some people take to it naturally, and

others do not; but I advise you to cultivate it, and endeavour to promote it in your minds. In order to do that you should read what amuses you and pleases you. You should not begin with difficult works, because, if you do, you will find the pursuit dry and tiresome. I would even say to you, read novels, read frivolous books, read anything that will amuse you and give you a taste for reading. On this point all persons could put themselves on an equality. Some persons would say they would rather spend their time in society; but it must be remembered that if they had cultivated a taste for reading beforehand they would be in a position to choose their society, whereas, if they had not, the probabilities were that they would have to mix with people inferior to themselves.

> Robert Lowe, Lord Sherbrooke, *Speech to the Students of the Croydon Science and Art Schools*, 1869

Books bear him up awhile, and make him try
To swim with bladders of philosophy.

> John Wilmot, Earl of Rochester, *A Satire against Mankind*

Books are men of higher stature,
And the only men that speak aloud for future times to hear.

> Elizabeth Barrett Browning, *Lady Geraldine's Courtship*

The Mood for Books

How the mood for a book sometimes rushes upon one, either one knows not why, or in consequence, perhaps, of some most trifling suggestion. Yesterday I was walking at dusk. I came to an old farmhouse; at the garden gate a vehicle stood waiting, and I saw it was our doctor's gig. Having passed, I turned to look back. There was a faint afterglow in the sky beyond the chimneys; a light twinkled at one of the upper windows. I said to myself, '*Tristram Shandy*,' and hurried home to plunge into a book which I have not opened for I dare say twenty years.

Not long ago, I awoke one morning and suddenly thought of the Correspondence between Goethe and Schiller; and so impatient did I become to open the book that I got up an hour earlier than usual. A book worth rising for; much better worth than old Burton, who pulled Johnson out of bed. A book which helps one to forget the idle or venomous chatter going on everywhere about us, and bids us cherish hope for a world 'which has such people in't'.

These volumes I had at hand; I could reach them down from my shelves at the moment when I hungered for them. But it often happens that the book which comes into my mind could only be procured with trouble and delay; I breathe regretfully and put aside the thought. Ah! the books that one will never read again. They gave delight, perchance something more; they left a perfume in the memory; but life has passed them by for ever. I have but to muse, and one after another they rise before me. Books gentle and quieting; books noble and inspiring; books that well merit to be pored over, not once but many a time. Yet never again shall I hold them in my hand; the years fly too quickly, and are too few. Perhaps when I lie waiting for the end, some of these lost books will come into my wandering thoughts, and I shall remember them as friends to whom I owed a kindness—friends passed upon the way. What regret in that last farewell!

George Gissing, *The Private Papers of Henry Ryecroft*

Permanence for Thought

I saw a man, who bore in his hands the same instruments as
our modern smith's, presenting a vase, which appeared to
be made of iron, amidst the acclamations of an assembled
multitude engaged in triumphal procession before the altars
dignified by the name of Apollo at Delphi; and I saw in the
same place men who carried rolls of papyrus in their hands
and wrote upon them with reeds containing ink made from
the soot of wood mixed with a solution of glue. 'See,' the
genius said, 'an immense change produced in the condition
of society by the two arts of which you here see the origin;
the one, that of rendering iron malleable, which is owing to a
single individual, an obscure Greek; the other, that of making
thought permanent in written characters, an art which
has gradually arisen from the hieroglyphics which you may
observe on yonder pyramids.'

Sir Humphry Davy, *Consolations in Travel*

Coats for Mackerel

I erect not here a statue to be set up in the market-place of a
town, or in a church, or in any other public place:

> *Non equidem hoc studeo, pullatis ut mihi nugis*
> *Pagina turgescat.* (PERS. *Sat.* v. 19.)

> I study not my written leaves should grow
> Big-swoln with bubbled toys, which vain breaths blow.

> *Secrete loquimur.* (PERS. *Sat.* v. 21.)

> We speak alone,
> Or one to one.

It is for the corner of a library, or to amuse a neighbour, a
kinsman, or a friend of mine withal, who by this image may
happily take pleasure to renew acquaintance and to reconverse
with me.... Notwithstanding if my posterity be of another

mind, I shall have wherewith to be avenged, for they cannot
make so little accompt of me, as then I shall do of them. All
the commerce I have in this with the world is that I borrow
the instruments of their writing, as more speedy and more
easy; in requital whereof I may peradventure hinder the
melting of some piece of butter in the market or a grocer
from selling an ounce of pepper.

> *Ne toga cordylis et paenula desit olivis.* (MARTIAL)
> Lest fish-fry should a fit gown want,
> Lest cloaks should be for Olives scant.

> *Et laxas scombris saepe dabo tunicas.* (CATULLUS)
> To long-tailed mackerels often I
> Will side-wide (paper) coats apply.

And if it happen no man read me, have I lost my time to have
entertained myself so many idle hours about so pleasing and
profitable thoughts? ... I have no more made my book than
my book hath made me. A book consubstantial to his author:
of a peculiar and fit occupation. A member of my life. Not
of an occupation and end strange and foreign, as all other
books.... What if I lend mine ears somewhat more attentively
unto books, sith I but watch if I can filch something from
them wherewith to enamel and uphold mine? I never study
to make a book, yet have I somewhat studied, because I had
already made it (if to nibble or pinch, by the head or feet,
now one author and then another, be in any sort to study),
but nothing at all to form my opinions.

Michel de Montaigne

Enduring Monuments

We see then how far the monuments of wit and learning are
more durable than the monuments of power or of the hands.
For have not the verses of Homer continued twenty-five
hundred years, or more, without the loss of a syllable or letter;

during which time infinite palaces, temples, castles, cities, have been decayed and demolished? It is not possible to have the true pictures or statues of Cyrus, Alexander, Caesar, no, nor of the kings or great personages of much later years; for the originals cannot last, and the copies cannot but leese of the life and truth. But the images of men's wits and knowledges remain in books, exempted from the wrong of time and capable of perpetual renovation. Neither are they fitly to be called images, because they generate still, and cast their seeds in the minds of others, provoking and causing infinite actions and opinions in succeeding ages. So that if the invention of the ship was thought so noble, which carrieth riches and commodities from place to place, and consociateth the most remote regions in participation of their fruits, how much more are letters to be magnified, which as ships pass through the vast seas of time, and make ages so distant to participate of the wisdom, illuminations, and inventions, the one of the other?

Francis Bacon, *Of the Advancement of Learning*

The Strange Quality of Books

Books have that strange quality, that being of the frailest and tenderest matter, they outlast brass, iron and marble; and though their habitations and walls, by uncivil hands, be many times overthrown; and they themselves, by foreign force, be turned prisoners, yet do they often, as their authors, keep their giver's names; seeming rather to change places and masters than to suffer a full ruin and total wreck. So, many of the books of Constantinople changed Greece for France and Italy; and in our time, that famous Library in the Palatinate changed Heidelberg for the Vatican. And this I think no small duty, nor meaner gift and retribution, which I render back again to my benefactor's honest fame, being a greater matter than riches; riches being momentany and evanishing, scarce possessed by the third heir; fame immortal, and almost everlasting; by fame

riches is often acquired, seldom fame by riches; except when
it is their good hap to fall in the possession of some generous-
minded man. And though a philosopher said of famous men,
disdainfully, that they died two deaths, one in their bodies,
another, long after, in their names, he must confess, that where
other men live but one life, famous men live two.

William Drummond, *Bibliotheca Edinburgena Lectori*

Books Are Not Dead Things

I deny not but that it is of greatest concernment in the
Church and Commonwealth to have a vigilant eye how books
demean themselves, as well as men; and thereafter to confine,
imprison, and do sharpest justice on them as malefactors: For
books are not absolutely dead things, but do contain a potency
of life in them to be as active as that soul was whose progeny
they are; nay, they do preserve, as in a vial, the purest ef-
ficacy and extraction of that living intellect that bred them. I
know they are as lively and as vigorously productive as those
fabulous dragon's teeth; and, being sown up and down, may
chance to spring up armed men. And yet, on the other hand,
unless wariness be used, as good almost kill a man as kill
a good book. Who kills a man kills a reasonable creature,
God's image; but he who destroys a good book, kills reason
itself; kills the image of God, as it were, in the eye. Many a
man lives a burden to the earth; but a good book is the precious life-blood of a master-spirit, embalmed and treasured up
on purpose to a life beyond life. 'Tis true no age can restore a
life, whereof, perhaps, there is no great loss; and revolutions
of ages do not oft recover the loss of a rejected truth, for the
want of which whole nations fare the worse. We should be
wary, therefore, what persecution we raise against the living
labours of public men, how we spill that seasoned life of man
preserved and stored up in books; since we see a kind of
homicide may be thus committed, sometimes a martyrdom,

and if it extend to the whole impression, a kind of massacre, whereof the execution ends not in the slaying of an elemental life, but strikes at that ethereal and fifth essence—the breath of reason itself; slays an immortality rather than a life.

John Milton, *Areopagitica*

Shakespeare in Heaven

BOSWELL 'There is a strange unwillingness to part with life, independent of serious fears as to futurity. A reverend friend of ours (naming him) tells me, that he feels an uneasiness at the thoughts of leaving his house, his study, his books.'

JOHNSON 'This is foolish in —— [Percy?]. A man need not be uneasy on these grounds; for, as he will retain his consciousness, he may say with the philosopher, *Omnia mea mecum porto.*'

BOSWELL 'True, Sir: we may carry our books in our heads; but still there is something painful in the thought of leaving for ever what has given us pleasure. I remember, many years ago, when my imagination was warm, and I happened to be in a melancholy mood, it distressed me to think of going into a state of being in which Shakespeare's poetry did not exist. A lady whom I then much admired, a very amiable woman, humoured my fancy, and relieved me by saying. "The first thing you will meet in the other world will be an elegant copy of Shakespeare's works presented to you."'

Dr. Johnson smiled benignantly at this, and did not appear to disapprove of the notion.

James Boswell, *Life of Johnson*

The Libraries of Heaven

I cannot think the glorious world of mind,
   Embalmed in books, which I can only see
In patches, though I read my moments blind,
   Is to be lost to me.

I have a thought that, as we live elsewhere,
   So will these dear creations of the brain;
That what I lose unread, I'll find, and there
   Take up my joy again.

O then the bliss of blisses, to be freed
   From all the wants by which the world is driven;
With liberty and endless time to read
   The libraries of Heaven!

                        Robert Leighton

The Only Things that Last for Ever

Actions pass away and are forgotten, or are only discernible
in their effects; conquerors, statesmen, and kings live but
by their names stamped on the page of history. Hume says
rightly that more people think about Virgil and Homer (and
that continually) than ever trouble their heads about Caesar or
Alexander. In fact, poets are a longer-lived race than heroes:
they breathe more of the air of immortality. They survive
more entire in their thoughts and acts. We have all that Virgil
or Homer did, as much as if we had lived at the same time
with them: we can hold their works in our hands, or lay them
on our pillows, or put them to our lips. Scarcely a trace of
what the others did is left upon the earth, so as to be visible
to common eyes. The one, the dead authors, are living men,
still breathing and moving in their writings. The others, the

conquerors of the world, are but the ashes in an urn. The sympathy (so to speak) between thought and thought is more intimate and vital than that between thought and action. Thought is linked to thought as flame kindles into flame: the tribute of admiration to the manes of departed heroism is like burning incense in a marble monument. Words, ideas, feelings, with the progress of time harden into substances: things, bodies, actions, moulder away, or melt into a sound, into thin air!—Yet though the schoolmen in the Middle Ages disputed more about the texts of Aristotle than the battle of Arbela, perhaps Alexander's Generals in his lifetime admired his pupil as much and liked him better. For not only a man's actions are effaced and vanish with him; his virtues and generous qualities die with him also: his intellect only is immortal and bequeathed unimpaired to posterity. Words are the only things that last for ever.

William Hazlitt, *Table Talk*

The Authors' Metamorphosis

How pleasant it is to reflect, that all these lovers of books have themselves become books! What better metamorphosis could Pythagoras have desired! How Ovid and Horace exulted in anticipating theirs! And how the world have justified their exultation! They had a right to triumph over brass and marble. It is the only visible change which changes no further; which generates and yet is not destroyed. Consider: mines themselves are exhausted; cities perish; kingdoms are swept away, and man weeps with indignation to think that his own body is not immortal.

Muoiono le città, muoiono i regni,
E l'uom d'esser mortal par che si sdegni.

Yet this little body of thought, that lies before me in the shape of a book, has existed thousands of years, nor since the invention of the press can anything short of an universal convulsion of nature abolish it. To a shape like this, so small yet so comprehensive, so slight yet so lasting, so insignificant yet so venerable, turns the mighty activity of Homer, and, so turning, is enabled to live and warm us for ever. To a shape like this turns the placid sage of Academus: to a shape like this the grandeur of Milton, the exuberance of Spenser, the pungent elegance of Pope, and the volatility of Prior. In one small room, like the compressed spirits of Milton, can be gathered together

The assembled souls of all that men held wise.

May I hope to become the meanest of these existences? This is a question which every author who is a lover of books asks himself some time in his life; and which must be pardoned, because it cannot be helped. I know not. I cannot exclaim with the poet,

Oh that my name were numbered among theirs,
Then gladly would I end my mortal days.

For my mortal days, few and feeble as the rest of them may be, are of consequence to others. But I should like to remain visible in this shape. The little of myself that pleases myself I could wish to be accounted worth pleasing others. I should like to survive so, were it only for the sake of those who love me in private, knowing as I do what a treasure is the possession of a friend's mind, when he is no more. At all events, nothing while I live and think can deprive me of my value for such treasures. I can help the appreciation of them while I last, and love them till I die; and perhaps, if fortune turns her face once more in kindness upon me before I go, I may chance, some quiet day, to lay my overheating temples on a book, and so have the death I most envy.

J.H. Leigh Hunt, *My Books*

A Lasting Link of Ages

But words are things, and a small drop of ink,
Falling, like dew, upon a thought, produces
That which makes thousands, perhaps millions, think;
'Tis strange, the shortest letter which man uses
Instead of speech, may form a lasting link
Of ages; to what straits old Time reduces
Frail man, when paper—even a rag like this,
Survives himself, his tomb, and all that's his!

And when his bones are dust, his grave a blank,
His station, generation, even his nation,
Become a thing, or nothing, save to rank
In chronological commemoration,
Some dull MS. oblivion long has sank,
Or graven stone found in a barrack's station
In digging the foundation of a closet,
May turn his name up, as a rare deposit.

And glory long has made the sages smile;
'Tis something, nothing, words, illusion, wind—
Depending more upon the historian's style
Than on the name a person leaves behind:
Troy owes to Homer what whist owes to Hoyle:
The present century was growing blind
To the great Marlborough's skill in giving knocks,
Until his late Life by Archdeacon Coxe.

                    George Gordon, Lord Byron, *Don Juan*

Though they [philosophers] write *contemptu gloriae*, yet, as
Hieron observes, they will put their names to their books.

                                        Robert Burton

Books of the Hour and of All Time

All books are divisible into two classes, the books of the hour, and the books of all time. Mark this distinction— it is not one of quality only. It is not merely the bad book that does not last, and the good one that does. It is a distinction of species. There are good books for the hour, and good ones for all time; bad books for the hour, and bad ones for all time. I must define the two kinds before I go farther.

The good book of the hour, then,—I do not speak of the bad ones—is simply the useful or pleasant talk of some person whom you cannot otherwise converse with, printed for you. Very useful often, telling you what you need to know; very pleasant often, as a sensible friend's present talk would be. These bright accounts of travels; good-humoured and witty discussions of question; lively or pathetic story-telling in the form of novel; firm fact-telling, by the real agents concerned in the events of passing history;—all these books of the hour, multiplying among us as education becomes more general, are a peculiar characteristic and possession of the present age: we ought to be entirely thankful for them, and entirely ashamed of ourselves if we make no good use of them. But we make the worst possible use, if we allow them to usurp the place of true books: for, strictly speaking, they are not books at all, but merely letters or newspapers in good print.... A book is written, not to multiply the voice merely, not to carry it merely, but to preserve it. The author has something to say which he perceives to be true and useful, or helpfully beautiful. So far as he knows, no one has yet said it; so far as he knows, no one else can say it. He is bound to say it, clearly and melodiously if he may; clearly, at all events. In the sum of his life he finds this to be the thing, or group of things, manifest to him;—this the piece of true knowledge, or sight, which his share of sunshine and earth has permitted him to seize. He would fain set it down for ever; engrave it on rock, if he could; saying, 'This is the best of me; for the rest, I ate, and drank, and slept, loved, and hated, like another; my life was as the vapour, and is not; but this I saw and knew: this, if anything of mine, is worth your memory.' That is his 'writing'; it is, in his small human way, and with whatever degree of true inspiration is in him, his inscription, or scripture. That is a 'Book'....

Now books of this kind have been written in all ages by their greatest men:—by great leaders, great statesmen, and great thinkers. These are all at your choice; and life is short. You have heard as much before; yet have you measured and mapped out this short life and its possibilities? Do you know, if you read this, that you cannot read that—that what you lose to-day you cannot gain to-morrow? Will you go and gossip with your housemaid, or your stable-boy, when you may talk with queens and kings; or flatter yourselves that it is with any worthy consciousness of your own claims to respect that you jostle with the common crowd for *entrée* here, and audience there, when all the while this eternal court is open to you, with its society wide as the world, multitudinous as its days, the chosen, and the mighty, of every place and time? Into that you may enter always; in that you may take fellowship and rank according to your wish; from that, once entered into it, you can never be outcast but by your own fault; by your aristocracy of companionship there, your own inherent aristocracy will be assuredly tested, and the motives with which you strive to take high place in the society of the living, measured, as to all the truth and sincerity that are in them, by the place you desire to take in this company of the Dead.

John Ruskin, Sesame and Lilies

Action and Reaction

Some of the well-puffed fashionable novels of eighteen
hundred and twenty-nine hold the pastry of eighteen hundred
and thirty; and others, which are now extolled in language
almost too high-flown for the merits of *Don Quixote*, will,
we have no doubt, line the trunks of eighteen hundred and
thirty-one.

Thomas Macaulay, *Mr. Robert Montgomery's Poems*

Who Will Believe My Verse

Who will believe my verse in time to come,
If it were filled with your most high deserts?
Though yet, heaven knows, it is but as a tomb
Which hides your life and shows not half your parts.
If I could write the beauty of your eyes
And in fresh numbers number all your graces,
The age to come would say, 'This poet lies;
Such heavenly touches ne'er touched earthly faces.'
So should my papers, yellowed with their age,
Be scorned, like old men of less truth than tongue,
And your true rights be termed a poet's rage
And stretchèd metre of an antique song:
   But were some child of yours alive that time,
   You should live twice,—in it and in my rhyme.

William Shakespeare

Immortality in Song

How many paltry, foolish, painted things,
That now in coaches trouble every street,
Shall be forgotten, whom no poet sings,
Ere they be well wrapped in their winding-sheet!

Where I to thee eternity shall give,
When nothing else remaineth of these days,
And queens hereafter shall be glad to live
Upon the alms of thy superfluous praise;
Virgins and matrons reading these my rhymes,
Shall be so much delighted with thy story,
That they shall grieve they lived not in these times,
To have seen thee, their sex's only glory:
   So shalt thou fly above the vulgar throng,
   Still to survive in my immortal song.

                            Michael Drayton

One Day I Wrote Her Name

One day I wrote her name upon the strand,
But came the waves and washed it away:
Again I wrote it with a second hand,
But came the tide and made my pains his prey.
'Vain man,' said she, 'that dost in vain essay
A mortal thing so to immortalize;
For I myself shall like to this decay,
And eke my name be wipèd out likewise
'Not so,' quoth I; 'let baser things devise
To die in dust, but you shall live by fame;
My verse your virtues rare shall eternize,
And in the heavens write your glorious name:
   Where, whenas Death shall all the world subdue,
   Our love shall live, and later life renew.'

                           Edmund Spenser

Well I Remember How You Smiled

Well I remember how you smiled
  To see me write your name upon
The soft sea-sand—*'O! what a child!*
  You think you're writing upon stone!'

I have since written what no tide
  Shall ever wash away, what men
Unborn shall read o'er ocean wide
  And find Ianthe's name again.

Walter Savage Landor

The Multiplicity of Books

Solomon saith truly, Of making many books there is no end, so insatiable is the thirst of men therein; as also endless is the desire of many in buying and reading them. But we come to our rules.

1. *It is a vanity to persuade the world one hath much learning, by getting a great library.* As soon shall I believe every one is valiant that hath a well-furnished armoury. I guess good housekeeping by the smoking, not the number of the tunnels, as knowing that many of them, built merely for uniformity, are without chimneys, and more without fires. Once a dunce void of learning but full of books flouted a libraryless scholar with these words: *Salve doctor sine libris.* But the next day the scholar coming into this jeerer's study, crowded with books; *Salvete libri*, saith he, *sine doctore.*

2. *Few books, well selected, are best.* Yet, as a certain fool bought all the pictures that came out, because he might have his choice, such is the vain humour of many men in gathering of books: yet when they have done all, they miss their end, it being in the editions of authors as in the fashions of clothes, when a man thinks he hath gotten the latest and newest, presently another newer comes out.

3. *Some books are only cursorily to be tasted of.* Namely, first, voluminous books, the task of a man's life to read them over; secondly, auxiliary books, only to be repaired to on occasions; thirdly, such as are mere pieces of formality, so that if you look on them, you look through them; and he that peeps through the casement of the index sees as much as if he were in the house. But the laziness of those cannot be excused who perfunctorily pass over authors of consequence, and only trade in their tables and contents. These, like city-cheaters, having gotten the names of all country gentlemen, make silly people believe they have long lived in those places where they never were, and flourish with skill in those authors they never seriously studied.

4. *The genius of the author is commonly discovered in the dedicatory epistle.* Many place the purest grain in the mouth of the sack for chapmen to handle or buy: and from the dedication one may probably guess at the work, saving some rare and peculiar exceptions. Thus, when once a gentleman admired how so pithy, learned, and witty a dedication was matched to a flat, dull, foolish book; *In truth,* said another, *they may be well matched together, for I profess they are nothing akin.*

5. *Proportion an hour's meditation to an hour's reading of a staple author.* This makes a man master of his learning, and dispirits the book into the scholar. The king of Sweden never filed his men above six deep in one company, because he would not have them lie in useless clusters in his army, but so that every particular soldier might be drawn out into service. Books that stand thin on the shelves, yet so as the owner of them can bring forth every one of them into use, are better than far greater libraries....

But what do I, speaking against multiplicity of books in this age, who trespass in this nature myself? What was a learned man's compliment, may serve for my confession and conclusion: *Multi mei similes hoc morbo laborant, ut cum scribere nesciant tamen a scribendo temperare non possint.*

Thomas Fuller, *The Holy State and the Profane State*

Multiplication is Vexation

The reason that books are multiplied, in spite of the general law that beings shall not be multiplied without necessity, is, that books are made from books. A new history of France or Spain is manufactured from several volumes already printed, without adding anything new. All dictionaries are made from dictionaries: almost all new geographical books are made from other books of geography; St. Thomas's dream has brought forth two thousand large volumes of divinity; and the same race of little worms that have devoured the parent are now gnawing the children.

Voltaire, *Philosophical Dictionary: Books*

The Multiplication of Originals

The invention of printing has not, perhaps, multiplied books, but only the copies of them; and if we believe there were six hundred thousand in the library of Ptolemy, we shall hardly pretend to equal it by any of ours, nor, perhaps, by all put together; I mean so many originals that have lived any time, and thereby given testimony to their having been thought worth preserving. For the scribblers are infinite, that like mushrooms or flies are born and die in small circles of time; whereas books, like proverbs, receive their chief value from the stamp and esteem of ages through which they have passed.

Sir William Temple, *Ancient and Modern Learning*

The Authors' Advantage

The circumstance which gives authors an advantage ... is this, that they can multiply their originals; or rather can make copies of their works, to what number they please, which shall be as valuable as the originals themselves. This gives a great author something like a prospect of eternity, but at the same time deprives him of those other advantages which artists meet with. The artist finds greater returns in profit, as the author in fame. What an inestimable price would a Virgil or a Homer, a Cicero or an Aristotle bear, were their works like a statue, a building, or a picture, to be confined only in one place, and made the property of a single person!

Joseph Addison, *Spectator*, 166

An Ignorant Age Hath Many Books

It is observed that *a corrupt society has many laws*; I know not whether it is not equally true, that *an ignorant age has many books*. When the treasures of ancient knowledge lie unexamined, and original authors are neglected and forgotten, compilers and plagiaries are encouraged who give us again what we had before, and grow great by setting before us what our own sloth had hidden from our view.

Samuel Johnson, *Idler*, 85

The Distraction of Choice

Under our present enormous accumulation of books, I do affirm, that a miserable distraction of choice (which is the germ of such a madness) must be very generally incident to the times; that the symptoms of it are, in fact, very prevalent; and that one of the chief symptoms is an enormous 'gluttonism' for books, and for adding language to language; and in this way it is that literature becomes much more a source of torment than of pleasure. Nay, I will go further, and will say that of many, who escape this disease, some owe their privilege simply to the narrowness of their minds and the contracted range of their sympathies with literature—which enlarged, they would soon lose it! others, again, owe it to their situation; as, for instance, in a country town, where, books being few, a man can use up all his materials, his appetite is unpalled—and he is grateful for the loan of a MS., &c.: but bring him up to London—show him the wagon-loads of unused stores—which he is at liberty to work up—tell him that these even are but a trifle, perhaps, to what he may find in the libraries of Paris, Dresden, Milan, &c.—of religious houses—of English noblemen, &c.; and this same man, who came up to London blithe and happy, will leave it pale and sad. You have ruined his peace of mind: a subject which he fancied himself capable of exhausting, he finds to be a labour for centuries: he has no longer the healthy pleasure of feeling himself master of his materials; he is degraded into their slave.

Thomas De Quincey, Letters to a Young Man

A Library of Twelve

You may get the whole of Sir Thomas Browne's works more easily than the *Hydrotaphia* in a single form.... If I were confined to a score of English books, this I think would be one of them; nay, probably, it would be one if the selection were cut down to twelve. My library, if reduced to those bounds, would consist of Shakespeare, Chaucer, Spenser, and Milton; Lord Clarendon; Jackson, Jeremy Taylor, and South; Isaac Walton, Sidney's *Arcadia*, Fuller's *Church History*, and Sir Thomas Browne; and what a wealthy and well-stored mind would that man have, what an inexhaustible reservoir, what a Bank of England to draw upon for profitable thoughts and delightful associations, who should have fed upon them.

Robert Southey, letter to G.C. Bedford

The Battle of the Books

Immediately the two main bodies withdrew, under their several ensigns, to the farther parts of the library, and there entered into cabals and consults upon the present emergency. The Moderns were in very warm debates upon the choice of their leaders; and nothing less than the fear impending from their enemies could have kept them from mutinies upon this occasion. The difference was greatest among the horse, where every private trooper pretended to the chief command, from Tasso and Milton to Dryden and Wither. The light-horse were commanded by Cowley and Despreaux. There came the bowmen under their valiant leaders, Descartes, Gassendi, and Hobbes; whose strength was such that they could shoot their arrows beyond the atmosphere, never to fall down again, but turn, like that of Evander, into meteors; or, like the cannon-ball, into stars. Paracelsus brought a squadron of stinkpot-flingers from the snowy mountains of Rhaetia. There came a vast body of dragoons, of different nations, under the leading of Harvey, their great aga: part armed with scythes, the weapons of death; part with lances and long knives, all steeped in poison; part shot bullets of a most malignant nature, and used white powder, which infallibly killed without report. There came several bodies of heavy-armed foot, all mercenaries, under the ensigns of Guiccardini, Davila, Polydore, Virgil, Buchanan, Mariana, Camden, and others. The engineers were commanded by Regiomontanus and Wilkins. The rest was a confused multitude, led by Scotus, Aquinas, and Bellarmine; of mighty bulk and stature, but without either arms, courage, or discipline. In the last place came infinite swarms of calones, a disorderly rout led by L'Estrange; rogues and ragamuffins, that follow the camp for nothing but the plunder, all without coats to cover them.

The Army of the Ancients was much fewer in number; Homer led the horse, and Pindar the light-horse; Euclid was chief engineer; Plato and Aristotle commanded the bowmen;

Herodotus and Livy the foot; Hippocrates, the dragoons; the allies, led by Vossius and Temple, brought up the rear.

All things violently tending to a decisive battle, Fame, who much frequented, and had a large apartment assigned her in the regal library, fled up straight to Jupiter, to whom she delivered a faithful account of all that passed between the two parties below; for among the Gods she always tells truth. Jove, in great concern, convokes a council in the Milky Way. The senate assembled, he declares the occasion of convening them; a bloody battle just impendent between two mighty armies of ancient and modern creatures, called books, wherein the celestial interest was but too deeply concerned. Momus, the patron of the Moderns, made an excellent speech in their favour, which was answered by Pallas, the protectress of the Ancients. The assembly was divided in their affections; when Jupiter commanded the Book of Fate to be laid before him. Immediately were brought by Mercury three large volumes in folio, containing memoirs of all things past, present, and to come. The clasps were of silver double gilt, the covers of celestial turkey leather, and the paper such as here on earth might almost pass for vellum. Jupiter, having silently read the decree, would communicate the import to none, but presently shut up the book. ...

Meanwhile Momus, fearing the worst, and calling to mind an ancient prophecy which bore no very good face to his children the Moderns, bent his flight to the region of a malignant deity called Criticism. She dwelt on the top of a snowy mountain in Nova Zembla; there Momus found her extended in her den, upon the spoils of numberless volumes, half devoured. At her right hand sat Ignorance, her father and husband, blind with age; at her left, Pride, her mother, dressing her up in the scraps of paper herself had torn. There was Opinion, her sister, light of foot, hood-winked, and headstrong, yet giddy and perpetually turning. About her played her children, Noise and Impudence, Dullness and Vanity, Positiveness, Pedantry, and Ill-manners.... 'Goddess,' said Momus, 'can you sit idly here while our devout worshippers, the Moderns, are this minute entering into a cruel battle, and perhaps now lying under the swords of their enemies? Who then hereafter will ever sacrifice or build altars to our divinities? Haste, therefore, to the British Isle, and, if possible, prevent their destruction; while I make factions among the gods, and gain them over to our party.' ...

The goddess and her train, having mounted the chariot, which was drawn by tame geese, flew over infinite regions, shedding her influence in due places, till at length she arrived at her beloved island of Britain; but in hovering over its metropolis, what blessings did she not let fall upon her seminaries of Gresham and Covent Garden! And now she reached the fatal plain of St. James's library, at what time the two armies were upon the point to engage; where, entering with all her caravan unseen, and landing upon a case of shelves, now desert, but once inhabited by a colony of virtuosos, she stayed awhile to observe the posture of both armies.

Jonathan Swift, *The Battle of the Books*

Old Authors to Read

Alonso of Aragon was wont to say, in commendation of Age, that Age appeared to be best in four things; Old wood best to burn, old wine to drink, old friends to trust, and old authors to read.

Francis Bacon, *Apophthegmes*

The Moons of Literature

Sir, ... we must read what the world reads at the moment. It
has been maintained that this superfoetation, this teeming of
the press in modern times, is prejudicial to good literature,
because it obliges us to read so much of what is of inferior
value, in order to be in the fashion; so that better works
are neglected for want of time, because a man will have
more gratification of his vanity in conversation, from having
read modern books than from having read the best books
of antiquity. But it must be considered, that we have now
more knowledge generally diffused; all our ladies read now,
which is a great extension. Modern writers are the moons of
literature; they shine with reflected light, with light borrowed
from the ancients. Greece appears to me to be the fountain of
knowledge; Rome of elegance.

Samuel Johnson, Boswell's Life

The Reading of New Books

*From Lien Chi Altangi to Fum Hoam, First President of the
Ceremonial Academy at Pekin, in China*

There are numbers in this city who live by writing new
books; and yet there are thousands of volumes in every large
library unread and forgotten. This, upon my arrival, was one
of those contradictions which I was unable to account for. Is
it possible, said I, that there should be any demand for new
books before those already published are read? Can there be
so many employed in producing a commodity with which the
market is overstocked; and with goods also better than any of
modern manufacture!

What at first view appeared an inconsistency is a proof at
once of this people's wisdom and refinement. Even allowing
the works of their ancestors better written than theirs, yet

those of the moderns acquire a real value, by being marked with the impression of the times. Antiquity has been in the possession of others; the present is our own: let us first therefore learn to know what belongs to ourselves, and then, if we have leisure, cast our reflections back to the reign of Shonsu, who governed twenty thousand years before the creation of the moon.

The volumes of antiquity, like medals, may very well serve to amuse the curious; but the works of the moderns, like the current coin of a kingdom, are much better for immediate use; the former are often prized above their intrinsic value, and kept with care, the latter seldom pass for more than they are worth, and are often subject to the merciless hands of sweating critics and clipping compilers: the works of antiquity were ever praised, those of the moderns read; the treasures of our ancestors have our esteem, and we boast the passion; those of contemporary genius engage our heart, although we blush to own it. The visits we pay the former resemble those we pay the great; the ceremony is troublesome, and yet such as we would not choose to forgo; our acquaintance with modern books is like sitting with a friend; our pride is not flattered in the interview, but it gives more internal satisfaction....

In England, where there are as many new books published as in all the rest of Europe together, a spirit of freedom and reason reigns among the people; they have been often known to act like fools, they are generally found to think like men.

Oliver Goldsmith, *Letters from a Citizen of the World*

The Classics Always Modern

In science read, by preference, the newest works; in literature, the oldest. The classic literature is always modern. New
books revive and re-decorate old ideas; old books suggest and
invigorate new ideas.

Edward Bulwer-Lytton, *Caxtoniana*

On Reading Old Books

I hate to read new books. There are twenty or thirty volumes
that I have read over and over again, and these are the only
ones that I have any desire ever to read at all. It was a long
time before I could bring myself to sit down to the *Tales
of My Landlord*, but now that author's works have made a
considerable addition to my scanty library.... Women judge
of books as they do of fashions or complexions, which are
admired only 'in their newest gloss'. That is not my way. I am
not one of those who trouble the circulating libraries much,
or pester the booksellers for mail-coach copies of standard
periodical publications. I cannot say that I am greatly addicted
to black-letter, but I profess myself well versed in the marble
bindings of Andrew Millar, in the middle of the last century;
nor does my taste revolt at Thurloe's *Stale Papers*, in russia
leather; or an ample impression of Sir William Temple's
Essays, with a portrait after Sir Godfrey Kneller in front. I do
not think altogether the worse of a book for having survived
the author a generation or two. I have more confidence in the
dead than the living.... When I take up a work that I have
read before (the oftener the better), I know what I have to
expect. The satisfaction is not lessened by being anticipated.
When the entertainment is altogether new, I sit down to it as
I should to a strange dish—turn and pick out a bit here and
there, and am in doubt what to think of the composition.
There is a want of confidence and security to second appetite.

New-fangled books are also like made-dishes in this respect, that they are generally little else than hashes and *rifaccimentos* of what has been served up entire and in a more natural state at other times. Besides, in thus turning to a well-known author, there is not only an assurance that my time will not be thrown away, or my palate nauseated with the most insipid or vilest trash, but I shake hands with, and look an old, tried, and valued friend in the face, compare notes, and chat the hours away. It is true, we form dear friendships with such ideal guests—dearer, alas! and more lasting, than those with our most intimate acquaintance. In reading a book which is an old favourite with me (say the first novel I ever read) I not only have the pleasure of imagination and of a critical relish of the work, but the pleasures of memory added to it. It recalls the same feelings and associations which I had in first reading it, and which I can never have again in any other way. Standard productions of this kind are links in the chain of our conscious being. They bind together the different scattered divisions of our personal identity. They are landmarks and guides in our journey through life. They are pegs and loops on which we can hang up, or from which we can take down, at pleasure, the wardrobe of a moral imagination, the relics of our best affections, the tokens and records of our happiest hours. They are 'for thoughts and for remembrance'! They are like Fortunatus's Wishing Cap—they give us the best riches—those of Fancy; and transport us, not over half the globe, but (which is better) over half our lives, at a word's notice!

My father Shandy solaced himself with Bruscambille. Give me for this purpose a volume of *Peregrine Pickle* or *Tom Jones*. Open either of them anywhere—at the memoirs of Lady Vane, or the adventures at the masquerade with Lady Bellaston, or the disputes between Thwackum and Square, or the escape of Molly Seagrim, or the incident of Sophia and her muff, or the edifying prolixity of her aunt's lecture—and there I find the same delightful, busy, bustling scene as ever,

and feel myself the same as when I was first introduced into
the midst of it. Nay, sometimes the sight of an odd volume of
these good old English authors on a stall, or the name lettered
on the back among others on the shelves of a library, answers
the purpose, revives the whole train of ideas, and sets 'the
puppets dallying'. Twenty years are struck off the list, and
I am a child again. A sage philosopher, who was not a very
wise man, said, that he should like very well to be young
again, if he could take his experience along with him. This
ingenious person did not seem to be aware, by the gravity
of his remark, that the great advantage of being young is to
be without this weight of experience, which he would fain
place upon the shoulders of youth, and which never comes
too late with years. Oh! what a privilege to be able to let this
hump, like Christian's burthen, drop from off one's back, and
transport oneself, by the help of a little musty duodecimo,
to the time when ignorance was bliss and when we first got
a peep at the raree-show of the world, through the glass of
fiction— gazing at mankind, as we do at wild beasts in a
menagerie, through the bars of their cages—or at curiosities
in a museum, that we must not touch! For myself, not only
are the old ideas of the contents of the work brought back
to my mind in all their vividness, but the old associations of
the faces and persons of those I then knew, as they were in
their lifetime—the place where I sat to read the volume, the
day when I got it, the feeling of the air, the fields, the sky—
return, and all my early impressions with them. This is better
to me—those places, those times, those persons, and those
feelings that come across me as I retrace the story and devour
the page, are to me better far than the wet sheets of the last
new novel.

William Hazlitt, The Plain Speaker

On Reading New Books

I cannot understand the rage manifested by the greater part
of the world for reading new books. If the public had read
all those that have gone before, I can conceive how they
should not wish to read the same work twice over; but
when I consider the countless volumes that lie unopened,
unregarded, unread, and unthought of, I cannot enter into
the pathetic complaints that I hear made that Sir Walter
writes no more—that the press is idle—that Lord Byron is
dead. If I have not read a book before, it is, to all intents and
purposes, new to me, whether it was printed yesterday or
three hundred years ago. If it be urged that it has no modern,
passing incidents, and is out of date and old-fashioned, then it
is so much the newer; it is farther removed from other works
that I have lately read, from the familiar routine of ordinary
life, and makes so much more addition to my knowledge. But
many people would as soon think of putting on old armour
as of taking up a book not published within the last month,
or year at the utmost. There is a fashion in reading as well
as in dress, which lasts only for the season. One would
imagine that books were, like women, the worse for being
old; that they have a pleasure in being read for the first time;
that they open their leaves more cordially; that the spirit of
enjoyment wears out with the spirit of novelty; and that,
after a certain age, it is high time to put them on the shelf.
This conceit seems to be followed up in practice.... The
knowledge which so many other persons have of its contents
deadens our curiosity and interest altogether. We set aside
the subject as one on which others have made up their minds
for us (as if we really could have ideas in their heads), and are
quite on the alert for the next new work, teeming hot from
the press, which we shall be the first to read, criticize, and
pass an opinion on. Oh, delightful! To cut open the leaves,
to inhale the fragrance of the scarcely dry paper, to examine
the type to see who is the printer (which is some clue to the

value that is set upon the work), to launch out into regions of thought and invention never trod till now, and to explore characters that never met a human eye before—this is a luxury worth sacrificing a dinner-party, or a few hours of a spare morning to. Who, indeed, when the work is critical and full of expectation, would venture to dine out, or to face a coterie of blue-stockings in the evening, without having gone through this ordeal, or at least without hastily turning over a few of the first pages, while dressing, to be able to say that the beginning does not promise much, or to tell the name of the heroine?

A new work is something in our power; we mount the bench, and sit in judgement on it; we can damn or recommend it to others at pleasure, can decry or extol it to the skies, and can give an answer to those who have not yet read it, and expect an account of it; and thus show our shrewdness and the independence of our taste before the world have had time to form an opinion. If we cannot write ourselves, we become, by busying ourselves about it, a kind of *accessories after the fact*.

William Hazlitt, Sketches and Essays

The Value of Modern Books

The great productions of Athenian and Roman genius are indeed still what they were. But though their positive value is unchanged, their relative value, when compared with the whole mass of mental wealth possessed by mankind, has been constantly falling. They were the intellectual all of our ancestors. They are but a part of our treasures. Over what tragedy could Lady Jane Grey have wept, over what comedy could she have smiled, if the ancient dramatists had not been in her library? A modern reader can make shift without *Oedipus* and *Medea*, while he possesses *Othello* and *Hamlet*. If he knows nothing of *Pyrgopolynices* and *Thraso*, he is familiar with *Bobadil*, and *Bessus*, and *Pistol*, and *Parolles*. If he cannot enjoy the delicious irony of Plato, he may find some compensation in that of Pascal. If he is shut out from *Nephelococcygia*, he may take refuge in *Lilliput* ... We believe that the books which have been written in the languages of Western Europe, during the last two hundred and fifty years—translations from the ancient languages of course included,—are of greater value than all the books which at the beginning of that period were extant in the world.

Thomas Macaulay, Lord Bacon

A Sort of Third Estate

Each age, it is found, must write its own books; or, rather, each generation for the next succeeding. The books of an older period will not fit this. Yet hence arises a grave mischief. The sacredness which attaches to the act of crea-tion—the act of thought—is transferred to the record. The poet chanting, was felt to be a divine man: henceforth the chant is divine also. The writer was a just and wise spirit; henceforward it is settled, the book is perfect; as love of the hero corrupts into worship of his statue. Instantly, the book becomes noxious: the guide is a tyrant. The sluggish and perverted mind of the multitude, slow to open to the incursions of Reason, having once so opened, having once received this book, stands upon it, and makes an outcry if it is disparaged. Colleges are built on it. Books are written on it by thinkers, not by Man Thinking; by men of talent, that is, who start wrong, who set out from accepted dogmas, not from their own sight of principles. Meek young men grow up in libraries, believing it their duty to accept the views which Cicero, which Locke, which Bacon, have given, forgetful that Cicero, Locke, and Bacon were only young men in libraries when they wrote these books.

Hence, instead of Man Thinking, we have the book-worm. Hence, the book-learned class, who value books as such; not as related to nature and the human constitution, but as making a sort of Third Estate with the world and the soul. Hence, the restorers of readings, the emendators, the bibliomaniacs of all degrees.

Books are the best of things, well used; abused, among the worst.

Ralph Waldo Emerson, The American Scholar

Old and New Books

Old books, as you well know, are books of the world's youth, and new books are fruits of its age. How many of all these ancient folios round me are like so many old cupels? The gold has passed out of these long ago, but their pores are full of the dross with which it was mingled.

Oliver Wendell Holmes,
The Professor at the Breakfast-Table

Security in Old Books

What a sense of security in an old book which Time has criticized for us! What a precious feeling of seclusion in having a double wall of centuries between us and the heats and clamours of contemporary literature! How limpid seems the thought, how pure the old wine of scholarship that has been settling for so many generations in those silent crypts and Falernian *amphorae* of the Past! No other writers speak to us with the authority of those whose ordinary speech was that of our translation of the Scriptures; to no modern is that frank unconsciousness possible which was natural to a period when reviews were not; and no later style breathes that country charm characteristic of days ere the metropolis drew all literary activity to itself, and the trampling feet of the multitude had banished the lark and the daisy from the fresh privacies of language. Truly, as compared with the present, these old voices seem to come from the morning fields and not the paved thoroughfares of thought....

There are volumes which have the old age of Plato, rich with gathering experience, meditation, and wisdom, which seem to have sucked colour and ripeness from the genial autumns of all the select intelligences that have steeped them in the sunshine of their love and appreciation;—these quaint freaks of russet tell of Montaigne; these stripes of crimson fire, of Shakespeare; this sober gold, of Sir Thomas Browne; this purpling bloom, of Lamb;—in such fruits we taste the legendary gardens of Alcinoüs and the orchards of Atlas; and there are volumes again which can claim only the inglorious senility of Old Parr or older Jenkins, which have outlived their half-dozen of kings to be the prize of showmen and treasuries of the born-to-be-forgotten trifles of a hundred years ago....

There is to us a sacredness in a volume, however dull; we live over again the author's lonely labours and tremulous hopes; we see him, on his first appearance after parturition, 'as well as could be expected,' a nervous sympathy yet surviving between the late-severed umbilical cord and the wondrous offspring, doubtfully entering the Mermaid, or the Devil Tavern, or the Coffee-house of Will or Button, blushing under the eye of Ben or Dryden or Addison, as if they must needs know him for the author of the *Modest Enquiry into the Present State of Dramatique Poetry*, or of the *Unities briefly considered by Philomusus*, of which they have never heard and never will so much as hear the names; we see the country-gentlemen (sole cause of its surviving to our day) who buy it as a book no gentleman's library can be complete without; we see the spendthrift heir, whose horses and hounds and Pharaonic troops of friends, drowned in a Red Sea of claret, bring it to the hammer, the tall octavo in tree-calf following

the ancestral oaks of the park. Such a volume is sacred to us.
But it must be the original foundling of the book-stall, the
engraved blazon of some extinct baronetcy within its cover,
its leaves enshrining memorial-flowers of some passion smoth-
ered while the Stuarts were not yet unkinged, suggestive
of the trail of laced ruffles, burnt here and there with ashes
from the pipe of some dozing poet, its binding worn and
weather-stained, that has felt the inquisitive finger, perhaps, of
Malone, or thrilled to the touch of Lamb, doubtful between
desire and the odd sixpence. When it comes to a question of
reprinting we are more choice. The new duodecimo is bald
and bare, indeed, compared with its battered prototype that
could draw us with a single hair of association.

J.R. Lowell, *Library of Old Authors*

To My Book

It will be looked for, book, when some but see
   Thy title, Epigrams, and named of me,
Thou shouldst be bold, licentious, full of gall,
   Wormwood and sulphur, sharp, and toothed withal,
Become a petulant thing, hurl ink and wit
   As madmen stones; not caring whom they hit.
Deceive their malice, who could wish it so;
   And by thy wiser temper let men know
Thou art not covetous of least self-fame,
   Made from the hazard of another's shame:
Much less with lewd, profane, and beastly phrase,
   To catch the world's loose laughter, or vain gaze.
He that departs with his own honesty
   For vulgar praise, doth it too dearly buy.

Ben Jonson

Books and Thieves

A good book steals the mind from vain pretences,
From wicked cogitations and offences;
It makes us know the world's deceiving pleasures,
And set our hearts on never-ending treasures.
So when thieves steal our cattle, coin, or ware,
It makes us see how mutable they are:
Puts us in mind that we should put our trust
Where felon cannot steal or canker rust.
Bad books through eyes and ears do break and enter,
And take possession of the heart's frail centre,
Infecting all the little kingdom man
With all the poisonous mischief that they can,
Till they have robbed and ransacked him of all
Those things which men may justly goodness call;
Rob him of virtue and of heavenly grace,
And leave him beggared in a wretched state.
So of our earthly goods, thieves steal the best.
And richest jewels, and leave us the rest.
Men know not thieves from true men by their looks.
Nor by their outsides no man can know books.
Both are to be suspected, all can tell.
And wise men, ere they trust, will try them well:
Some books not worth the reading for their fruits,
Some thieves not worth the hanging, for their suits.
And as with industry, and art, and skill
One thief doth daily rob another still,
So one book from another, in this age,
Steals many a line, a sentence, or a page.
And as the veriest thief may have some friend
So the worst books some knave will still defend.
...
Still books and thieves in one conceit do join,
For, if you mark them, they are all for coin.

John Taylor, An Arrant Thief

Mountebank Authors

They [the Stationers] have so pestered their printing-
houses and shops with fruitless volumes that the ancient
and renowned authors are almost buried among them as
forgotten; and that they have so much work to prefer their
termly pamphlets, which they provide to take up the people's
money and time, that there is neither of them left to bestow
on a profitable book; so they who desire knowledge are still
kept ignorant; their ignorance increaseth their affection to
vain toys; their affection makes the stationer to increase his
provision of such stuff, and at last you shall see nothing to be
sold amongst us but Curranto's *Bevis of Southampton* or such
trumpery. The Arts are already almost lost among the writings of mountebank authors. For if any one among us would
study Physic, the Mathematics, Poetry, or any of the liberal
sciences, they have in their warehouses so many volumes of
quack-salving receipts; of false propositions; and of inartificial
rhymings (of which last sort they have some of mine there,
God forgive me!) that unless we be directed by some artist,
we shall spend half our age before we can find those authors
which are worth our readings. For what need the stationer
be at the charge of printing the labours of him that is master
of his art, and will require that respect which his pain
deserveth, seeing he can hire for a matter of forty shillings
some needy ignoramus to scribble upon the same subject, and
by a large promising title, make it as vendible for an impression or two, as though it had the quintessence of all art?

George Wither, The Scholler's Purgatory

Printers Gain by Bad Books

Learning hath gained most by those books by which the printers have lost. Arius Montanus, in printing the Hebrew Bible, commonly called the Bible of the king of Spain, much wasted himself, and was accused in the court of Rome for his good deed, and being cited thither, *Pro tantorum laborum praemio vix veniam impetravit.* Likewise Christopher Plantin, by printing of his curious interlineary Bible in Antwerp, through the unseasonable exactions of the king's officers, sunk and almost ruined his estate. And our worthy English knight, who set forth the golden-mouthed father in a silver print, was a loser by it.

Whereas foolish pamphlets prove most beneficial to the printers. When a French printer complained that he was utterly undone by printing a solid serious book of Rabelais concerning physic, Rabelais, to make him recompense, made that his jesting scurrilous work, which repaired the printer's loss with advantage. Such books the world swarms too much with. When one had set out a witless pamphlet, writing *finis* at the end thereof, another wittily wrote beneath it:

———*Nay there thou liest, my friend,*
In writing foolish books there is no end.

And surely such scurrilous scandalous papers do more than conceivable mischief. First, their lusciousness puts many palates out of taste, that they can never after relish any solid and wholesome writers; secondly, they cast dirt on the faces of many innocent persons, which dried on by continuance of time can never after be washed off; thirdly, the pamphlets of this age may pass for records with the next, because publicly uncontrolled, and what we laugh at, our children may believe: fourthly, grant the things true they jeer at, yet this music is unlawful in any Christian church, to play upon the sins and miseries of others, the fitter object of the elegies than the satires of all truly religious.

Thomas Fuller, *The Holy State and the Profane State*

The Evil that Men Do

If writings are thus durable, and may pass from age to age throughout the whole course of time, how careful should an author be of committing anything to print that may corrupt posterity, or poison the minds of men with vice and error! Writers of great talents, who employ their parts in propagating immorality, and seasoning vicious sentiments with wit and humour, are to be looked upon as the pests of society and the enemies of mankind: they leave books behind them, as it is said of those who die in distempers which breed an ill will towards their own species, to scatter infection and destroy their posterity. They act the counterparts of a Confucius or a Socrates; and seem to have been sent into the world to deprave human nature, and sink it into the condition of brutality.

Joseph Addison, *Spectator*, 166

He who has published an injurious book, sins, as it were, in his very grave; corrupts others while he is rotting himself.

Robert South

On Certain Books

Faith and fixed hope these pages may peruse,
And still be faith and hope; but, O ye winds!
Blow them far off from all unstable minds,
And foolish grasping hands of youth! Ye dews
Of heaven! be pleased to rot them where they fall,
Lest loitering boys their fancies should abuse,
And they get harm by chance, that cannot choose;
So be they stained and sodden, each and all!
And if, perforce, on dry and gusty days,

Upon the breeze some truant leaf should rise,
Brittle with many weathers, to the skies,
Or flit and dodge about the public ways—
Man's choral shout, or organ's peal of praise
Shall shake it into dust, like older lies.

C. Tennyson Turner

To the Pure All Things are Pure

'To the pure all things are pure'; not only meats and drinks,
but all kind of knowledge, whether of good or evil; the
knowledge cannot defile, nor consequently the books, if the
will and conscience be not defiled. For books are as meats
and viands are, some of good, some of evil substance; and
yet God, in that unapocryphal vision, said without exception,
'Rise, Peter, kill and eat'; leaving the choice to each man's
discretion. Wholesome meats to a vitiated stomach differ
little or nothing from unwholesome; and best books to a
naughty mind are not unapplicable to occasions of evil. Bad
meats will scarce breed good nourishment in the healthiest
concoction; but herein the difference is of bad books, that
they to a discreet and judicious reader serve in many respects
to discover to confute, to forewarn and to illustrate.... If it
be true that a wise man, like a good refiner, can gather gold
out of the drossiest volume, and that a fool will be a fool
with the best book, yea, or without book, there is no reason
that we should deprive a wise man of any advantage to his
wisdom, while we seek to restrain from a fool that which
being restrained will be no hindrance to his folly.

John Milton, Areopagitica

Liberty and Bad Books

The men who died to buy us liberty knew that it was better
to let in a thousand bad books than shut out one good one.
We cannot, then, silence evil books, but we can turn away
our eyes from them; we can take care that what we read, and
what we let others read, should be good and wholesome.

Charles Kingsley, *Village Sermons: On Books*

Bad Books and Debauched Minds

Books will perhaps be found, in a less degree than is commonly imagined, the corrupters of the morals of mankind.
They form an effective subsidiary to events and the contagion
of vicious society; but, taken by themselves, they rarely
produce vice and profligacy where virtue existed before.
Everything depends upon the spirit in which they are read.
He that would extract poison from them, must for the most
part come to them with a mind already debauched. The
power of books in generating virtue is probably much greater
than in generating vice.

William Godwin, *The Inquirer: Of Choice in Reading*

Virginibus Puerisque

To read my book, the virgin shy
May blush, while Brutus standeth by:
But when he's gone, read through what's writ,
And never stain a cheek for it.

Robert Herrick, *Hesperides*

A Whimsical Surprise

I should not care to be caught in the serious avenues of some cathedral alone, and reading *Candide*.

I do not remember a more whimsical surprise than having been once detected—by a familiar damsel—reclined at my ease upon the grass, on Primrose Hill (her Cythera), reading—*Pamela*. There was nothing in the book to make a man seriously ashamed at the exposure; but as she seated herself down by me, and seemed determined to read in company, I could have wished it had been—any other book. We read on very sociably for a few pages; and, not finding the author much to her taste, she got up, and—went away. Gentle casuist, I leave it to thee to conjecture, whether the blush (for there was one between us) was the property of the nymph or the swain in this dilemma. From me you shall never get the secret.

Charles Lamb, *Detached Thoughts on Books and Reading*

Romances are Pernicious

Make careful choice of the books which you read. Let the Holy Scriptures ever have the pre-eminence, and next them, the solid, lively, heavenly treatises which best expound and apply the Scriptures; and next those, the credible histories, especially of the Church, and tractates upon inferior sciences and arts: but take heed of the poison of the writings of false teachers, which would corrupt your understandings: and of vain romances, play-books, and false stories, which may bewitch your fantasies and corrupt your hearts.

To a very judicious able reader, who is fit to censure all he reads, there is no great danger in the reading of the Books of any seducers: it doth but show him how little and thin a cloak is used to cover a bad cause. But alas, young soldiers, not used to such wars, are startled at a very sophism, or at a terrible threatening of damnation to dissenters (which every censorious sect can use) or at every confident triumphant boast, or at everything that hath a fair pretence of truth or godliness ... Meddle not therefore with poison, till you better know how to use it, and may do it with less danger; as long as you have no need.

As for play-books, and romances, and idle tales, I have already showed, in my *Book of Self-denial*, how pernicious they are, especially to youth, and to frothy, empty, idle wits, that know not *what a man is*, nor what he hath to do in the world. They are powerful baits of the Devil, to keep more necessary things out of their minds, and better books out of their hands, and to poison the mind so much the more dangerously, as they are read with more delight and pleasure.

Richard Baxter, Christian Directory

The Danger of Poets and Romances

It is impossible for me, by any words that I can use, to express, to the extent of my thoughts, the danger of suffering young people to form their opinions from the writings of poets and romances. Nine times out of ten, the morality they teach is bad, and must have a bad tendency. Their wit is employed to *ridicule virtue*, as you will almost always find, if you examine the matter to the bottom. The world owes a very large part of its sufferings to tyrants; but what tyrant was there amongst the ancients, whom the poets did not place *amongst the gods?* Can you open an English poet without, in some part or other of his works, finding the grossest flatteries of royal and noble persons? How are young people not to think that the praises bestowed on these persons are just? Dryden, Parnell, Gay, Thomson, in short, what poet have we had, or have we, Pope only excepted, who was not, or is not, a pensioner, or a sinecure placeman, or the wretched dependant of some part of the Aristocracy? Of the extent of the power of writers in producing mischief to a nation, we have two most striking instances in the cases of Dr. Johnson and Burke.... It is, therefore, the duty of every father, when he puts a book into the hands of his son or daughter, to give the reader a true account of *who* and *what* the writer of the book was, or is.

> William Cobbett, *Advice to Young Men and (incidentally)*
> *to Young Women in the Middle and Higher Ranks of Life*

A Daughter's Favourite Novels

I could make neither head nor tail of it; it was neither fish, flesh, nor good red herring: it was all about my Lord, and Sir Harry, and the Captain ... The people talk such wild gibberish as no folks in their sober senses ever did talk; and the things that happen to them are not like the things that ever happen to me or any of my acquaintance. They are at home one minute, and beyond the sea the next; beggars to-day, and lords to-morrow; waiting-maids in the morning, and duchesses at night ... One would think every man in these books had the bank of England in his escritoire ... In these books (except here and there one, whom they make worse than Satan himself), every man and woman's child of them, are all wise, and witty, and generous, and rich, and handsome, and genteel, and all to the last degree. Nobody is middling, or good in one thing and bad in another, like my live acquaintance; but it is all up to the skies, or down to the dirt. I had rather read *Tom Hickathrift*, or *Jack the Giant Killer*, a thousand times.

> Hannah More, *The Two Wealthy Farmers*

Only a Novel

'What are you reading, Miss ——?' 'Oh! It's only a novel!' replies the young lady; while she lays down her book with affected indifference, or momentary shame. 'It is only *Cecilia*, or *Camilla*, or *Belinda*'; or, in short, only some work in which the greatest powers of the mind are displayed; in which the most thorough knowledge of human nature, the happiest delineation of its varieties, the liveliest effusions of wit or humour, are conveyed to the world in the best chosen language.

Jane Austen, *Northanger Abbey*

Novels as Engines of Civilization

The listlessness and want of sympathy with which most of the works written expressly for circulation among the labouring classes are read by them, if read at all, arises mainly from this—that the story told, or the lively or friendly style assumed, is *manifestly* and *palpably* only a cloak for the instruction intended to be conveyed—a sort of gilding of what they cannot well help fancying must be a pill, when they see so much and such obvious pains taken to wrap it up ... You will find that in the higher and better class of works of fiction and imagination duly circulated, you possess all that you require to strike your grappling-iron into their souls, and chain them, willing followers, to the car of civilization ... The novel, in its best form, I regard as one of the most powerful engines of civilization ever invented.

Sir John Herschel, *Address to the Subscribers to the Windsor Public Library*

A Novel of High Life

Lord Harry has written a novel,
    A story of elegant life;
No stuff about love in a hovel,
    No sketch of a commoner's wife:
No trash, such as pathos and passion,
    Fine feelings, expression, and wit;
But all about people of fashion,
    Come look at his caps—how they fit!

O Radcliffe! thou once wert the charmer
    Of girls who sat reading all night;
Thy heroes were striplings in armour,
    Thy heroines damsels in white.
But past are thy terrible touches,
    Our lips in derision we curl,
Unless we are told how a Duchess
    Conversed with her cousin the Earl.

We now have each dialogue quite full
    Of titles—'I give you my word,
My lady, you're looking delightful';
    'O dear, do you think so, my lord!'
'You've heard of the marquis's marriage.
    The bride with her jewels new set,
Four horses, new travelling carriage,
    And *déjeuner à la fourchette?'*

Haut Ton finds her privacy broken,
    We trace all her ins and her outs;
The very small talk that is spoken
    By very great people at routs,
At Tenby Miss Jinks asks the loan of
    The book from the innkeeper's wife,
And reads till she dreams she is one of
    The leaders of elegant life.

T.H. Bayly

Lady Constance ... guanoed her mind by reading French novels.

Benjamin Disraeli, Tancred

Novels are Sweets

Novels are sweets. All people with healthy literary appetites love them—almost all women;—a vast number of clever, hard-headed men. Why, one of the most learned physicians in England said to me only yesterday, 'I have just read *So-and-So* for the second time' (naming one of Jones's exquisite fictions). Judges, bishops, chancellors, mathematicians, are notorious novel-readers; as well as young boys and sweet girls, and their kind, tender mothers.

William Makepeace Thackeray,
Roundabout Papers: On a Lazy Idle Boy

Plagiarie

He [King Charles I, in his *Eikon Basilike*] borrows David's Psalmes, as he charges the Assembly of Divines in his twentieth Discourse, To *have set forth old Catechisms and confessions of faith new drest*. Had he borrowed David's heart, it had been much the holier theft. For such kind of borrowing as this, if it be not bettered by the borrower, among good Authors is accounted Plagiarie. However, this was more tolerable than Pamela's prayer, stolen out of Sir Philip.

John Milton, Eikonoklastes

Transplantation

I number not my borrowings, but I weigh them. And if I
would have made their number to prevail, I would have had
twice as many. They are all, or almost all, of so famous and
ancient names, that methinks they sufficiently name themselves without me. If in reasons, comparisons, and arguments,
I transplant any into my soil, or confound them with mine
own, I purposely conceal the author, thereby to bridle the
rashness of these hasty censures that are so headlong cast
upon all manner of compositions, namely, young writings
of men yet living. ... I will have them to give Plutarch a bob
upon mine own lips, and vex themselves in wronging Seneca
in me.

Michel de Montaigne

Book-Makers and Plagiarists

Some that turn over all books, and are equally searching
in all papers; that write out of what they presently find or
meet, without choice; by which means it happens that what
they have discredited and impugned in one work, they have
before or after extolled the same in another. Such are all the
Essayists, even their master Montaigne. These in all they
write confess still what books they have read last, and therein
their own folly so much that they bring it to the stake raw
and undigested; not that the place did need it neither, but that
they thought themselves furnished and would vent it.

Some again, who, after they have got authority, or, which
is less, opinion, by their writings, to have read much, dare
presently to feign whole books and authors, and lie safely.
For what never was will not easily be found, not by the most
curious.

And some, by a cunning protestation against all reading,
and false venditation of their own naturals, think to divert the

sagacity of their readers from themselves, and cool the scent of their fox-like thefts, when yet they are so rank as a man may find whole pages together usurped from one author.

Ben Jonson, Timber

A Learned Plagiary

The greatest man of the last age, Ben Jonson, was willing to give place to the classics in all things: he was not only a professed imitator of Horace, but a learned plagiary of all the others; you track him everywhere in their snow. If Horace, Lucan, Petronius Arbiter, Seneca, and Juvenal had their own from him, there are few serious thoughts which are new in him.... But he has done his robberies so openly, that one may see he fears not to be taxed by any law. He invades authors like a monarch and what would be theft in other poets, is only victory in him.

John Dryden, Essay of Dramatic Poesy

Hidden Treasure

Writers ... are apter to be beholding to books than to men, not only as the first are more in their possession, being more constant companions than dearest friends, but because they commonly make such use of treasure found in books as of other treasure belonging to the dead and hidden under ground; for they dispose of both with great secrecy, defacing the shape or images of the one as much as of the other, through fear of having the original of their stealth or abundance discovered. And the next cause why writers are more in libraries than in company is that books are easily opened, and learned men are usually shut up by a froward or envious humour of retention, or else unfold themselves so as we may read more of their weakness and vanity than wisdom, imitating the holiday-custom in great cities, where the shops of chandlery and slight wares are familiarly open, but those of solid and staple merchandise are proudly locked up.

Sir William Davenant, Gondibert

Literary Cookery

We have been reading a treatise on the morality of Shakespeare; it is a happy and easy way of filling a book, that the present race of authors have arrived at—that of criticizing the works of some eminent poet: with monstrous extracts and short remarks. It is a species of cookery I begin to grow tired of; they cut up their authors into chops, and by adding a little crumbled bread of their own, and tossing it up a little, they present it as a fresh dish; you are to dine upon the poet;—the critic supplies the garnish; yet has the credit, as well as profit, of the whole entertainment.

Hannah More, Memoirs

The Manufactory of Books

To a veteran like myself, who have watched the books of forty seasons, there is nothing so old as a new book. An astonishing sameness and want of individuality pervades modern books. The ideas they contain do not seem to have passed through the mind of the writer. They have not even that originality—the only originality which John Mill in his modesty would claim for himself—'which every thoughtful mind gives to its own mode of conceiving and expressing truths which are common property'—(*Autobiography*). When you are in London step into the reading-room of the British Museum. There is the great manufactory out of which we turn the books of the season. It was so before there was any British Museum. It was so in Chaucer's time—

For out of the old fields, as men saith,
Cometh all this new corn from year to year,
And out of old books in good faith
Cometh all this new science that men lere.

It continued to be so in Cervantes' day. 'There are,' says he in *Don Quixote*, 'men who will make you books and turn them loose in the world, with as much dispatch as they would do a dish of fritters.'

It is not, then, any wonder that De Quincy should account it 'one of the misfortunes of life that one must read thousands of books only to discover that one need not have read them'.... And I cannot doubt that Bishop Butler had observed the same phenomenon when he wrote, in 1729: 'The great number of books of amusement which daily come in one's way, have in part occasioned this idle way of considering things. By this means time, even in solitude, is happily got rid of without the pain of attention; neither is any part of it more put to the account of idleness, one can scarce forbear saying is spent with less thought, than great part of that which is spent in reading.'

Mark Pattison, Fortnightly Review: Books and Critics

How Volumes Swell

The muse shall tell
How science dwindles, and how volumes swell;
How commentators each dark passage shun,
And hold their farthing candles to the sun;
How tortured texts to speak our sense are made,
And every vice is to the scripture laid.

Edward Young, Love of Fame

Recipe for an Anthology

Our modern wits are not to reckon upon the infinity of
matter for a constant supply. What remains, therefore, but
that our last recourse must be had to large indexes and little
compendiums? quotations must be plentifully gathered, and
booked in alphabet; to this end, though authors need to be
little consulted, yet critics, and commentators, and lexicons
carefully must. But, above all, those judicious collectors of
bright parts, and flowers, and *observandas*, are to be nicely
dwelt on; by some called the sieves and coulters of learning,
though it is left undetermined whether they dealt in pearls
or meal, and consequently, whether we are more to value
that which passed through, or what stayed behind. By these
methods, in a few weeks, there starts up many a writer
capable of managing the profoundest and most universal
subjects. For what though his head be empty, provided his
commonplace book be full? And if you will bate him but
the circumstances of method, and style, and grammar, and
invention; allow him but the common privileges of transcrib-
ing from others, and digressing from himself, as often as he
shall see occasion; he will desire no more ingredients towards
fitting up a treatise that shall make a very comely figure on
a bookseller's shelf; there to be preserved neat and clean for
a long eternity, adorned with the heraldry of its title fairly
inscribed on a label; never to be thumbed or greased by
students, nor bound to everlasting chains of darkness in a
library.

Jonathan Swift, A *Tale of a Tub*

His Invention is no more than the finding out of his papers,
and his few gleanings there, and his disposition of them is just
as the book-binder's, a setting or glueing of them together.

John Earle, *Microcosmographie*

Good God! how many dungboats full of fruitless works do they yearly foist on his Majesty's subjects; how many hundred reams of foolish, profane, and senseless ballads do they quarterly disperse abroad.

George Wither

Our Master, Meleager

Our master, Meleager, he who framed
    The first Anthology and daintiest,
Mated each minstrel with a flower, and named
    For each the blossom that beseemed him best.
'Twas then as now; garlands were somewhat rare,
    Candidates many: one in doleful strain
Lamented thus, 'This is a sad affair;
    How shall I face my publisher again?
Lacking some emblem suitable for me,
    My book's undone; I shall not sell a copy.'
'Take courage, son,' quoth Phoebus, 'there must be
    Somewhere or other certainly a poppy.'

Richard Garnett

'Tis pleasant, sure, to see one's name in print;
A book's a book, although there's nothing in 't.

George Gordon, Lord Byron

That Invention of the Enemy—An Abridgement

All my life long I have delighted in voluminous works; in other words, I have delighted in that sort of detail which permits so intimate a familiarity with the subjects of which it treats ...
Even in this world of Beauties, and of Extracts, I do not believe myself quite alone in my love of the elaborate and the minute;

and yet I doubt if many people contemplate very long very
big books with the sense of coming enjoyment which such a
prospect gives me; and few shrink, as I do, with aversion and
horror from that invention of the enemy—an Abridgement.
I never shall forget the shock I experienced in seeing Bruce,
that opprobrium of an unbelieving age, that great and graphic
traveller, whose eight or nine goodly volumes took such
possession of me, that I named a whole colony of Bantams after
his Abyssinian princes and princesses, calling a little golden
strutter of a cock after that arch-tyrant the Ras Michael; and a
speckled hen, the beauty of the poultry-yard, Ozoro Ester, in
honour of the Ras's favourite wife— I never felt greater disgust
than at seeing this magnificent work cut down to a thick,
dumpy volume, seven inches by five; except, perhaps, when
I happened to light upon another pet book—Drinkwater's
Siege of Gibraltar, where I had first learned to tremble at the
grim realities of war, had watched day by day the firing of the
red-hot balls, had groped my way through the galleries, and
taken refuge in the casemates,—degraded from the fair proportions of a goodly quarto into the thin and meagre pamphlet
of a lending library, losing a portion of its lifelike truth with
every page that was cut away.

Mary Russell Mitford, *Recollections of a Literary Life*

Original Editions

We love, we own, to read the great productions of the human
mind as they were written. We have this feeling even about
scientific treatises; though we know that the sciences are
always in a state of progression, and that the alterations made
by a modern editor in an old book on any branch of natural
or political philosophy are likely to be improvements. Some
errors have been detected by writers of this generation in the
speculations of Adam Smith. A short cut has been made to
much knowledge at which Sir Isaae Newton arrived through

arduous and circuitous paths. Yet we still look with peculiar veneration on the *Wealth of Nations* and on the *Principia*, and should regret to see either of those great works garbled even by the ablest hands. But in works which owe much of their interest to the character and situation of the writers the case is infinitely stronger. What man of taste and feeling can endure *rifacimenti*, harmonies, abridgements, expurgated editions? Who ever reads a stage-copy of a play when he can procure the original? Who ever cut open Mrs. Siddons's *Milton*? Who ever got through ten pages of Mr. Gilpin's translation of John Bunyan's *Pilgrim* into modern English? Who would lose, in the confusion of a *Diatessaron*, the peculiar charm which belongs to the narrative of the disciple whom Jesus loved? The feeling of a reader who has become intimate with any great original work is that which Adam expressed towards his bride:

> Should God create another Eve, and I
> Another rib afford, yet loss of thee
> Would never from my heart.

No substitute, however exquisitely formed, will fill the void left by the original. The second beauty may be equal or superior to the first; but still it is not she.

Thomas Macaulay, *Boswell's Life of Johnson*

Dedications

Above all the rest, the gross and palpable flattery whereunto many not unlearned have abased and abused their wits and pens, turning (as Du Bartas saith) Hecuba into Helena, and Faustina into Lucretia, hath most diminished the price and estimation of learning. Neither is the modern dedication of books and writings, as to patrons, to be commended: for that books (such as are worthy the name of books) ought to have no patrons but truth and reason.

Francis Bacon, *Of the Advancement of Learning*

Presentation Copies

I want to read you some new passages from an interleaved copy of my book. You haven't read the printed part yet. I gave you a copy of it, but nobody reads a book that is given to him. Of course not. Nobody but a fool expects him to. He reads a little in it here and there, perhaps, and he cuts all the leaves if he cares enough about the writer, who will be sure to call on him some day, and if he is left alone in his library for five minutes will have hunted every corner of it until he has found the book he sent,—if it is to be found at all, which doesn't always happen, if there's a penal colony anywhere in a garret or closet for typographical offenders and vagrants.

Oliver Wendell Holmes, *The Poet at the Breakfast-Table*

Poets and their Bibliographies

Old poets fostered under friendlier skies,
    Old Virgil who would write ten lines, they say,
    At dawn, and lavish all the golden day
To make them wealthier in his readers' eyes;
And you, old popular Horace, you the wise
    Adviser of the nine-years-pondered lay.
    And you, that wear a wreath of sweeter bay,
Catullus, whose dead songster never dies;
If glancing downward on the kindly sphere
    That once had rolled you round and round the Sun,
    You see your Art still shrined in human shelves,
You should be jubilant that you flourished here
    Before the Love of Letters, overdone,
Had swampt the sacred poets with themselves.

Alfred, Lord Tennyson

Men in their Nightgowns

Writing of Lives is very profitable, both to the memory of
the party, and to posterity. They do better lance into secret
humours, and present men in their nightgowns, when they are
truly themselves. A general may be more perfectly discovered
on his pallet, than when he appears in the head of an army.

John Hall, *Horae Vacivae*

Biography

Oh, that mine enemy had written a book!—and that it were
my life; unless indeed it provoked my friend to write another.

It has always appeared to me a strong argument for the
non-existence of spirits that these friendly microscopic biographers are not haunted by the ghosts of the unfortunate men
whom they persist in holding up to public contempt.

Sir Arthur Helps, *Thoughts in the Cloister*

Biography Preferred to History

Read French authors. Read Rochefoucauld. The French
writers are the finest in the world, for they clear our heads of
all ridiculous ideas....

Read no history, nothing but biography, for that is life
without theory.

Benjamin Disraeli, *Contarini Fleming*

On Reading Translations

The respectable and sometimes excellent translations of
Bohn's Library have done for literature what railroads have
done for internal intercourse. I do not hesitate to read all
the books I have named, and all good books, in translations.
What is really best in any book is translatable,—any real
insight or broad human sentiment. Nay, I observe that, in
our Bible, and other books of lofty moral tone, it seems
easy and inevitable to render the rhythm and music of the
original into phrases of equal melody. The Italians have a
fling at translators,—*i traditori traduttori*; but I thank them.
I rarely read any Latin, Greek, German, Italian, sometimes
not a French book in the original, which I can procure in a
good version. I like to be beholden to the great metropolitan
English speech, the sea which receives tributaries from every
region under heaven. I should as soon think of swimming
across the Charles River when I wish to go to Boston, as of
reading all my books in originals, when I have them rendered
for me in my mother-tongue.

Ralph Waldo Emerson, *Books*

Translations from the Classics

Others again here lived in my days
That have of us deservèd no less praise
For their translations than the daintiest wit
That on Parnassus thinks he highest doth sit.
And for a chair may 'mongst the Muses call
As the most curious maker of them all:
As reverent Chapman, who hath brought to us
Musaeus, Homer, and Herodotus
Out of the Greek, and by his skill hath reared
Them to that height and to our tongue endeared

That, were those poets at this day alive
To see their books thus with us to survive,
They would think, having neglected them so long,
They had been written in the English tongue.

Michael Drayton, *To Henry Reynolds*

It is good to have translations, because they serve as a
comment, so far as the judgement of one man goes.

John Selden

On First Looking into Chapman's Homer

Much have I travelled in the realms of gold,
And many goodly states and kingdoms seen;
Round many western islands have I been
Which bards in fealty to Apollo hold.
Oft of one wide expanse had I been told
That deep-browed Homer ruled as his demesne;
Yet did I never breathe its pure serene
Till I heard Chapman speak out loud and bold:
Then felt I like some watcher of the skies
When a new planet swims into his ken;
Or like stout Cortez when with eagle eyes
He stared at the Pacific—and all his men
Looked at each other with a wild surmise—
Silent, upon a peak in Darien.

John Keats

To My Worthy and Honoured Friend
Master George Chapman

Whose work could this be, Chapman, to refine
Old Hesiod's ore, and give it thus! but thine,
Who hadst before wrought in rich Homer's mine.

What treasure hast thou brought us! and what store
Still, still, dost thou arrive with at our shore,
To make thy honour and our wealth the more!

If all the vulgar tongues that speak this day
Were asked of thy discoveries, they must say,
To the Greek coast thine only knew the way.

Such passage hast thou found, such returns made,
As now of all men, it is called thy trade,
And who make thither else, rob or invade.

Ben Jonson

When Translations are to be Preferred

The reason the classics are not read is because there still
lingers a tradition, handed down from the eighteenth century,
that it is useless to read them unless in the original. A tone of
sarcastic contempt is maintained towards the person who shall
presume to peruse Xenophon not in the original Greek, or
Virgil not in the original Latin.

In the view of these critics it is the Greek, it is the Latin,
that is valuable, not the contents of the volume. Shakespeare,
however, the greatest genius of England, thought otherwise.
It is known that his ideas of Grecian and Roman history were
derived from somewhat rude translations, yet it is acknowledged that the spirit of the ancient warriors and of the ancient
luxury lives in his *Antony and Cleopatra*, and nowhere in all the

ancient writers is there a poem breathing the idea of Aphrodite like his *Venus and Adonis*. The example of so great a genius may shield us in an effort to free the modern mind from this eighteenth-century incubus.

The truth is, the classics are much better understood in a good translation than in the original. To obtain a sufficient knowledge of Greek, for instance, to accurately translate is almost the work of a lifetime. Concentration upon this one pursuit gradually contracts the general perceptions, and it has often happened that an excellent scholar has been deficient in common knowledge, as shown by the singular character of his own notes. But his work of translation in itself is another matter.

It is a treasure; from it poets derive their illustrations; dramatists their plots; painters their pictures. A young mind full of intelligence, coming to such a translation, enters at once into the spirit of the ancient writer. A good translation is thus better than the original.

Richard Jefferies, The Dewy Morn

Quotation

In quoting of books, quote such authors as are usually read; others you may read for your own satisfaction, but not name them.

Quoting of authors is most for matter of fact; and then I write them as I would produce a witness; sometimes for a free expression, and then I give the author his due, and gain myself praise by reading him.

To quote a modern Dutchman where I may use a classic author, is as if I were to justify my reputation, and I neglect all persons of note and quality that know me, and bring the testimonial of the scullion in the kitchen.

John Selden, Table Talk

Merit in Quotation

Next to the originator of a good sentence is the first quoter of it.... We are as much informed of a writer's genius by what he selects as by what he originates. We read the quotation with his eyes, and find a new and fervent sense; as a passage from one of the poets, well recited, borrows new interest from the rendering. As the journals say, 'the italics are ours.' The profit of books is according to the sensibility of the reader. The profoundest thought or passion sleeps as in a mine, until an equal mind and heart finds and publishes it. The passages of Shakespeare that we most prize were never quoted until within this century; and Milton's prose, and Burke, even, have their best fame within it. Every one, too, remembers his friends by their favourite poetry or other reading.

Observe, also, that a writer appears to more advantage in the pages of another book than in his own. In his own, he waits as a candidate for your approbation; in another's he is a lawgiver.

Ralph Waldo Emerson, *Quotation and Originality*

On the Portrait of Shakespeare

This figure that thou here seest put,
It was for gentle Shakespeare cut,
Wherein the graver had a strife
With Nature, to outdo the life.
Oh, could he but have drawn his wit
As well in brass, as he has hit
His face, the print would then surpass
All that was ever writ in brass.
But, since he cannot, reader, look
Not on his picture, but his book.

Ben Jonson

Shakespeare's Livelong Monument

What needs my Shakespeare for his honoured bones,
The labour of an age in pilèd stones.
Or that his hallowed relics should be hid
Under a star-ypointing pyramid?
Dear son of Memory, great heir of Fame,
What need'st thou such weak witness of thy name?
Thou in our wonder and astonishment
Hast built thyself a livelong monument.
For whilst to the shame of slow-endeavouring art,
Thy easy numbers flow, and that each heart
Hath from the leaves of thy unvalued book,
Those Delphic lines with deep impression took,
Then thou our fancy of itself bereaving,
Dost make us marble with too much conceiving;
And so sepulchred in such pomp dost lie,
That kings for such a tomb would wish to die.

John Milton

Under Mr Milton's Picture
before his 'Paradise Lost'

Three Poets, in three distant ages born,
Greece, Italy, and England did adorn.
The first in loftiness of thought surpassed,
The next in majesty, in both the last:
The force of Nature could no farther go;
To make a third she joined the former two.

John Dryden

Books of Morality

Books of morality are daily written, yet its influence is still little in the world; so the ground is annually ploughed, and yet multitudes are in want of bread. But, surely, neither the labours of the moralist nor of the husbandman are vain: let them for a while neglect their tasks and their usefulness will be known; the wickedness that is now frequent would become universal, the bread that is now scarce would wholly fail.

Samuel Johnson, *Adventurer*, 137

The Secret Influence of Books

Books have always a secret influence on the understanding: we cannot at pleasure obliterate ideas; he that reads books of science, though without any fixed desire of improvement, will grow more knowing; he that entertains himself with moral or religious treatises will imperceptibly advance in goodness; the ideas which are often offered to the mind will at last find a lucky moment when it is disposed to receive them.

Samuel Johnson, *Adventurer*, 137

Dead Counsellors are Safest

It was the maxim, I think, of Alphonsus of Aragon that *dead counsellors are safest*. The grave puts an end to flattery and artifice, and the information that we receive from books is pure from interest, fear, or ambition. Dead counsellors are likewise most instructive, because they are heard with patience and with reverence. We are not unwilling to believe that man wiser than ourselves from whose abilities we may receive advantage without any danger of rivalry or opposition, and who affords us the light of his experience without hurting our eyes by flashes of insolence.

Samuel Johnson, *Rambler*, 87

The Real Working Effective Church

But to the Church itself, as I hinted already, all is changed, in its preaching, in its working, by the introduction of Books. The Church is the working recognized Union of our Priests or Prophets, of those who by wise teaching guide the souls of men. While there was no Writing, even while there was no Easy-writing, or *Printing*, the preaching of the voice was the natural sole method of performing this. But now with Books!—He that can write a true Book, to persuade England, is not he the Bishop and Archbishop, the Primate of England and of all England? I many a time say, the writers of News-papers, Pamphlets, Poems, Books, these *are* the real working effective Church of a modern country. Nay, not only our preaching, but even our worship, is not it too accomplished by means of Printed Books?... Fragments of a real 'Church Liturgy 'and 'Body of Homilies', strangely disguised from the common eye, are to be found weltering in that huge froth-ocean of Printed Speech we loosely call Literature! Books are our Church too.

On all sides, are we not driven to the conclusion that, of the things which man can do or make here below, by far the most momentous, wonderful and worthy are the things we call Books! Those poor bits of rag-paper with black ink on them;—from the Daily Newspaper to the sacred Hebrew Book, what have they not done, what are they not doing!— For indeed, whatever be the outward form of the things (bits of paper, as we say, and black ink), is it not verily, at bottom, the highest act of man's faculty that produces a Book? It is the *Thought* of man; the true thaumaturgic virtue; by which man works all things whatsoever. All that he does, and brings to pass, is the vesture of a Thought. This London City, with all its houses, palaces, steam-engines, cathedrals, and huge immeasurable traffic and tumult, what is it but a Thought, but millions of Thoughts made into One;—a huge immeasurable Spirit of a Thought, embodied in brick, iron, smoke, dust, Palaces, Parliaments, Hackney Coaches, Katherine Docks, and the rest of it! Not a brick was made but some man had to *think* of the making of that brick.—The thing we called 'bits of paper with traces of black ink', is the *purest* embodiment a Thought of man can have. No wonder it is, in all ways, the activest and noblest.

Thomas Carlyle, Heroes and Hero-Worship

Books as Sign-posts

The modern scholars have their usual recourse to the Universities of their countries; some few, it may be, to those of their neighbours; and this in quest of books rather than men for their guides, though these are living and those in comparison but dead instructors, which, like a hand with an inscription, can point out the straight way upon the road, but can neither tell you the next turnings, resolve your doubts, or answer your questions, like a guide that has traced it over, and perhaps knows it as well as his chamber. And who are these dead guides we seek in our journey? They are at best but some few authors that remain among us of a great many that wrote in Greek and Latin from the age of Hippocrates to that of Marcus Antoninus, which reaches not much above six hundred years.

Sir William Temple, Ancient and Modern Learning

The Need of a Guide to Books

The colleges, whilst they provide us with libraries, furnish
no professor of books; and, I think, no chair is so much
wanted. In a library we are surrounded by many hundreds
of dear friends, but they are imprisoned by an enchanter
in these paper and leathern boxes; and, though they know
us, and have been waiting two, ten, or twenty centuries for
us,—some of them,—and are eager to give us a sign, and
unbosom themselves, it is the law of their limbo that they
must not speak until spoken to; and as the enchanter has
dressed them, like battalions of infantry, in coat and jacket of
one cut, by the thousand and ten thousand, your chance of
hitting on the right one is to be computed by the arithmetical
rule of Permutation and Combination,—not a choice out of
three caskets, but out of half a million caskets all alike. But
it happens in our experience, that in this lottery there are
at least fifty or a hundred blanks to a prize. It seems, then,
as if some charitable soul, after losing a great deal of time
among the false books, and alighting upon a few true ones
which made him happy and wise, would do a right act in
naming those which have been bridges or ships to carry him
safely over dark morasses and barren oceans, into the heart
of sacred cities, into palaces and temples. This would be best
done by those great masters of books who from time to time
appear,—the Fabricii, the Seldens, Magliabecchis, Scaligers,
Mirandolas, Bayles, Johnsons, whose eyes sweep the whole
horizon of learning. But private readers, reading purely for
love of the book, would serve us by leaving each the shortest
note of what he found.

Ralph Waldo Emerson, Books

The True University of these Days

To look at Teaching, for instance. Universities are a notable, respectable product of the modern ages. Their existence too is modified, to the very basis of it, by the existence of Books. Universities arose while there were yet no Books procurable; while a man, for a single Book, had to give an estate of land. That, in those circumstances, when a man had some knowledge to communicate, he should do it by gathering the learners round him, face to face, was a necessity for him. If you wanted to know what Abelard knew, you must go and listen to Abelard. Thousands, as many as thirty thousand, went to hear Abelard and that metaphysical theology of his. And now for any other teacher who had also something of his own to teach, there was a great convenience opened: so many thousands eager to learn were already assembled yonder; of all places the best place for him was that. For any third teacher it was better still; and grew ever the better, the more teachers there came. It only needed now that the King took notice of this new phenomenon; combined or agglomerated the various schools into one school; gave it edifices, privileges, encouragements, and named it *Universitas*, or School of all Sciences: the University of Paris, in its essential characters, was there. The model of all subsequent Universities; which down even to these days, for six centuries now, have gone on to found themselves. Such, I conceive, was the origin of Universities. It is clear, however, that with this simple circumstance, facility of getting Books, the whole conditions of the business from top to bottom were changed. Once invent Printing, you metamorphosed all Universities, or superseded them! The Teacher needed not now to gather men personally round him, that he might *speak* to them what he knew: print it in a Book, and all learners far and wide, for a trifle, had it each at his own fireside, much more effectually to learn it!—Doubtless there is still peculiar virtue in Speech; even writers of Books may still, in some circumstances, find it convenient to speak also,—witness our present meeting here! There is, one would say, and must ever remain while man has a tongue, a distinct province for Speech as well as for Writing and Printing. In regard to all things this must remain; to Universities among others. But the limits of the two have nowhere yet been pointed out, ascertained; much less put in practice: the University which would completely take-in that great new fact, of the existence of Printed Books, and stand on a clear footing for the Nineteenth Century as the Paris one did for the Thirteenth, has not yet come into existence. If we think of it, all that a University, or final highest School, can do for us, is still but what the first School began doing—teach us to *read*. We learn to *read*, in various languages, in various sciences; we learn the alphabet and letters of all manner of Books. But the place where we are to get knowledge, even theoretic knowledge, is the Books themselves! It depends on what we read, after all manner of Professors have done their best for us. The true University of these days is a Collection of Books.

Thomas Carlyle, *Heroes and Hero-Worship*

Oxford and Cambridge: Two Epigrams

The King observing with judicious eyes
The state of both his Universities,
To one he sent a regiment: for why?
That learned body wanted loyalty.
To the other he sent books, as well discerning
How much that loyal body wanted learning.

Joseph Trapp

The King to Oxford sent his troop of horse,
For Tories own no argument but force;
With equal care to Cambridge books he sent,
For Whigs allow no force but argument.

Sir William Browne

Books will speak plain, when counsellors blanch.

Francis Bacon, *Of Counsell*

Against Writers that Carp at Other Men's Books

The readers and the hearers like my books,
And yet some writers cannot them digest;
But what care I? for when I make a feast,
I would my guests should praise it, not the cooks.

Sir John Harington

A Critic

is one that has spelt over a great many of books, and his
observation is the orthography. He is the surgeon of old
authors, and heals the wounds of dust and ignorance. He
converses much in fragments and *Desunt multa*'s, and if he
piece it up with two lines, he is more proud of that book than
the author. He runs over all sciences to peruse their syntaxes,
and thinks all learning comprised in writing Latin. He tastes
styles, as some discreeter palaters do wine; and tells you
which is genuine, which sophisticate and bastard. His own
phrase is a miscellany of old words, deceased long before the
Caesars, and entombed by Varro, and the modernest man he
follows is Plautus. He writes *Omneis* at length, and *quicquid*,
and his gerund is most inconformable. He is a troublesome
vexer of the dead, which after so long sparing must rise up
to the judgement of his castigations. He is one that makes all
books sell dearer, whilst he swells them into folios with his
comments.

John Earle, *Microcosmographie*

Style v. Sense

Others for language all their care express,
And value books, as women men, for dress:
Their praise is still,—the style is excellent:
The sense, they humbly take upon content.
Words are like leaves; and where they most abound,
Much fruit of sense beneath is rarely found.

Alexander Pope, *Essay on Criticism*

Where Fools Rush In

The bookful blockhead, ignorantly read,
With loads of learned lumber in his head,
With his own tongue still edifies his ears,
And always listening to himself appears.
All books he reads, and all he reads assails,
From Dryden's *Fables* down to D'Urfey's *Tales*.
With him, most authors steal their works, or buy;
Garth did not write his own *Dispensary*.
Name a new play, and he's the poet's friend,
Nay, showed his faults—but when would poets mend?
No place so sacred from such fops is barred,
Nor is Paul's church more safe than Paul's churchyard.
Nay, fly to altars; there they'll talk you dead:
For fools rush in where angels fear to tread.

Alexander Pope, *Essay on Criticism*

Literary Hypocrisy

There are some subjects of which almost all the world perceive the futility; yet all combine in imposing upon each other as worthy of praise. But chiefly this imposition obtains in literature, where men publicly contemn what they relish with rapture in private, and approve abroad what has given them disgust at home.

Oliver Goldsmith, *Letters from a Citizen of the World*

In the Seat of the Scorner

They who are in the habit of passing sentence upon books,— and what ignoramus in our days does not deem himself fully qualified for sitting in the seat of the scorner?—are apt to think that they have condemned a work irretrievably, when they have pronounced it to be unintelligible. Unintelligible to whom? To themselves, the self-constituted judges. So that their sentence presumes their competency to pronounce it: and this, to every one save themselves, may be exceedingly questionable.

It is true, the very purpose for which a writer publishes his thoughts, is, that his readers should share them with him. Hence the primary requisite of a style is its intelligibleness: that is to say, it must be capable of being understood. But intelligibleness is a relative quality, varying with the capacity of the reader. The easiest book in a language is inaccessible to those who have never set foot within the pale of that language. The simplest elementary treatise in any science is obscure and perplexing, until we become familiar with the terminology of that science. Thus every writer is entitled to demand a certain amount of knowledge in those for whom he writes, and a certain degree of dexterity in using the implements of thought....

When a man says he sees nothing in a book, he very often means that he does not see himself in it: which, if it is not a comedy or a satire, is likely enough.

A.W. and J.C. Hare, *Guesses at Truth*

The Final Verdict upon Books

They who make up the final verdict upon every book are not the partial and noisy readers of the hour when it appears; but a court as of angels, a public not to be bribed, not to be entreated, and not to be overawed, decides upon every man's title to fame. Only those books come down which deserve to last. Gilt edges, vellum, and morocco, and presentation copies to all the libraries, will not preserve a book in circulation beyond its intrinsic date. It must go with all Walpole's Noble and Royal Authors to its fate. Blackmore, Kotzebue, or Pollock may endure for a night, but Moses and Homer stand for ever. There are not in the world at any one time more than a dozen persons who read and understand Plato: never enough to pay for an edition of his works; yet to every generation these come duly down, for the sake of those few persons, as if God brought them in his hand. 'No book,' said Bentley, 'was ever written down by any but itself.' The permanence of all books is fixed by no effort friendly or hostile, but by their own specific gravity, or the intrinsic importance of their contents to the constant mind of man.

Ralph Waldo Emerson, *Spiritual Laws*

Talent alone cannot make a writer. There must be a man behind the book.

Ralph Waldo Emerson, *Goethe*

The Critics' Influence on the Public

The opinion of the great body of the reading public is very
materially influenced even by the unsupported assertions
of those who assume a right to criticize. Nor is the public
altogether to blame on this account. Most even of those who
have really a great enjoyment in reading are in the same state,
with respect to a book, in which a man who has never given
particular attention to the art of painting is with respect to a
picture. Every man who has the least sensibility or imagination derives a certain pleasure from pictures. Yet a man of the
highest and finest intellect might, unless he had formed his
taste by contemplating the best pictures, be easily persuaded
by a knot of connoisseurs that the worst daub in Somerset
House was a miracle of art.

   Just such is the manner in which nine readers out of ten
judge of a book. They are ashamed to dislike what men who
speak as having authority declare to be good.

Thomas Macaulay, Mr. Robert Montgomery's Poems

Taste in Literature and Art

I know many persons who have the purest taste in literature,
and yet false taste in art, and it is a phenomenon which
puzzles me not a little; but I have never known any one with
false taste in books, and true taste in pictures. It is also of
the greatest importance to you, not only for art's sake, but
for all kinds of sake, in these days of book deluge, to keep
out of the salt swamps of literature, and live on a little rocky
island of your own, with a spring and a lake in it, pure and
good. I cannot, of course, suggest the choice of your library
to you: every several mind needs different books; but there
are some books which we all need, and assuredly, if you read
Homer, Plato, Aeschylus, Herodotus, Dante, Shakespeare,

and Spenser, as much as you ought you will not require wide
enlargement of shelves to right and left of them for purposes
of perpetual study.

John Ruskin, *The Elements of Drawing*

'There is no book so bad,' said the bachelor, 'but something
good may be found in it.'

Miguel de Cervantes

The Filial Piety of Books

Nor is there any paternal fondness which seems to savour
less of absolute instinct, and which may be so well reconciled
to worldly wisdom, as this of authors for their books. These
children may most truly be called the riches of their father,
and many of them have with true filial piety fed their parent
in his old age; so that not only the affection but the interest
of the author may be highly injured by those slanderers whose
poisonous breath brings his book to an untimely end.

Lastly, the slanderer of a book is, in truth, the slanderer of
the author ... neither can any one give the names of sad stuff,
horrid nonsense, &e., to a book, without calling the author
a blockhead; which, though in a moral sense it is a preferable
appellation to that of villain, is, perhaps, rather more injurious to his worldly interest.

Henry Fielding, *Tom Jones*

The Mote and the Beam

To complain in print of the multitude of books seems to me
a self-accusing vanity, whilst the querulous reprehenders add
to the cause of complaint and transgress themselves in that
which they seem to wish amended. 'Tis true, the births of the

press are numerous, nor is there less variety in the humours and fancies of perusers, and while the number of the one exceeds not the diversity of the other some will not think that too much which others judge superfluous. The genius of one approves what another disregardeth. And were nothing to pass the press but what were suited to the universal gusto, farewell, typography! ... I seek no applause from the disgrace of others, nor will I, huckster-like, discredit any man's ware to recommend mine own. I am not angry that there are so many books already (bating only the anomalies of impiety and irreligion), nor will I plead the necessity of publishing mine from feigned importunities.

Joseph Glanvill, The Vanity of Dogmatizing

The foolishest book is a kind of leaky boat on the sea of wisdom; some of the wisdom will get in, anyhow.

Oliver Wendell Holmes, The Poet at the Breakfast-Table

Censorship

Popish books teach and inform; what we know, we know much out of them. The fathers, church story, school-men, all may pass for popish books; and if you take away them, what learning will you leave? Besides, who must be judge? The customer or the waiter? If he disallows a book it must not be brought into the kingdom; then Lord have mercy upon all scholars! These puritan preachers, if they have anything good, they have it out of popish books, though they will not acknowledge it, for fear of displeasing the people. He is a poor divine that cannot sever the good from the bad.

John Selden, Table Talk

The Imprimatur

Learning hath of late years met with an obstruction in many
places which suppresses it from flourishing or increasing, in
spite of all its other helps, and that is the inquisition upon the
press, which prohibits any book from coming forth without
an imprimatur; an old relic of popery, only necessary for the
concealing of such defects of government which of right ought
to be discovered and amended.

Charles Blount, *A Just Vindication of Learning*, 1693

A Great Book is a Great Evil

Μέγα βιβλίον μέγα κακόν

A man who publishes his works in a volume has an infinite
advantage over one who communicates his writings to the
world in loose tracts and single pieces. We do not expect
to meet with anything in a bulky volume till after some
heavy preamble, and several words of course, to prepare the
reader for what follows: nay, authors have established it as
a kind of rule, that a man ought to be dull sometimes, as
the most severe reader makes allowances for many rests and
nodding-places in a voluminous writer. This gave occasion to
the famous Greek proverb which I have chosen for my motto,
That a great book is a great evil....

An essay writer must practise in the chemical method
and give the virtue of a full draught in a few drops. Were
all books reduced thus to their quintessence, many a bulky
author would make his appearance in a penny-paper: there
would be scarce such a thing in nature as a folio: the works of
an age would be contained on a few shelves, not to mention
millions of volumes that would be utterly annihilated....

When knowledge, instead of being bound up in books, and
kept in libraries and retirements, is thus obtruded upon the
public; when it is canvassed in every assembly, and exposed

upon every table; I cannot forbear reflecting upon that passage in the Proverbs, 'Wisdom crieth without, she uttereth her voice in the streets.'

Joseph Addison, Spectator, 124

A Little Book the Most Excellent

For books we shall generally find that the most excellent in any art or science have been still the smallest and most compendious; and this not without ground, for it is an argument that the author was a master of what he wrote, and had a clear notion and a full comprehension of the subject before him. For the reason of things lies in a little compass, if the mind could at any time be so happy as to light upon it. Most of the writings and discourses in the world are but illustration and rhetoric, which signifies as much as nothing to a mind eager in pursuit after the causes and philosophical truth of things.... The truth is, there could be no such thing as art or science, could not the mind of man gather the general natures of things out of the heap of numberless particulars, and then bind them up into such short aphorisms or propositions, that so they may be made portable to the memory, and thereby become ready and at hand for the judgement to apply and make use of as there shall be occasion.

Robert South, Sermon against Long Extempore Prayers

There are many books written by many men, from which two truths only arc discoverable by the readers; namely, that the writers thereof wanted two things,—principle and preferment.

C.C. Colton, Lacon

Books of One Thought

Few books have more than one thought: the generality indeed have not quite so many. The more ingenious authors of the former seem to think that, if they once get their candle lighted, it will burn on for ever. Yet even a candle gives a sorry, melancholy light unless it has a brother beside it, to shine on it and keep it cheerful. For lights and thoughts are social and sportive: they delight in playing with and into each other. One can hardly conceive a duller state of existence than sitting at whist with three dummies: and yet many of our prime philosophers have seldom done anything else.

A.W. and J.C. Hare, *Guesses at Truth*

Inductive Criticism

A heedy reader shall often discover in other men's compositions perfections far differing from the author's meaning, and such as haply he never dreamed of, and illustrateth them with richer senses and more excellent constructions.

Michel de Montaigne

Reading between Lines

In hours of high mental activity we sometimes do the book too much honour, reading out of it better things than the author wrote,—reading, as we say, between the lines. You have had the like experience in conversation: the wit was in what you heard, not in what the speakers said. Our best thought came from others. We heard in their words a deeper sense than the speakers put into them, and could express ourselves in other people's phrases to finer purpose than they knew.

Ralph Waldo Emerson, *Quotation and Originality*

Purple Patches

There are some fine passages, I am told, in that book.

Are there? Then beware of them. Fine passages are mostly *culs de sac*. For in books also does one see

Rich windows that exclude the light
And passages that lead to nothing.

A.W. and J.C. Hare, Guesses at Truth

There's more ado to interpret interpretations than to interpret things, and more books upon books than upon any other subject. We do but inter-glose ourselves. All swarmeth with commentaries; of authors there is great penury.

Michel de Montaigne

The Royal Road

ERASMUS I am told there is a certain compendious art, that will help a man to accomplish himself with all the liberal sciences by a very little labour.

DESIDERIUS What is that you talk of? Did you ever see the book?

ERASMUS I did see it, and that was all, having nobody to instruct me in the use of it.

DESIDERIUS What was the subject of the book?

ERASMUS It treated of various forms of dragons, lions, leopards; and various circles, and words written in them, some in Greek, some in Latin, and some in Hebrew and other barbarous languages.

DESIDERIUS Pray, in how many days' time did the title-page promise you the knowledge of the arts and sciences?

ERASMUS In fourteen.

DESIDERIUS In truth, a very noble promise. But did you ever know anybody that has become learned by that notable art?

ERASMUS No.

DESIDERIUS No, nor nobody ever did, or ever will, till we can see an alchemist grow rich.

ERASMUS Why, is there no such art then? I wish with all my heart there was.

DESIDERIUS Perhaps you do, because you would not be at the pains which are required to become learned.

ERASMUS You are right.

DESIDERIUS It seemed meet to the Divine Being that the common riches, gold, jewels, silver, palaces, and kingdoms should be bestowed on the slothful and undeserving; but the true riches, and such as are properly our own, must be gotten by labour.

Erasmus, *Colloquies*: *The Notable Art*

Readers and Writers

Many books require no thought from those who read them, and for a very simple reason;—they made no such demand on those who wrote them. Those works therefore are the most valuable, that set our thinking faculties in the fullest operation.

C.C. Colton, *Lacon*

Studies

Studies serve for delight, for ornament, and for ability. Their chief use for delight, is in privateness and retiring; for ornament, is in discourse; and for ability, is in the judgement and disposition of business; for expert men can execute, and perhaps judge of particulars, one by one; but the general counsels, and the plots and marshalling of affairs come best from those that are learned. To spend too much time in studies, is sloth; to use them too much for ornament, is affectation; to make judgement wholly by their rules, is the humour of a scholar: they perfect nature, and are perfected by experience: for natural abilities are like natural plants, that need pruning by study; and studies themselves do give forth directions too much at large, except they be bounded in by experience. Crafty men contemn studies, simple men admire them, and wise men use them; for they teach not their own use; but that is a wisdom without them and above them, won by observation. Read not to contradict and confute, nor to believe and take for granted, nor to find talk and discourse, but to weigh and consider. Some books are to be tasted, others to be swallowed, and some few to be chewed and digested: that is, some books are to be read only in parts; others to be read, but not curiously; and some few to be read wholly, and with diligence and attention. Some books also may be read by deputy, and extracts made of them by others; but that would be only in the less important arguments, and the meaner sort of books; else distilled books are, like common distilled waters, flashy things. Reading maketh a full man; conference a ready man; and writing an exact man; and, therefore, if a man write little, he had need have a great memory; if he confer little, he had need have a present wit; and if he read little, he had need have much cunning, to seem to know that he doth not. Histories make men wise; poets, witty; the mathematics, subtile; natural philosophy, deep; moral, grave; logic and rhetoric, able to contend: *Abeunt studio, in mores*; nay, there is no stand or impediment in the wit, but may be wrought out by fit studies: like as diseases of the body may have appropriate exercises; bowling is good for the stone and reins, shooting for the lungs and breast, gentle walking for the stomach, riding for the head and the like; so if a man's wit be wandering, let him study the mathematics; for in demonstrations, if his wit be called away never so little, he must begin again; if his wit be not apt to distinguish or find difference, let him study the schoolmen, for they are *Cymini sectores*. If he be not apt to beat over matters, and to call up one thing to prove and illustrate another, let him study the lawyers' cases: so every defect of the mind may have a special receipt.

Francis Bacon, Essays

The Choice of Books

In study there must be an expulsive virtue to shun all that is erroneous; and there is no science but is full of such stuff, which by direction of tutor and choice of good books must be excerned. Do not confound yourself with multiplicity of authors; two is enough upon any science, provided they be plenary and orthodox; *Philosophy* should be your substantial food, *Poetry* your banqueting stuff; *Philosophy* hath more of reality in it than any Knowledge, the *Philosopher* can fathom the deep, measure mountains, reach the stars with a staff, and bless heaven with a girdle.

But among these Studies you must not forget the *unicum necessarium*; on Sundays and Holidays let *Divinity* be the sole object of your speculation, in comparison whereof all other knowledge is but cobweb-learning.

James Howell, Familiar Letters

Chewing the Cud

Reading furnishes the mind only with materials of knowledge; it is thinking makes what we read ours. We are of the ruminating kind, and it is not enough to cram ourselves with a great load of collections; unless we chew them over again they will not give us strength and nourishment.... The memory may be stored, but the judgement is little better, and the stock of knowledge not increased, by being able to repeat what others have said or produce the arguments we have found in them. Such a knowledge as this is but knowledge by hearsay, and the ostentation of it is at best but talking by rote, and very often upon weak and wrong principles. For all that is to be found in books is not built upon true foundations, nor always rightly deduced from the principles it is pretended to be built on.... The mind is backward in itself to be at the pains to trace every argument to its original, and to see upon what basis it stands, and how firmly; but yet it is this that gives so much the advantage to one man more than another in reading. The mind should, by severe rules, be tied down to this at first uneasy task; use and exercise will give it facility. So that those who are accustomed to it, readily, as it were with one cast of the eye, take a view of the argument, and presently, in most cases, see where it bottoms. Those who have got this faculty, one may say, have got the true key of books, and the clue to lead them through the mizmaze of variety of opinions and authors to truth and certainty. This young beginners should be entered in, and showed the use of, that they might profit by their reading.... This way of thinking on and profiting by what we read will be a clog and rub to any one only in the beginning; when custom and exercise has made it familiar, it will be dispatched in most occasions, without resting or interruption in the course of our reading.

John Locke, *Conduct of the Understanding*

The Sufficiency of Homer

Read Homer once, and you can read no more;
For all books else appear so mean, so poor,
Verse will seem prose, but still persist to read,
And Homer will be all the books you need.

John Sheffield, Duke of Buckingham, *Essay on Poetry*

Homer and Virgil

Be Homer's works your study and delight,
Read them by day, and meditate by night;
Thence form your judgement, thence your maxims bring,
And trace the Muses upward to their spring.
Still with itself compared, his text peruse;
And let your comment be the Mantuan Muse.
   When first young Maro in his boundless mind
A work to outlast immortal Rome designed,
Perhaps he seemed above the critic's law,
And but from Nature's fountains scorned to draw:
But when to examine every part he came,
Nature and Homer were, he found, the same.
Convinced, amazed, he checks the bold design;
And rules as strict his laboured work confine,
As if the Stagirite o'erlooked each line.
Learn hence for ancient rules a just esteem:
To copy nature is to copy them.

Alexander Pope, *Essay on Criticism*

Reading According to Inclination

He [Dr. Johnson] said, that for general improvement, a man
should read whatever his immediate inclination prompts him
to; though, to be sure, if a man has a science to learn, he
must regularly and resolutely advance. He added, 'what we
read with inclination makes a much stronger impression. If
we read without inclination, half the mind is employed in
fixing the attention; so there is but one half to be employed
on what we read.' He told us, he read Fielding's *Amelia*
through without stopping. He said, 'If a man begins to read
in the middle of a book, and feels an inclination to go on, let
him not quit it, to go to the beginning. He may perhaps not
feel again the inclination.'

Dr. Johnson advised me to-day, to have as many books about me as I could; that I might read upon any subject upon which l had a desire for instruction at the time. 'What you read *then* (said he) you will remember; but if you have not a book immediately ready, and the subject moulds in your mind, it is a chance if you again have a desire to study it.' He added, 'If a man never has an eager desire for instruction, he should prescribe a task for himself. But it is better when a man reads from immediate inclination.'

Another admonition of his was, never to go out without some little book or other in the pocket. 'Much time,' added he, 'is lost by waiting, by travelling, &c., and this may be prevented, by making use of every possible opportunity for improvement.'

James Boswell, *Life of Johnson*

Read Few Books Well

Read few books well. We forget names and dates; and reproach our memory. They are of little consequence. We feel our limbs enlarge and strengthen; yet cannot tell the dinner or the dish that caused the alteration. Our minds improve though we cannot name the author and have forgotten the particulars.

Read all books through; and bad books most carefully, lest you should lose one good thought, being determined never to look into them again. A man may read a great deal too much.

J. Horne Tooke, *Recollections of S. Rogers*

Books as Fruitful Trees

Under a strong persuasion that little of real value is derived
by persons in general from a wide and various reading; but
still more deeply convinced as to the actual mischief of
unconnected and promiscuous reading, and that it is sure, in
a greater or less degree, to enervate even where it does not
likewise inflate; I hope to satisfy many an ingenious mind,
seriously interested in its own development and cultivation,
how moderate a number of volumes, if only they be ju-
diciously chosen, will suffice for the attainment of every wise
and desirable purpose; that is, in addition to those which
he studies for specific and professional purposes. It is saying
less than the truth to affirm that an excellent book (and the
remark holds almost equally good of a Raphael as of a Milton)
is like a well-chosen and well-tended fruit-tree. Its fruits are
not of one season only. With the due and natural intervals,
we may recur to it year after year, and it will supply the same
nourishment and the same gratification, if only we ourselves
return to it with the same healthful appetite.

S.T. Coleridge, *Prospectus to a Course of Lectures*

Reading Several Books at a Time

The advice I would give to any one who is disposed really
to read for the sake of knowledge is, that he should have
two or three books in course of reading at the same time.
He will read a great deal more in that time and with much
greater profit. All travels are worth reading, as subsidiary to
reading, and in fact essential parts of it: old or new, it matters
not—something is to be learnt from all. And the custom of
making brief notes of reference to everything of interest or
importance would be exceedingly useful.

Robert Southey, letter to Henry Taylor

When and Where to Read

Much depends upon *when* and *where* you read a book. In the five or six impatient minutes, before the dinner is quite ready, who would think of taking up the *Fairy Queen* for a stop-gap, or a volume of Bishop Andrewes' sermons?

Milton almost requires a solemn service of music to be played before you enter upon him. But he brings his music, to which, who listens, had need bring docile thoughts, and purged ears.

Winter evenings—the world shut out—with less of ceremony the gentle Shakespeare enters. At such a season, the *Tempest*, or his own *Winter's Tale.*—

These two poets you cannot avoid reading aloud—to yourself, or (as it chances) to some single person listening. More than one—and it degenerates into an audience.

Books of quick interest, that hurry on for incidents, are for the eye to glide over only. It will not do to read them out. I could never listen to even the better kind of modern novels without extreme irksomeness.

A newspaper, read out, is intolerable.

Charles Lamb, *Detached Thoughts
on Books and Reading*

Small Authors Dangerous

It is dangerous to have any intercourse or dealing with small authors. They are as troublesome to handle, as easy to dis-compose, as difficult to pacify, and leave as unpleasant marks on you, as small children. Cultivate on the other hand the society and friendship of the higher; first that you may learn to reverence them, which of itself is both a pleasure and a virtue, and then that on proper occasions you may defend them against the malevolent, which is a duty. And this duty cannot be well and satisfactorily performed with an imperfect knowledge, or with an inadequate esteem.

Walter Savage Landor, Imaginary Conversations

Books that Provoke Thought

It is wholesome and bracing for the mind, to have its faculties kept on the stretch. It is like the effect of a walk in Switzerland upon the body. Reading an Essay of Bacon's, for instance, or a chapter of Aristotle or of Butler, if it be well and thoughtfully read, is much like climbing up a hill, and may do one the same sort of good.... For my own part, I have ever gained the most profit and the most pleasure also, from the books which have made me think the most: and, when the difficulties have once been overcome, these are the books which have struck the deepest root, not only in my memory and understanding, but likewise in my affections. For this point too should be taken into account. We are wont to think slightly of that, which it costs us a slight effort to win. When a maiden is too forward, her admirer deems it time to draw back. Whereas whatever has associated itself with the arousal and activity of our better nature, with the important and memorable epochs in our lives, whether moral or intellectual, is,—to cull a sprig from the beautiful passage in which Wordsworth describes the growth of Michael's love for his native hills—

> Our living being, even more
> Than our own blood,—and could it less?—retains
> Strong hold on our affections, is to us
> A pleasurable feeling of blind love,
> The pleasure which there is in life itself.

If you would fertilize the mind, the plough must be driven over and through it. The gliding of wheels is easier and rapider, but only makes it harder and more barren. Above all, in the present age of light reading, that is, of reading hastily, thoughtlessly, indiscriminately, unfruitfully, when most books are forgotten as soon as they are finished, and very many sooner, it is well if something heavier is cast now and then into the midst of the literary public. This may scare and repel the weak: it will rouse and attract the stronger, and increase their strength by making them exert it. In the sweat of the brow is the mind as well as the body to eat its bread.

A.W. and J.C. Hare, Guesses at Truth

Rules for Reading

The best rule of reading will be a method from nature, and not a mechanical one of hours and pages. It holds each student to a pursuit of his native aim, instead of a desultory miscellany. Let him read what is proper to him, and not waste his memory on a crowd of mediocrities. As whole nations have derived their culture from a single book,—as the Bible has been the literature as well as the religion of large portions of Europe,—as Hafiz was the eminent genius of the Persians, Confucius of the Chinese, Cervantes of the Spaniards; so, perhaps, the human mind would be a gainer, if all the secondary writers were lost—say, in England, all but Shakespeare, Milton, and Bacon—through the profounder study so drawn to those wonderful minds. With this pilot of his own genius, let the student read one, or let him read many, he will read advantageously. . . .

The three practical rules, then, which I have to offer, are,—1. Never read any book that is not a year old. 2. Never read any but famed books. 3. Never read any but what you like; or, in Shakespeare's phrase,

No profit goes where is no pleasure ta'en:
In brief, sir, study what you most affect.

Montaigne says, 'Books are a languid pleasure;' but I find certain books vital and spermatic, not leaving the reader what he was: he shuts the book a richer man. I would never willingly read any others than such.

Ralph Waldo Emerson, Books

A Diet of Books

I would not be hurried by any love of system, by any exaggeration of instincts, to underrate the Book. We all know, that, as the human body can be nourished on any food, though it were boiled grass and the broth of shoes, so the human mind can be fed by any knowledge. And great and heroic men have existed, who had almost no other information than by the printed page. I only would say, that it needs a strong head to bear that diet. One must be an inventor to read well. As the proverb says, 'He that would bring home the wealth of the Indies must carry out the wealth of the Indies.' There is, then, creative reading as well as creative writing. When the mind is braced by labour and invention, the page of whatever book we read becomes luminous with manifold allusion. Every sentence is doubly significant, and the sense of our author is as broad as the world. We then see, what is always true, that, as the seer's hour of vision is short and rare among heavy days and months, so is its record, perchance, the least part of his volume. The discerning will read, in his Plato or Shakespeare, only that least part,—only the authentic utterances of the oracle; all the rest he rejects, were it never so many times Plato's and Shakespeare's.

Ralph Waldo Emerson, The American Scholar

A Course of Reading

Let us turn our attention to the intellectual advantages accompanying the pursuit, since the proper function of books is in the general case associated with intellectual culture and occupation. It would seem that, according to a received prejudice or opinion, there is one exception to this general connexion, in the case of the possessors of libraries, who are under a vehement suspicion of not reading their books. Well, perhaps it is true in the sense in which those who utter the taunt understand the reading of a book. That one should possess no books beyond his power of perusal—that he should buy no faster than as he can read straight through what he has already bought—is a supposition alike preposterous and unreasonable. 'Surely you have far more books than you can read,' is sometimes the inane remark of the barbarian who gets his books, volume by volume, from some circulating library or reading club, and reads them all through, one after the other, with a dreary dutifulness, that he may be sure that he has got the value of his money.

It is true that there are some books—as Homer, Virgil, Horace, Milton, Shakespeare, and Scott—which every man should read who has the opportunity—should read, mark, learn, and inwardly digest.... But is one next to read through the sixty and odd folio volumes of the Bollandist *Lives of the Saints*, and the new edition of the Byzantine historians, and the State Trials, and the *Encyclopedia Britannica*, and Moreri, and the Statutes at large, and the *Gentleman's Magazine* from the beginning, each separately, and in succession? Such a course of reading would certainly do a good deal towards weakening the mind, if it did not create absolute insanity.

But in all these just named, even in the Statutes at large, and in thousands upon thousands of other books, there is precious honey to be gathered by the literary busy bee, who passes on from flower to flower. In fact, 'a course of reading,' as it is sometimes called, is a course of regimen for dwarfing the mind, like the drugs which dog-breeders give to King Charles spaniels to keep them small. Within the span of life allotted to man there is but a certain number of books that it is practicable to read through, and it is not possible to make a selection that will not, in a manner, wall in the mind from a free expansion over the republic of letters. The being chained, as it were, to one intellect in the perusal straight on of any large book, is a sort of mental slavery superinducing imbecility. Even Gibbon's *Decline and Fall*, luminous and comprehensive as its philosophy is, and rapid and brilliant the narrative, will become deleterious mental food if consumed straight through without variety. It will be well to relieve it occasionally with a little Boston's *Fourfold State*, or Hervey's *Meditations*, or Sturm's *Reflections for Every Day in the Year*, or *Don Juan*, or Ward's *History of Stoke-upon-Trent*.

J.H. Burton, *The Book-Hunter*

Poets as Commentators

I hold that no man can have any just conception of the history of England who has not often read, and meditated, and learnt to love the great poets of England. The greatest of them, such as Chaucer, Shakespeare, Massinger, George Herbert, Milton, Cowley, Dryden, Pope, and Burns, often throw more rich and brilliant colours, and sometimes even more clear and steady lights, on the times and doings of our forefathers, than are to be gathered out of all the chroniclers together, from the Venerable Bede to the philosophical Hume. They are at least the greatest and best commentators on those chroniclers.

Sir James Stephen, *Desultory and Systematic Reading*

The Method of Reading Profane History

In perusal of history, first, provide you some writers in chronology and cosmography. For if you be ignorant of the times and places when and where the things you read were done, it cannot choose but breed confusion in your reading, and make you many times grossly to slip and mistake in your discourse. When, therefore, you set to your book, have by you Helvicus, his *Chronology*, and a map of the country in which you are conversant; and repair unto them to acquaint you with time and place, when and where you are. If you be versing the ancient histories, then provide you Ptolemy's maps, or Ortelius, his *Conatus Geographiei:* if the latter, then some of the modern cards...

Before you come to read the acts of any people, as those that intend to go to bowls will first see and view the ground upon which they are to play, so it shall not be amiss for you first to take a general view of that ground, which you mean more particularly to traverse, by reading some short epitome.... This will give you a general taste of your business, and add light unto particular authors....

From the order of reading and the matters in reading to be observed, we come to the method of observation. What order we are for our best use to keep in entering our notes into our paper-books.

The custom which hath most prevailed hitherto was commonplacing, a thing at the first original very plain and simple; but by after-times much increased, some augmenting the number of the heads, others inventing quainter forms of disposing them: till at length commonplace books became like unto the Roman Breviary or Missal. It was a great part of clerkship to know how to use them. The vastness of the volumes, the multitude of heads, the intricacy of disposition, the pains of committing the heads to memory, and last, of the labour of so often turning the books to enter the observations in their due places, are things so expensive of

time and industry, that although at length the work comes
to perfection, yet it is but like the silver mines in Wales, the
profit will hardly quit the pains. I have often doubted with
myself whether or no there were any necessity of being so
exactly methodical. First, because there hath not yet been
found a method of that latitude, but little reading would
furnish you with some things, which would fall without the
compass of it. Secondly, because men of confused, dark and
cloudy understandings, no beam or light of order and method
can ever rectify; whereas men of clear understanding, though
but in a mediocrity, if they read good books carefully, and
note diligently, it is impossible but they should find incredible profit, though their notes lie never so confusedly. The
strength of our natural memory, especially if we help it, by
revising our own notes; the nature of things themselves,
many times ordering themselves, and *tantum non*, telling us
how to range them; a mediocrity of care to see that matters
lie not too chaos-like, will with very small damage save us
this great labour of being over-superstitiously methodical.
And what though peradventure something be lost, *Exilis domus
est*, &c. It is a sign of great poverty of scholarship, where
everything that is lost is missed; whereas rich and well-
accomplished learning is able to lose many things with little
or no inconvenience.

John Hales, *Golden Remains*

Abstracts of Books

My abstracts of each book were made in the French language:
my observations often branched into particular essays; and
I can still read, without contempt, a dissertation of eight
folio pages on eight lines (287–94) of the fourth *Georgic* of
Virgil....

This various reading, which I now conducted with discretion, was digested, according to the precept and model of Mr.

Locke, into a large commonplace book; a practice, however, which I do not strenuously recommend. The action of the pen will doubtless imprint an idea on the mind as well as on the paper: but I much question whether the benefits of this laborious method are adequate to the waste of time; and I must agree with Dr. Johnson (*Idler*, No. 74), 'that what is twice read is commonly better remembered than what is transcribed'....

I will embrace this occasion of recommending to the young student a practice which about this time [1759] I myself adopted. After glancing my eye over the design and order of a new book, I suspended the perusal till I had finished the task of self-examination, till I had revolved, in a solitary walk, all that I knew, or believed, or had thought on the subject of the whole work, or of some particular chapter: I was then qualified to discern how much the author added to my original stock; and if I was sometimes satisfied by the agreement, I was sometimes armed by the opposition of our ideas.

Edward Gibbon, *Autobiography*

Bescribbling with Notes

Somewhat to aid the weakness of my memory and to assist her great defects; for it hath often been my chance to light upon books which I supposed to be new and never to have read, which I had, not understanding, diligently read and run over many years before, and all bescribbled with my notes: I have a while since accustomed myself to note at the end of my book (I mean such as I purpose to read but once) the time I made an end to read it, and to set down what censure or judgement I gave of it; that so it may at least at another time represent unto my mind the air and general idea I had conceived of the author in reading him.

Michel de Montaigne

Books to be Marked

If the books which you read are your own, mark with a pen or pencil the most considerable things in them which you desire to remember. Then you may read that book the second time over with half the trouble, by your eye running over the paragraphs which your pencil has noted. It is but a very weak objection against this practice to say, 'I shall spoil my book;' for I persuade myself that you did not buy it as a bookseller, to sell it again for gain, but as a scholar, to improve your mind by it; and if the mind be improved, your advantage is abundant, though your book yields less money to your executors.

Isaac Watts, *Logic*

Underscoring

On a subsequent evening, when I called by invitation to consult some other volumes, the conversation turned on the practice of underscoring books of study. Sir William spoke highly of the practice, as attended with many advantages, especially in the saving of time and labour. Intelligent under-lining gave a kind of abstract of an important work, and by the use of different coloured inks to mark a difference of contents, and discriminate the doctrinal from the historical or illustrative elements of an argument or exposition, the abstract became an analysis very serviceable for ready refer-ence. He mentioned that this principle had been carried to a ludicrous extreme in the publication of a coloured New Testament by an Anglicized German, Wirgmann by name. ... In this book, entitled *Divarication of the New Testament into Doctrine and History*, the pages were all coloured, most of them parti-coloured, the doctrine being throughout visually separated from the history by this device; the doctrine being, if I remember rightly, blue, and the history red. The author expressed his belief that all the sects of Christendom had arisen from a confusion of these elements, and that his grand discovery in the 'Divarication' would annihilate sects, establish pure Christianity as a sacred science, and become hereafter a Euclid in Theology.

Sir William Hamilton, *Life* by J. Veitch

The Parson's Accessory Knowledge

The Country Parson hath read the Fathers also, and the Schoolmen, and the later writers, or a good proportion of all, out of all which he hath compiled a book, and Body of Divinity, which is the storehouse of his sermons, and which he preacheth all his life; but diversely clothed, illustrated, and enlarged. For though the world is full of such composures, yet every man's own is fittest, readiest, and most savoury to him. Besides, this being to be done in his younger and pre-paratory times, it is an honest joy ever after to look upon his well-spent hours.

George Herbert, *A Priest to the Temple*

Commonplace Books

For the disposition and collocation of that knowledge which we preserve in writing, it consisteth in a good digest of commonplaces, wherein I am not ignorant of the prejudice imputed to the rise of commonplace books, as causing a re-tardation of reading, and some sloth or relaxation of memory. But because it is but a counterfeit thing in knowledges to be forward and pregnant, except a man be deep and full, I hold the entry of commonplaces to be a matter of great use and essence in studying, as that which assureth copy of invention, and contracteth judgement to a strength. But this is true, that of the methods of commonplaces that I have seen, there is none of any sufficient worth: all of them carrying merely the face of a school, and not of a world; and referring to vulgar matters and pedantical divisions, without all life or respect to action.

Francis Bacon, *Of the Advancement of Learning*

A New Method of a Commonplace Book

I take a paper book of what size I please. I divide the two first pages that face one another by parallel lines into five-and-twenty equal parts, every fifth line black, the other red. I then cut them perpendicularly by other lines that I draw from the top to the bottom of the page. I put about the middle of each five spaces one of the twenty letters I design to make use of, and, a little forward in each space, the five vowels, one below another, in their natural order. This is the index to the whole volume, how big soever it may be.

The index being made after this manner, I leave a margin in all the other pages of the book, of about the largeness of an inch, in a volume in folio, or a little larger; and, in a less volume, smaller in proportion.

If I would put anything in my Commonplace Book, I find out a head to which I may refer it. Each head ought to be some important and essential word to the matter in hand, and in that word regard is to be had to the first letter, and the vowel that follows it; for upon these two letters depends all the use of the index.

I omit three letters of the alphabet as of no use to me, viz. K, Y, W, which are supplied by C, I, U, that are equivalent to them. I put the letter Q that is always followed with an u in the fifth space of Z. By throwing Q last in my index, I preserve the regularity of my index, and diminish not in the least its extent; for it seldom happens that there is any head begins with Zu. I have found none in the five-and-twenty years I have used this method.... When I meet with anything that I think fit to put into my commonplace book, I first find a proper head. Suppose, for example, that the head be EPISTOLA, I look into the index for the first letter and the following vowel, which in this instance are E i; if in the space marked E i there is any number that directs me to the page designed for words that begin with an E, and whose first vowel after the initial letter is I, I must then write under the word Epistola, in that page, what I have to remark. I write the head in large letters and begin a little way out into the margin, and I continue on the line, in writing what I have to say. I observe constantly this rule that only the head appears in the margin, and that it be continued on, without ever doubling the line in the margin, by which means the heads will be obvious at first sight....

If the head is a monosyllable and begins with a vowel, that vowel is at the same time both the first letter of the word and the characteristic vowel. Therefore I write the word Ars in A a and Os in O o....

As to the language in which one ought to express the heads I esteem the Latin tongue most commodious, provided the nominative case be always kept to.... But it is not of much consequence what language is made use of, provided there be no mixture in the heads of different languages.

John Locke, letter to Mr. Toignard

A commonplace book contains many notions in garrison, whence the owner may draw out an army into the field on competent warning.

Thomas Fuller, *The Holy and the Profane State*

Reading without thinking may indeed make a rich commonplace, but 'twill never make a clear head.

John Norris, *On the Advantages of Thinking*

Marginal Notes and Commonplace Books

It is the practice of many readers to note, in the margin of their books, the most important passages, the strongest arguments, or the brightest sentiments. Thus they load their minds with superfluous attention, repress the vehemence of curiosity by useless deliberation, and by frequent interruption break the current of narration or the chain of reason, and at last close the volume, and forget the passages and marks together.

Others I have found unalterably persuaded that nothing is certainly remembered but what is transcribed; and they have therefore passed weeks and months in transferring large quotations to a commonplace book. Yet, why any part of a book, which can be consulted at pleasure, should be copied, I was never able to discover. The hand has no closer correspondence with the memory than the eye. The act of writing itself distracts the thoughts, and what is read twice is commonly better remembered than what is transcribed. This method therefore consumes time without assisting memory.

The true art of memory is the art of attention. No man will read with much advantage, who is not able, at pleasure, to evacuate his mind, or who brings not to his author an intellect defecated and pure, neither turbid with care, nor agitated by pleasure. If the repositories of thought are already full, what can they receive? If the mind is employed on the past or the future, the book will be held before the eyes in vain. What is read with delight is commonly retained, because pleasure always secures attention: but the books which are consulted by occasional necessity, and perused with impatience, seldom leave any traces on the mind.

Samuel Johnson, *Idler,* 74

The Bee and the Butterfly

More is got from one book on which the thought settles for a definite end in knowledge, than from libraries skimmed over by a wandering eye. A cottage flower gives honey to the bee, a king's garden none to the butterfly.

Edward Bulwer-Lytton, *Caxtoniana*

Chance Readings

Interdum speciosa locis morataque recte
Fabula nullius veneris, sine pondere et arte,
Valdius oblectat populum meliusque moratur
Quam versus inopes rerum nugaeque canorae.—HORACE

It is the custom of the Mahometans, if they see any printed or written paper upon the ground, to take it up and lay it aside carefully, as not knowing but it may contain some piece of their Alcoran. I must confess I have so much of the Mussul-man in me, that I cannot forbear looking into every printed paper which comes in my way, under whatsoever despicable circumstances it may appear; for as no mortal author, in the ordinary fate and vicissitude of things, knows to what use his works may some time or other be applied, a man may often meet with very celebrated names in a paper of tobacco. I have lighted my pipe more than once with the writings of a prelate; and know a friend of mine, who, for these several years, has converted the essays of a man of quality into a kind of fringe for his candlesticks. I remember in particular, after having read over a poem of an eminent author on a victory, I met with several fragments of it upon the next rejoicing day, which had been employed in squibs and crackers, and by that means celebrated its subject in a double capacity. I once met with a page of Mr. Baxter under a Christmas pie. Whether or no the pastry-cook had made use of it through chance or waggery, for the defence of that superstitious *viande*, I know not; but upon the perusal of it, I conceived so good an idea of the author's piety, that I bought the whole book. I have often profited by these accidental readings, and have sometimes found very curious pieces, that are either out of print, or not to be met with in the shops of our London booksellers. For this reason, when my friends take a survey of my library, they are very much surprised to find, upon the shelf of folios, two long bandboxes standing upright among my books, till I let them see that they are both of them lined with deep erudition and abstruse literature.

Joseph Addison, Spectator, 85

Appetite and Satiety

The library at Waverley-Honour, a large Gothic room, with double arches and a gallery, contained such a miscellaneous and extensive collection of volumes as had been assembled together, during the course of two hundred years, by a family which had been always wealthy, and inclined, of course, as a mark of splendour, to furnish their shelves with the current literature of the day, without much scrutiny, or nicety of discrimination. Throughout this ample realm Edward was permitted to roam at large.... With a desire of amusement, therefore, which better discipline might soon have converted into a thirst for knowledge, young Waverley drove through the sea of books, like a vessel without a pilot or a rudder. Nothing perhaps increases by indulgence more than a desultory habit of reading, especially under such opportunities of gratifying it. I believe one reason why such numerous instances of erudition occur among the lower ranks is, that, with the same powers of mind, the poor student is limited to a narrow circle for indulging his passion for books, and must necessarily make himself master of the few he possesses ere he can acquire more. Edward, on the contrary, like the epicure who only deigned to take a single morsel from the sunny side of a peach, read no volume a moment after it ceased to excite his curiosity or interest; and it necessarily happened, that the habit of seeking only this sort of gratification rendered it daily more difficult of attainment, till the passion for reading, like other strong appetites, produced by indulgence a sort of satiety.

Sir Walter Scott, Waverley

The Habit of Casual Reading

Not to mention the multitudes who read merely for the sake of talking, or to qualify themselves for the world, or some such kind of reasons; there are, even of the few who read for their own entertainment, and have a real curiosity to see what is said, several, which is prodigious, who have no sort of curiosity to see what is true....

For the sake of this whole class of readers, for they are of different capacities, different kinds, and get into this way from different occasions, I have often wished that it had been the custom to lay before people nothing in matters of argument but premises, and leave them to draw conclusions themselves; which, though it could not be done in all cases, might in many.

The great number of books and papers of amusement, which, of one kind or another, daily come in one's way, have in part occasioned, and most perfectly fall in with and humour, this idle way of reading and considering things. By this means, time even in solitude is happily got rid of, without the pain of attention; neither is any part of it more put to the account of idleness, one can scarce forbear saying, is spent with less thought, than great part of that which is spent in reading.

Joseph Butler, Preface to Sermons

Johnson's Cursory Reading

Mr. Elphinston talked of a new book that was much admired,
and asked Dr. Johnson if he had read it. Johnson: 'I have
looked into it.' 'What (said Elphinston), have you not read
it through?' Johnson, offended at being thus pressed, and so
obliged to own his cursory mode of reading, answered tartly,
'No, Sir, do *you* read books *through?*'

James Boswell, *Life of Johnson*

Desultory Reading

Desultory reading is indeed very mischievous, by fostering habits of loose, discontinuous thought, by turning the
memory into a common sewer for rubbish of all sorts to float
through, and by relaxing the power of attention, which of
all our faculties most needs care, and is most improved by it.
But a well-regulated course of study will no more weaken the
mind, than hard exercise will weaken the body: nor will a
strong understanding be weighed down by its knowledge, any
more than an oak is by its leaves, or than Samson was by his
locks. He whose sinews are drained by his hair, must already
be a weakling.

A.W. and J.C. Hare, *Guesses at Truth*

A Bookish Ambition

Affect not, as some do, that bookish ambition, to be stored
with books and have well-furnished libraries, yet keep their
heads empty of knowledge: to desire to have many books,
and never to use them, is like a child that will have a candle
burning by him, all the while he is sleeping.

Henry Peacham, *The Compleat Gentleman*

Full Libraries and Empty Heads

We have a generation of people in the world, that are so far
from putting themselves upon the hazard of knowing too
much, that they affect a kind of Socratical knowledge (though
it be the clear contrary way), a knowledge of knowing
nothing; they hate learning, and wisdom, and understanding
with that perfect hatred, that if one could fancy such things
to be in paradise, one would think (if I may speak it, as I
mean it without profaneness) that the Devil could not tempt
them to come near the tree of knowledge; I cannot say these
are in a state of innocency, but I am sure they are in a state of
simplicity. But among those few persons (especially those of
quality) that pretend to look after books, how many are there
that affect rather to look upon them, than in them? Some
covet to have libraries in their houses, as ladies desire to have
cupboards of plate in their chambers, only for show; as if
they were only to furnish their rooms, and not their minds;
if the only having of store of books were sufficient to improve
a man, the stationers would have the advantage of all others;
but certainly books were made for use, and not for ostentation; in vain do they boast of full libraries that are contented
to live with empty heads.

Sir William Waller, *Divine Meditations*

A Pretender to Learning

... is oftener in his study than at his book.... His table is
spread wide with some classic folio, which is as constant to
it as the carpet, and hath lain open in the same page this half
year.... He walks much alone in the posture of meditation,
and has a book still before his face in the fields. His pocket is
seldom without a Greek Testament, or Hebrew Bible, which
he opens only in the church, and this when some stander-by

looks over.... He is a great nomenclator of authors, whom he has read in general in the catalogue, and in particular in the title, and goes seldom so far as the dedication.

John Earle, Microcosmographie

Superficial Readers

Man has a natural desire to know,
But the one half is for interest, the other show:
As scriveners take more pains to learn the slight
Of making knots than all the hands they write:
So all his study is not to extend
The bounds of knowledge, but some vainer end;
To appear and pass for learnèd, though his claim
Will hardly reach beyond the empty name:
For most of those that drudge and labour hard,
Furnish their understandings by the yard,
As a French library by the whole is,
So much an ell for quartos and for folios;
To which they are the indexes themselves,
And understand no further than the shelves;
But smatter with their tables and editions,
And place them in their classical partitions;
When all a student knows of what he reads
Is not in 's own but under general heads
Of commonplaces not in his own power,
But, like a Dutchman's money, i' th' cantore;
Where all he can make of it, at the best,
Is hardly three per cent. for interest;
And whether he will ever get it out
Into his own possession is a doubt:
Affects all books of past and modern ages,
But reads no further than the title-pages,
Only to con the author's names by rote,
Or, at the best, those of the books they quote

Enough to challenge intimate acquaintance
With all the learnèd Moderns and the Ancients.
As Roman noblemen were wont to greet,
And compliment the rabble in the street,
Had nomenclators in their trains, to claim
Acquaintance with the meanest by his name,
And by so mean contemptible a bribe
Trepanned the suffrages of every tribe;
So learned men, by authors' names unknown,
Have gained no small improvement to their own,
And he's esteemed the learnedest of all others
That has the largest catalogue of authors.

Samuel Butler, *Satire upon the Imperfection*
and Abuse of Human Learning

Talking from Books

Dr. Johnson this day, when we were by ourselves [on the journey to the Hebrides] observed, how common it was for people to talk from books; to retail the sentiments of others, and not their own; in short, to converse without any originality of thinking. He was pleased to say, 'You and I do not talk from books.'

James Boswell, *Life of Johnson*

There are no race of people who talk about books, or perhaps, who read books, so little as literary men.

William Makepeace Thackeray

A Short Cut to Fame

There is a sort of vanity some men have, of talking of and
reading obscure and half-forgotten authors, because it passes
as a matter of course, that he who quotes authors which are
so little read, must be completely and thoroughly acquainted
with those authors which are in every man's mouth. For
instance, it is very common to quote Shakespeare; but it
makes a sort of stare to quote Massinger. I have very little
credit for being well acquainted with Virgil; but if I quote
Silius Italicus, I may stand some chance of being reckoned a
great scholar. In short, whoever wishes to strike out of the
great road, and to make a short cut to fame, let him neglect
Homer, and Virgil, and Horace, and Ariosto and Milton, and,
instead of these, read and talk of Frascatorius, Sannazarius,
Lorenzini, Pastorini, and the thirty-six primary sonneteers
of Bettinelli;—let him neglect everything which the suffrage
of ages has made venerable and grand, and dig out of their
graves a set of decayed scribblers, whom the silent verdict of
the public has fairly condemned to everlasting oblivion. If he
complain of the injustice with which they have been treated,
and call for a new trial with loud and importunate clamour,
though I am afraid he will not make much progress in the
estimation of men of sense, he will be sure to make some
noise in the crowd, and to be dubbed a man of very curious
and extraordinary erudition.

> Sydney Smith, *Moral Philosophy*, Lecture IX,
> *On the Conduct of the Understanding*

The author who speaks about his own books is almost as bad
as a mother who talks about her own children.

> Benjamin Disraeli

Title-Readers

Some read to think,—these are rare; some to write,—these are common; and some read to talk,—and these form the great majority. The first page of an author not unfrequently suffices for all the purposes of this latter class: of whom it has been said, that they treat books as some do lords; they inform themselves of their *titles*, and then boast of an intimate acquaintance.

C.C. Colton, *Lacon*

The Burning of Don Quixote's Books

The priest and the barber of the place, who were Don Quixote's great friends, happened to be there [at Don Quixote's house]; and the housekeeper was saying to them aloud: What is your opinion, Señor Licentiate Pero Perez (for that was the priest's name) of my master's misfortune? for neither he, nor his horse, nor the target, nor the lance, nor the armour have been seen these six days past. Woe is me! I am verily persuaded, and it is as certainly true as I was born to die, that these cursed books of knight-errantry which he keeps, and is so often reading, have turned his brain; and now I think of it, I have often heard him say, talking to himself, that he would turn knight-errant, and go about the world in quest of adventures. The devil and Barabbas take all such books, that have thus spoiled the finest understanding in all La Mancha. The niece joined with her, and said moreover: Know, master Nicholas (for that was the barber's name), that it has often happened, that my honoured uncle has continued poring on these confounded books of disadventures two whole days and nights.... But I take the blame of all this to myself, that I did not advertise you, gentlemen, of my dear uncle's extravagances, before they were come to the height that they now are, that you might have prevented them by

burning all those cursed books, of which he has so great a
store, and which as justly deserve to be committed to the
flames, as if they were heretical....

Whilst Don Quixote still slept on, the priest asked the
niece for the keys of the chamber where the books were,
those authors of the mischief; and she delivered them with a
very good will. They all went in, and the housekeeper with
them. They found above a hundred volumes in folio, very
well bound, besides a great many small ones. And no sooner
did the housekeeper see them, than she ran out of the room
in great haste, and immediately returned with a pot of holy
water and a bunch of hyssop, and said: Señor Licentiate, take
this and sprinkle the room, lest some enchanter, of the many
these books abound with, should enchant us in revenge for
what we intend to do, in banishing them out of the world.
The priest smiled at the housekeeper's simplicity, and ordered
the barber to reach him the books one by one, that they
might see what they treated of; for, perhaps, they might find
some that might not deserve to be chastised by fire. No,
said the niece, there is no reason why any of them should be
spared.... The housekeeper said the same; so eagerly did they
both thirst for the death of those innocents. But the priest
would not agree to that, without first reading the titles at
least....

That night the housekeeper set fire to, and burnt all the
books that were in the yard [whither they had been cast], and
in the house too; and some must have perished, that deserved
to be treasured up in perpetual archives.

Miguel de Cervantes, Don Quixote

Brains Squashed by Books

There have indeed been minds overlaid by much reading,
men who have piled such a load of books on their heads, their
brains have seemed to be squashed by them.

A.W. and J.C. Hare, Guesses at Truth

Deep-Versed in Books and Shallow in Himself

Many books,
Wise men have said, are wearisome; who reads
Incessantly, and to his reading brings not
A spirit and judgement, equal or superior,
(And what he brings, what needs he elsewhere seek?)
Uncertain and unsettled still remains,
Deep-versed in books, and shallow in himself;
Crude or intoxicate, collecting toys
And trifles for choice matters, worth a sponge;
As children gathering pebbles on the shore.

John Milton, Paradise Regained

Swallowing the Husks

The heart
May give an useful lesson to the head,
And learning wiser grow without his books.
Knowledge and wisdom, far from being one,
Have oft-times no connexion. Knowledge dwells
In heads replete with thoughts of other men;
Wisdom in minds attentive to their own.
Knowledge, a rude unprofitable mass,
The mere materials with which Wisdom builds,
Till smoothed and squared and fitted to its place,
Does but encumber whom it seems to enrich.

Knowledge is proud that he has learned so much;
Wisdom is humble that he knows no more.
   Books are not seldom talismans and spells,
By which the magic art of shrewder wits
Holds an unthinking multitude enthralled.
Some to the fascination of a name
Surrender judgement, hood-winked. Some the style
Infatuates, and through labyrinths and wilds
Of error leads them by a tune entranced.
While sloth seduces more, too weak to bear
The insupportable fatigue of thought,
And swallowing, therefore, without pause or choice.
The total grist unsifted, husks and all.
But trees, and rivulets whose rapid course
Defies the check of winter, haunts of deer,
And sheep-walks populous with bleating lambs.
And lanes in which the primrose ere her time
Peeps through the moss that clothes the hawthorn root,
Deceive no student. Wisdom there, and truth,
Not shy, as in the world, and to be won
By slow solicitation, seize at once
The roving thought, and fix it on themselves.

William Cowper, *The Winter Walk at Noon*

Much reading is like much eating, wholly useless without
digestion.

Robert South

If I had read as much as other men, I should have been as
ignorant as they.

Thomas Hobbes

Reading and Illiteracy

You might read all the books in the British Museum (if you could live long enough) and remain an utterly 'illiterate', uneducated person; but ... if you read ten pages of a good book, letter by letter,—that is to say, with real accuracy,—you are for evermore in some measure an educated person.

John Ruskin, *Sesame and Lilies*

Reading as Intellectual Indolence

Do I boast of my omnivorousness of reading, even apart from romances? Certainly no!—never, except in joke. It's against my theories and ratiocinations, which take upon themselves to assert that we all generally err by *reading too much*, or out of proportion to what we *think*. I should be wiser, I am persuaded, if I had not read half as much—should have had stronger and better exercised faculties. The fact is, that the *ne plus ultra* of intellectual indolence is this reading of books. It comes next to what the Americans call 'whittling'.

Elizabeth Barrett Browning,
letter to R.H. Horne

Books and Men

He that sets out on the journey of life, with a profound knowledge of books, but a shallow knowledge of men, with much sense of others, but little of his own, will find himself as completely at a loss on occasions of common and of constant recurrence, as a Dutchman without his pipe, a Frenchman without his mistress, an Italian without his fiddle, or an Englishman without his umbrella.

C.C. Colton, *Lacon*

Study is like the heaven's glorious sun,
    That will not be deep-searched with saucy looks;
Small have continual plodders ever won,
    Save base authority from others' books.

William Shakespeare, *Love's Labour's Lost*

The Mighty Dead

        Studious let me sit,
And hold high converse with the mighty dead—
Sages of ancient time, as gods revered,
As gods beneficent, who blessed mankind
With arts and arms, and humanized a world.
Roused at the inspiring thought, I throw aside
The long-lived volume.

James Thomson, *The Seasons*

The Message of Books

If books are only dead things, if they do not speak to one, or
answer one when one speaks to them, if they have nothing to
do with the common things that we are busy with—with the
sky over our head, and the ground under our feet—I think
that they had better stay on the shelves.... What I regret is
that many of us spend much of our time in reading books,
and in talking of books—that we like nothing worse than the
reputation of being indifferent to them, and nothing better
than the reputation of knowing a great deal about them; and
yet that, after all, we do not know them in the same way as
we know our fellow-creatures, not even in the way we know
any dumb animal that we walk with or play with. This is a
great misfortune, in my opinion, and one which I am afraid is
increasing as what we call 'the taste for literature' increases.
It is very pleasant to think in what distant parts of the earth

it [the English language] is spoken, and that in all those parts these books which are friends of ours are acknowledged as friends. And there is a living and productive power in them. They have produced an American literature, which is coming back to instruct us. They will produce by and by an Australian literature, which will be worth all the gold that is sent to us from the diggings.

F.D. Maurice, *The Friendship of Books*

Overrating the Virtue of Books

In modern times instruction is communicated chiefly by means of Books. Books are no doubt very useful helps to knowledge, and in some measure also, to the practice of useful arts and accomplishments, but they are not, in any case, the primary and natural sources of culture, and, in my opinion, their virtue is not a little apt to be overrated, even in those branches of acquirement where they seem most indispensable. They are not creative powers in any sense; they are merely helps, instruments, tools; and even as tools they are only artificial tools, superadded to those with which the wise prevision of Nature has equipped us, like telescopes and microscopes, whose assistance in many researches reveals unimagined wonders, but the use of which should never tempt us to undervalue or to neglect the exercise of our own eyes. The original and proper sources of knowledge are not books, but life, experience, personal thinking, feeling, and acting. When a man starts with these, books can fill up many gaps, correct much that is inaccurate, and extend much that is inadequate; but, without living experience to work on, books are like rain and sunshine fallen on unbroken soil.

J.S. Blackie, *On Self-culture*

What Profits It

And yet, alas! when all our lamps are burned,
   Our bodies wasted, and our spirits spent,
When we have all the learnèd volumes turned,
   Which yield men's wits both help and ornament,
What can we know or what can we discern?

Sir John Davies, *On the Immortality of the Soul*

How well he's read, to reason against reading!

William Shakespeare, *Love's Labour's Lost*

Books and Eyesight

Why, all delights are vain; but that most vain
Which, with pain purchased doth inherit pain:
As, painfully to pore upon a book,
   To seek the light of truth; while truth the while
Doth falsely blind the eyesight of his look:
   Light seeking light doth light of light beguile:
So, ere you find where light in darkness lies,
Your light grows dark by losing of your eyes.

William Shakespeare, *Love's Labour's Lost*

Books Instead of Stimulants

I know what it is to have had to toil when the brain was
throbbing, the mind incapable of originating a thought, and
the body worn and sore with exhaustion; and I know what it
is in such an hour, instead of having recourse to those gross
stimulants to which all worn men, both of the higher and
lower classes, are tempted, to take down my Sophocles or
my Plato (for Plato was a poet), my Goethe, or my Dante,

Shakespeare, Shelley, Wordsworth, or Tennyson; and I know
what it is to feel the jar of nerve gradually cease, and the
darkness in which all life had robed itself to the imagination
become light, discord pass into harmony, and physical exhaustion rise by degrees into a consciousness of power.

F.W. Robertson, *Lectures and Addresses*

A Literatura Hilaris

Cast your eyes down any list of English writers ... and almost
the only names that strike you as belonging to personally
cheerful men are Beaumont and Fletcher, Suckling, Fielding,
Farquhar, Steele, O'Keefe, Andrew Marvell, and Sterne....
I am only speaking of the rarity of a certain kind of sunshine
in our literature, and expressing a little rainy-day wish that
we had a little more of it. It ought to be collected. There
should be a joyous set of elegant extracts—a *Literatura
Hilaris* or *Gaudens*,—in a score of volumes, that we could
have at hand, like a cellaret of good wine, against April or
November weather. Fielding should be the port, and Farquhar
the champagne, and Sterne the malmsey; and whenever the
possessor cast an eye on his stock he should know that he had
a choice draught for himself after a disappointment, or for a
friend after dinner,—some cordial extract of Parson Adams,
or Plume, or Uncle Toby, generous as heart could desire, and
as wholesome for it as laughter for the lungs.

J.H. Leigh Hunt, *Cheerful Poets*

The Blessed Chloroform of the Mind

A congenial book can be taken up by any lover of books,
with the certainty of its transporting the reader within a few
minutes to a region immeasurably removed from that which
he desires to quit. The shape or pattern of the magic carpet

whereon he flies through space and time, is of no consequence. The son of science is rapt by a problem; the philosopher by an abstruse speculation; the antiquary is carried centuries back into the chivairic past; the lover of poetry is borne upon glittering wings into the future. The charm works well for all. Books are the blessed chloroform of the mind.... It is not a very high claim that is here set forth on behalf of Literature—that of Pass-time, and yet what a blessed boon even that is! Conceive the hours of *inertia* (a thing different from idleness) that it has mercifully consumed for us! hours wherein nothing could be done, nothing, perhaps, be *thought*, of our own selves, by reason of some impending calamity. Wisely does the dentist furnish his hateful antechamber with books of all sorts. Who could abide for an hour in such an apartment with nothing to occupy his thoughts save the expectation of that wrench to come! ... Indeed, it must be confessed that where Books fail as an anodyne, is rather in cases of physical than of mental pain. Through the long watches of the night, and by the bedside of some slowly dying dear one, it is easier to obtain forgetfulness—the only kind of rest that it may be safe or possible to take—by means of reading, than to do so when one is troubled with mere toothache. Nor does this arise from selfishness—since we would endure twenty toothaches, if they might give ease to the sufferer—but because the sharpness of the pang prevents our applying our mind to anything else; while the deep dull sorrow of the soul permits an intervening thought, and over it slides another, and then another, until a layer of such is formed, and the mind of the reader gets wholly free, for a brief but blessed time, partitioned off, as it were, from his real trouble.

James Payn, *Chambers's Journal*, 1864

Lounging Books

I sometimes wish for a catalogue of lounging books—books that one takes up in the gout, low spirits, *ennui*, or when in waiting for company. Some novels, gay poetry, odd whimsical authors, as Rabelais, &c. A catalogue raisonné of such might be itself a good lounging book.

Horace Walpole, *Letters*

To Drive the Night Away

So whan I saw I might not slepe,
Til now late, this other night,
Upon my bedde I sat upright,
And bad oon reche me a book,
A romaunce, and he hit me took
To rede and dryve the night away;
For me thoghte it better play
Than playen either at chesse or tables.

Geoffrey Chaucer, *The Book of the Duchesse*

Proof of Good Matter

If you find the Miltons in certain parts dirtied and soiled with a crumb of right Gloucester, blacked in the candle (my usual supper), or peradventure a stray ash of tobacco wafted into the crevices, look to that passage more especially: depend upon it, it contains good matter.

Charles Lamb, letter to S.T. Coleridge

The Dog and the Bone

At Mr. Dilly's to-day [April 15, 1778] ... before dinner Dr.
Johnson seized upon Mr. Charles Sheridan's *Account of the late
Revolution in Sweden*, and seemed to read it ravenously, as if
he devoured it, which was to all appearance his method of
studying. 'He knows how to read better than any one (said
Mrs. Knowles); he gets at the substance of a book directly; he
tears out the heart of it.' He kept it wrapt up in the tablecloth
in his lap during the time of dinner, from an avidity to have
one entertainment in readiness when he should have finished
another; resembling (if I may use so coarse a simile) a dog
who holds a bone in his paws in reserve, while he eats something else which has been thrown to him.

James Boswell, *Life of Johnson*

Writing at Meal Times

... Albeit, when I did dictate [these Chronicles], I thought
thereof no more than you, who possibly were drinking the
whilst, as I was. For in the composing of this lordly book I
never lost nor bestowed any more, nor any other time, than
what was appointed to serve me for taking of my bodily refec-
tion, that is, whilst I was eating and drinking. And, indeed,
that is the fittest and most proper hour, wherein to write
these high matters and deep sentences: as Homer knew very
well, the paragon of all philologues, and Ennius, the father
of the Latin poets, as Horace calls him, although a certain
sneaking jobbernol alleged that his verses smelled more of the
wine than oil.

François Rabelais, *The Life of Gargantua and Pantagruel*

Out-of-Doors Reading

I am not much a friend to out-of-doors reading. I cannot
settle my spirits to it. I knew a Unitarian minister, who was
generally to be seen upon Snow-hill (as yet Skinner's-street
was not), between the hours of ten and eleven in the morning,
studying a volume of Lardner. I own this to have been a strain
of abstraction beyond my reach. I used to admire how he
sidled along, keeping clear of secular contacts. An illiterate
encounter with a porter's knot, or a bread basket, would have
quickly put to flight all the theology I am master of, and have
left me worse than indifferent to the five points.

> Charles Lamb, *Detached Thoughts on Books and Reading*

O for a Booke

O for a Booke and a shadie nooke,
    Eyther in-a-doore or out,
With the greene leaves whisp'ring overhede,
    Or the Streete cryes all about,
Where I may Reade all at my ease,
    Both of the Newe and Olde,
For a jollie goode Booke whereon to looke,
    Is better to me than golde.

> John Wilson

Farewell to Books in Springtime

Than mote we to bokes that we finde,
Through which that olde thinges been in minde,
And to the doctrine of these olde wyse,
Yeven credence, in every skilful wyse,
And trowen on these olde aproved stories
Of holinesse, of regnes, of victories,

Of love, of hate, of other sundry thinges,
Of whiche I may not maken rehersinges,
And if that olde bokes were a-weye,
Y-loren were of remembraunce the keye.
Wel oghte us than on olde bokes leve,
Ther-as ther is non other assay by preve,
    And, as for me, though that my wit be lyte,
On bokes for to rede I me delyte,
And in myn herte have hem in reverence;
And to hem yeve swich lust and swich credence,
That ther is wel unethe game noon
That from my bokes make me to goon,
But hit be other up-on the haly-day,
Or elles in the joly tyme of May;
Whan that I here the smale foules singe,
And that the floures ginne for to springe,
Farwel my studie, as lasting that sesoun!

Geoffrey Chaucer, *The Legend of Good Women*

The Tables Turned

Up! up! my Friend, and quit your books;
Or surely you'll grow double:
Up! up! my Friend, and clear your looks;
Why all this toil and trouble?

The sun, above the mountain's head,
A freshening lustre mellow
Through all the long green fields has spread,
His first sweet evening yellow.

Books! 'tis a dull and endless strife:
Come, hear the woodland linnet,
How sweet his music! on my life,
There's more of wisdom in it.

And hark! how blithe the throstle sings!
He, too, is no mean preacher:
Come forth into the light of things,
Let Nature be your Teacher.

She has a world of ready wealth,
Our minds and hearts to bless—
Spontaneous wisdom breathed by health,
Truth breathed by cheerfulness.

One impulse from a vernal wood
May teach you more of man,
Of moral evil and of good,
Than all the sages can.

Sweet is the love which Nature brings;
Our meddling intellect
Mis-shapes the beauteous forms of things:—
We murder to dissect.

Enough of Science and of Art;
Close up those barren leaves;
Come forth, and bring with you a heart
That watches and receives.

William Wordsworth

Picture Books in Winter

Summer fading, winter comes—
Frosty mornings, tingling thumbs,
Window robins, winter rooks,
And the picture story-books.

Water now is turned to stone
Nurse and I can walk upon;
Still we find the flowing brooks
In the picture story-books.

All the pretty things put by,
Wait upon the children's eye,
Sheep and shepherds, trees and crooks,
In the picture story-books.

We may see how all things are,
Seas and cities, near and far,
And the flying fairies' looks
In the picture story-books.

How am I to sing your praise,
Happy chimney-corner days,
Sitting safe in nursery nooks,
Reading picture story-books?

Robert Louis Stevenson, *A Child's Garden of Verses*

Old Story Books

Old Story Books! Old Story Books! we owe ye much,
    old friends,
Bright-coloured threads in Memory's warp, of which Death
    holds the ends.
Who can forget ye? who can spurn the ministers of joy
That waited on the lisping girl and petticoated boy?
I know that ye could win my heart when every bribe or threat
Failed to allay my stamping rage, or break my sullen pet:
A 'promised story' was enough, and I turned, with eager smile,
To learn about the naughty 'pig that would not mount
    the stile'.

There was a spot in days of yore whereon I used to stand,
With mighty question in my head and penny in my hand;
Where motley sweets and crinkled cakes made up a
    good show,
And 'story books' upon a string appeared in brilliant row.
What should I have? the peppermint was incense in my nose,
But I had heard of 'hero Jack', who slew his giant foes
My lonely coin was balanced long, before the tempting stall,
'Twixt book and bull's eye—but, forsooth! 'Jack' got it
    after all.

Talk of your 'vellum, gold embossed', 'morocco', 'roan',
    and 'calf',
The blue and yellow wraps of old were prettier by half;
And as to pictures—well we know that never one was made
Like that where 'Bluebeard' swings aloft his wife-destroying
    blade.
'Hume's England'—pshaw! what history of battles, states,
    and men,
Can vie with Memoirs 'all about sweet little Jenny Wren'?
And what are all the wonders that e'er struck a nation dumb,
To those recorded as performed by 'Master Thomas Thumb'?

Miss 'Riding Hood', poor luckless child! my heart grew big
  with dread
When the grim 'wolf', in 'grandmamma's' best bonnet,
  showed his head;
I shuddered when, in innocence, she meekly peeped beneath,
And made remarks about 'great eyes', and wondered at
  'great teeth'.
And then the 'House that Jack built', and the 'Beanstalk'
  Jack cut down,
And 'Jack's eleven brothers', on their travels of renown;
And 'Jack', whose cracked and plastered head ensured him
  lyric fame,
These, these, methinks, make 'vulgar Jack' a rather
  classic name.

Fair 'Valentine', I loved him well; but, better still the bear
That hugged his brother in her arms with tenderness and care.
I lingered spellbound o'er the page, though eventide wore late,
And left my supper all untouched to fathom 'Orson's' fate.
Then 'Robin with his merry men', a noble band were they,
We'll never see the like again, go hunting where we may.
In Lincoln garb, with bow and barb, rapt Fancy bore me on,
Through Sherwood's dewy forest paths, close after
  'Little John'.

Miss 'Cinderella' and her 'shoe' kept long their reigning
  powers,
Till harder words and longer themes beguiled my flying hours;
And 'Sinbad', wondrous sailor he, allured me on his track,
And set me shouting when he flung the old man from his back.
And oh! that tale—the matchless tale that made me dream
  at night—
Of 'Crusoe's' shaggy robe of fur, and 'Friday's' death-spurred
  flight;
Nay, still I read it, and again, in sleeping visions, see
The savage dancers on the sand—the raft upon the sea.

Old Story Books! Old Story Books! I doubt if 'Reason's Feast'
Provides a dish that pleases more than 'Beauty and the Beast';
I doubt if all the ledger-leaves that bear a sterling sum,
Yield happiness like those that told of 'Master Horner's plum'.
Old Story Books! Old Story Books! I never pass ye by
Without a sort of furtive glance—right loving, though 'tis sly;
And fair suspicion may arise—that yet my spirit grieves
For dear 'Old Mother Hubbard's Dog' and 'Ali Baba's Thieves'.

Eliza Cook

The First Authors for Youth

And as it is fit to read the best authors to youth first, so let
them be of the openest and clearest: as Livy before Sallust,
Sidney before Donne; and beware of letting them taste
Gower or Chaucer at first, lest falling too much in love with
antiquity, and not apprehending the weight, they grow rough
and barren in language only. When their judgements are firm
and out of danger, let them read both the old and the new;
but no less take heed that their new flowers and sweetness
do not as much corrupt as the others' dryness and squalor, if
they choose not carefully. Spenser, in affecting the ancients,
writ no language: yet I would have him read for his matter,
but as Virgil read Ennius. The reading of Homer and Virgil is
counselled by Quintilian as the best way of informing youth
and confirming man. For, besides that the mind is raised
with the height and sublimity of such a verse, it takes spirit
from the greatness of the matter, and is tincted with the best
things. Tragic and lyric poetry is good too; and comic with
the best, if the manners of the reader be once in safety.

Ben Jonson, Timber

Advice to Mothers

Mr. B——— has just put into my hands Mr. Locke's *Treatise on Education*, and he commands me to give him my thoughts upon it in writing. He has a very high regard for this author, and tells me that my tenderness for Billy will make me think some of the first advice given in it a little harsh, perhaps; but, although he has not read it through, only having dipped into it here and there, he believes, from the name of the author, I cannot have a better directory; and my opinion of it, after I have well considered it, will inform him, he says, of my own capacity and prudence, and how far he may rely upon both in the point of a first education.

Samuel Richardson, Pamela

Getting a Boy Forward

I am always for getting a boy forward in his learning; for that is a sure good. I would let him at first read *any* English book which happens to engage his attention; because you have done a great deal when you have brought him to have entertainment from a book. He'll get better books afterwards.

Samuel Johnson, Boswell's Life

At Large in the Library

I would put a child into a library (where no unfit books are) and let him read at his choice. A child should not be discouraged from reading anything that he takes a liking to, from a notion that it is above his reach. If that be the case, the child will soon find it out and desist; if not, he of course gains the instruction; which is so much the more likely to come, from the inclination with which he takes up the study.

Samuel Johnson, Boswell's Life

The Best Books the Commonest

Books are but one inlet of knowledge; and the powers of
the mind, like those of the body, should be left open to all
impressions. I applied too close to my studies, soon after I
was of your age, and hurt myself irreparably by it. Whatever
may be the value of learning, health and good spirits are of
more.... By conversing with the *mighty dead*, we imbibe sentiment with knowledge. We become strongly attached to those
who can no longer either hurt or serve us, except through
the influence which they exert over the mind. We feel the
presence of that power which gives immortality to human
thoughts and actions, and catch the flame of enthusiasm from
all ages and nations.... As to the books you will have to read
by choice or for amusement, the best are the commonest.
The names of many of them are already familiar to you. Read
them as you grow up with all the satisfaction in your power,
and make much of them. It is, perhaps, the greatest pleasure
you will have in life; the one you will think of longest, and
repent of least. If my life had been more full of calamity than
it has been (much more than I hope yours will be), I would
live it over again, my poor little boy, to have read the books I
did in my youth.

William Hazlitt, *On the Conduct of Life;*
or Advice to a Schoolboy

Montaigne's Early Reading

The first taste or feeling I had of books, was of the pleasure I
took in reading the fables of Ovid's *Metamorphoses*; for, being
but seven or eight years old, I would steal and sequester myself
from all other delights, only to read them: Forsomuch as the
tongue wherein they were written was to me natural; and
it was the easiest book I knew, and by reason of the matter
therein contained most agreeing with my young age. For of

King Arthur, of Lancelot du Lake, of Amadis, of Huon of
Bordeaux, and such idle time-consuming and wit-besotting
trash of books wherein youth doth commonly amuse itself, I
was not so much as acquainted with their names, and to this
day know not their bodies, nor what they contain, so exact
was my discipline. Whereby I became more careless to study
my other prescript lessons. And well did it fall out for my
purpose that I had to deal with a very discreet master, who
out of his judgement could with such dexterity wink at and
second my untowardliness, and such other faults that were
in me. For by that means I read over Virgil's *Aeneas*, Terence,
Plautus, and other Italian comedies, allured thereunto by the
pleasantness of their several subjects: Had he been so foolishly-
severe, or so severely froward as to cross this course of mine,
I think, verily, I had never brought anything from the college
but the hate and contempt of books, as doth the greatest part
of our nobility. Such was his discretion, and so warily did
he behave himself, that he saw and would not see: he would
foster and increase my longing: suffering me but by stealth and
by snatches to glut myself with those books, holding ever a
gentle hand over me, concerning other regular studies.

Michel de Montaigne

Johnson's Early Reading

Sir, in my early years I read very hard. It is a sad reflection,
but a true one, that I knew almost as much at eighteen as I do
now [then aged fifty-four]. My judgement, to be sure, was not
so good; but I had all the facts. I remember very well, when I
was at Oxford, an old gentleman said to me, 'Young man, ply
your book diligently now and acquire a stock of knowledge;
for when years come upon you, you will find that poring
upon books will be but an irksome task.'

Samuel Johnson, Boswell's *Life*

Gibbon's Early Reading

The perusal of the Roman classics was at once my exercise and reward. Dr. Middleton's *History*, which I then appreciated above its true value, naturally directed me to the writings of Cicero. The most perfect editions, that of Olivet, which may adorn the shelves of the rich, that of Ernesti, which should lie on the table of the learned, were not within my reach. For the familiar epistles I used the text and English commentary of Bishop Ross; but my general edition was that of Verburgius, published at Amsterdam in two large volumes in folio, with an indifferent choice of various notes.... Cicero in Latin, and Xenophon in Greek, are indeed the two ancients whom I would first propose to a liberal scholar....

In the infancy of my reason I turned over, as an idle amusement, the most serious and important treatise: in its maturity, the most trifling performance could exercise my taste or judgement; and more than once I have been led by a novel into a deep and instructive train of thinking.

Edward Gibbon, *Autobiography*

A Birth of Intellect

When only eleven years old, with three pence in my pocket—my whole fortune—I perceived, at Richmond, in a bookseller's window, a little book, marked 'Price Threepence'—Swift's *Tale of a Tub*. Its odd title excited my curiosity; I bought it in place of my supper. So impatient was I to examine it, that I got over into a field at the upper corner of Kew Gardens, and sat down to read, on the shady side of a haystack. The book was so different from anything I had read before—it was something so new to my mind, that, though I could not at all understand some parts of it, still it delighted me beyond measure, and produced, what I have always considered, a sort of birth of intellect. I read on till it was dark, without any thought of supper or bed. When I could see no longer, I put it into my pocket, and fell asleep beside the stack, till the birds awaked me in the morning; and then I started off, still reading my little book. I could relish nothing beside; I carried it about with me wherever I went, till, when about twenty years old, I lost it in a box that fell overboard in the Bay of Fundy.

William Cobbett

Wordsworth's Early Reading

A precious treasure had I long possessed,
A little yellow, canvas-covered book,
A slender abstract of the Arabian Tales;
And, from companions in a new abode,
When first I learnt, that this dear prize of mine
Was but a block hewn from a mighty quarry—
That there were four large volumes, laden all
With kindred matter, 'twas to me, in truth,
A promise scarcely earthly. Instantly,
With one not richer than myself, I made
A covenant that each should lay aside
The moneys he possessed, and hoard up more,
Till our joint savings had amassed enough
To make this book our own. Through several months,
In spite of all temptations, we preserved
Religiously that vow; but firmness failed,
Nor were we ever masters of our wish.

And when thereafter to my father's house
The holidays returned me, there to find
That golden store of books which I had left,
What joy was mine! How often in the course
Of those glad respites, though a soft west wind
Ruffled the waters to the angler's wish,
For a whole day together, have I lain
Down by thy side, O Derwent! murmuring stream,

On the hot stones, and in the glaring sun,
And there have read, devouring as I read,
Defrauding the day's glory, desperate!
Till with a sudden bound of smart reproach,
Such as an idler deals with in his shame,
I to the sport betook myself again.

A gracious spirit o'er this earth presides,
And o'er the heart of man: invisibly
It comes, to works of unreproved delight,
And tendency benign, directing those
Who care not, know not, think not what they do.
The tales that charm away the wakeful night
In Araby, romances; legends penned
For solace by dim light of monkish lamps;
Fictions, for ladies of their love, devised
By youthful squires; adventures endless, spun
By the dismantled warrior in old age,
Out of the bowels of those very schemes
In which his youth did first extravagate;
These spread like day, and something in the shape
Of these will live till man shall be no more.
Dumb yearnings, hidden appetites, are ours,
And *they must* have their food. Our childhood sits,
Our simple childhood, sits upon a throne
That hath more power than all the elements.
I guess not what this tells of Being past,
Nor what it augurs of the life to come;
But so it is, and, in that dubious hour,
That twilight when we first begin to see
This dawning earth, to recognise, expect,
And, in the long probation that ensues,
The time of trial, ere we learn to live
In reconcilement with our stinted powers;
To endure this state of meagre vassalage,
Unwilling to forgo, confess, submit,

Uneasy and unsettled, yoke-fellows
To custom, mettlesome, and not yet tamed
And humbled down;—oh! then we feel, we feel,
We know where we have friends. Ye dreamers, then,
Forgers of daring tales! we bless you then,
Impostors, drivellers, dotards, as the ape
Philosophy will call you: *then* we feel
With what, and how great might ye are in league,
Who make our wish, our power, our thought a deed,
An empire, a possession,—ye whom time
And seasons serve; all Faculties to whom
Earth crouches, the elements are potter's clay,
Space like a heaven filled up with northern lights,
Here, nowhere, there, and everywhere at once.

William Wordsworth, *The Prelude*

Old-Fashioned Verse

In verse alone I ran not wild
When I was hardly more than child.
Contented with the native lay
Of Pope or Prior, Swift or Gay,
Or Goldsmith, or that graver bard
Who led me to the lone churchyard.
    Then listened I to Spenser's strain,
Till Chaucer's Canterbury train
Came trooping past, and carried me
In more congenial company.
Soon my soul was hurried o'er
This bright scene: the 'solemn roar'
Of organ, under Milton's hand.
Struck me mute: he bade me stand
Where none other ambled near....
I obeyed, with love and fear.

Walter Savage Landor

Leigh Hunt's Early Reading

Cowley says that even when he was 'a very young boy at school, instead of his running about on holidays, and playing with his fellows, he was wont to steal from them and walk into the fields, either alone with a book, or with some one companion, if he could find one of the same temper'. When I was at school, I had no fields to run into, or I should certainly have gone there; and I must own to having played a great deal; but then I drew my sports as much as possible out of books, playing at Trojan wars, chivalrous encounters with coal-staves, and even at religious mysteries. When I was not at these games I was either reading in a corner, or walking round the cloisters with a book under one arm and my friend linked with the other, or with my thoughts. It has since been my fate to realize all the romantic notions I had of a friend at that time.

J.H. Leigh Hunt, *My Books*

A Kindly Tie

Then, above all, we had Walter Scott, the kindly, the generous, the pure—the companion of what countless delightful hours; the purveyor of how much happiness; the friend whom we recall as the constant benefactor of our youth! How well I remember the type and the brownish paper of the old duodecimo *Tales of My Landlord*! ... Oh! for a half-holiday, and a quiet corner, and one of those books again! Those books, and perhaps those eyes with which we read them; and, it may be, the brains behind the eyes! It may be the tart was good; but how fresh the appetite was! ... The boy critic loves the story; grown up, he loves the author who wrote the story. Hence the kindly tie is established between writer and reader, and lasts pretty nearly for life.

William Makepeace Thackeray, *Roundabout Papers*

Charles Dickens's Early Reading

My father had left a small collection of books in a little room upstairs, to which I had access (for it adjoined my own), and which nobody else in our house ever troubled. From that blessed little room, Roderick Random, Peregrine Pickle, Humphrey Clinker, Tom Jones, the Vicar of Wakefield, Don Quixote, Gil Blas, and Robinson Crusoe, came out, a glorious host, to keep me company. They kept alive my fancy, and my hope of something beyond that place and time,—they, and the Arabian Nights, and the Tales of the Genii—and did me no harm; for whatever harm was in some of them was not there for me; *I* knew nothing of it. It is astonishing to me now, how I found time, in the midst of my porings and blunderings over heavier themes, to read those books as I did. It is curious to me how I could ever have consoled myself under my small troubles (which were great troubles to me), by impersonating my favourite characters in them—as I did—and by putting Mr. and Miss Murdstone into all the bad ones—which I did too. I have been Tom Jones (a child's Tom Jones, a harmless creature) for a week together. I have sustained my own idea of Roderick Random for a month at a stretch, I verily believe. I had a greedy relish for a few volumes of Voyages and Travels—I forget what, now—that were on those shelves; and for days and days I can remember to have gone about my region of our house, armed with the centre-piece out of an old set of boot-trees—the perfect realization of Captain Somebody, of the Royal British Navy, in danger of being beset by savages, and resolved to sell his life at a great price. The Captain never lost dignity, from having his ears boxed with the Latin grammar. I did; but the Captain was a Captain and a hero, in despite of all the grammars of all the languages in the world, dead or alive.

This was my only and my constant comfort. When I think of it, the picture always rises in my mind, of a summer evening, the boys at play in the churchyard, and I sitting on

my bed, reading as if for life. Every barn in the neighbourhood, every stone in the church, and every foot of the
churchyard, had some association of its own, in my mind,
connected with these books, and stood for some locality made
famous in them.

Charles Dickens, *David Copperfield*

The Visionary Gleam

Books have in a great measure lost their power over me; nor
can I revive the same interest in them as formerly. I perceive
when a thing is good, rather than feel it. It is true, '"Marcian
Colonna" is a dainty book'; and the reading of Mr. Keats's *Eve
of St. Agnes* lately made me regret that I was not young again.
The beautiful and tender images there conjured up, 'come
like shadows—so depart.' The 'tiger-moth's wings', which
he has spread over his rich poetic blazonry, just flit across my
fancy; the gorgeous twilight window which he has painted
over again in his verse, to me 'blushes' almost in vain 'with
blood of queens and kings'. I know how I should have felt at
one time in reading such passages; and that is all. The sharp
luscious flavour, the fine *aroma* is fled, and nothing but the
stalk, the bran, the husk of literature is left.

William Hazlitt, *On Reading Old Books*

Reading for Love's Sake

If thou survive my well-contented day,
When that churl Death my bones with dust shall cover,
And shalt by fortune once more re-survey
These poor rude lines of thy deceasèd lover.
Compare them with the bettering of the time,
And though they be outstripped by every pen,
Reserve them for my love, not for their rime,

Exceeded by the height of happier men.
O! then vouchsafe me but this loving thought:
'Had my friend's Muse grown with this growing age,
A dearer birth than this his love had brought.
To march in ranks of better equipage:
   But since he died, and poets better prove,
   Theirs for their style I'll read, his for his love.'

William Shakespeare,
Sonnet XXXII

Valediction to His Book

I'll tell thee now (dear love) what thou shalt do
   To anger destiny, as she doth us;
   How I shall stay, though she eloign me thus,
And how posterity shall know it too;
      How thine may out-endure
      Sibyl's glory, and obscure
      Her who from Pindar could allure,
And her, through whose help Lucan is not lame,
And her, whose book (they say) Homer did find, and name.

Study our manuscripts, those myriads
   Of letters, which have passed 'twixt thee and me;
   Thence write our annals, and in them will be
To all whom love's subliming fire invades
      Rule and example found;
      There the faith of any ground
      No schismatic will dare to wound,
That sees how Love this grace to us affords,
To make, to keep, to use, to be these his records.

This book, as long-lived as the elements,
   Or as the world's form, this all-gravèd tome
   In cypher writ, or new-made idiom;

We for Love's clergy only are instruments;
    When this book is made thus,
    Should again the ravenous
    Vandals and the Goths invade us,
Learning were safe; in this our universe,
Schools might learn sciences, spheres music, angels verse.

Here Love's divines—since all divinity
    Is love or wonder—may find all they seek,
    Whether abstract spiritual love they like,
Their souls exhaled with what they do not see;
    Or, loth so to amuse
    Faith's infirmity, they choose
    Something which they may see and use;
For, though mind be the heaven, where love doth sit,
Beauty a convenient type may be to figure it.

Here more than in their books may lawyers find,
    Both by what titles mistresses are ours,
    And how prerogative these states devours,
Transferred from Love himself to womankind;
    Who, though from heart and eyes,
    They exact great subsidies,
    Forsake him who on them relies;
And for the cause, honour or conscience give;
Chimeras vain as they or their prerogative.

Here statesmen—or of them, they which can read—
    May of their occupation find the grounds;
    Love, and their art, alike it deadly wounds,
If to consider what 'tis, one proceed.
    In both they do excel,
    Who the present govern well,
    Whose weakness none doth, or dares, tell;
In this thy book, such will there something see,
As in the Bible some can find out alchemy.

Thus vent thy thoughts; abroad I'll study thee,
   As he removes far off, that great heights takes;
   How great love is, presence best trial makes,
But absence tries how long this love will be;
     To take a latitude
     Sun, or stars, are fitliest viewed
     At their brightest, but to conclude
Of longitudes, what other way have we,
But to mark when and where the dark eclipses be?

                     John Donne

The Book of the Brain

     From the table of my memory
I'll wipe away all trivial fond records,
All saws of books, all forms, all pressures past,
That youth and observation copied there;
And thy commandment all alone shall live
Within the book and volume of my brain.

           William Shakespeare, *Hamlet*

Love's Purveyor

No greater grief than to remember days
Of joy, when misery is at hand. That kens
Thy learned instructor. Yet so eagerly
If thou art bent to know the primal root,
From whence our love gat being, I will do
As one, who weeps and tells his tale. One day,
For our delight we read of Lancelot,
How him love thralled. Alone we were, and no
Suspicion near us. Oft-times by that reading
Our eyes were drawn together, and the hue
Fled from our altered cheek. But at one point

Alone we fell. When of that smile we read,
The wishèd smile so rapturously kissed
By one so deep in love, then he, who ne'er
From me shall separate, at once my lips
All trembling kissed. The book and writer both
Were love's purveyors. In its leaves that day
We read no more.

Dante Alighieri, Inferno

The Double Lesson

Maiden of Padua, on thy lap
   Thus lightly let the volume lie;
And as within some pictured map
   Fair isles and waters we descry.
Trace out, with white and gliding finger,
   Along the truth-illumined page,
Its golden lines and words that linger
   In memory's cell, from youth to age.

The young Preceptor at thy side
   Had pupil ne'er before so fair;
And though that scholar be thy guide,
   He sits that fellow-learner there.
As every page unfolds its meaning,
   As every rustling leaf turns o'er,
He finds, whilst o'er thy studies leaning,
   Beauty where all was dull before.

Familiar is the book to him,
   A record of heroic deed;
Yet deems he now his eyes were dim,
   And thine have taught them first to read.
Now fades in him the scholar's glory;

For he would give the fame he sought,
With thee to read the simplest story,
   And learn what sages never taught.

The precious wealth of countless books,
   Lies stowed within his grasping mind;
Yet should he not peruse thy looks,
   He now were more than Ignorance blind.
From many a language, old, enchanting,
   Rare truths to nations he enrolls;
But one old language yet was wanting,
   The one you teach him—tis the soul's.
. . .

Full long this lesson, Pupil fair!
   All pupils else hath he forsook;
He draws still nearer to thy chair,
   And bends yet closer o'er the book.
As time flies on, now fast, now fleeter,
   More slowly is the page turned o'er;
The lesson seems to both the sweeter,
   And more enchanting grows the lore.

The book now yields a tenderer theme;
   The Master loses all his art,
The Pupil droops as in a dream,
   And both are reading with one heart.
His eyes upraised a moment glisten
   With hope, and joy, and fear profound;
While thine, oh, Maiden! do they *listen*?
   They seem to *hear* his sigh's faint sound.

But hark! what sound indeed breaks through
   The silence of that life-long hour!
Melodious tinklings, such as sue
   For favour near a lady's bower.

Ah! Maid of Padua, music swelling
   In tribute to thy radiant charms,
Now greets thee in thy father's dwelling,
   To woo thee from a father's arms.

The suitor comes with song and lute,
   Youth, riches, pleasures, round him wait;
Go bid him, Paduan Maid, be mute,
   Thy lot is cast, he comes too late!
One lesson given, and one received,
   The Book prevails, the Lute's denied;
With love thy inmost heart has heaved,
   And thou shalt be a student's bride.

Samuel Laman Blanchard

Cupid and the Book of Poems

Cadenus many things had writ:
Vanessa much esteemed his wit,
And called for his Poetic Works:
Meantime the boy in secret lurks;
And, while the book was in her hand,
The urchin from his private stand
Took aim, and shot with all his strength
A dart of such prodigious length,
It pierced the feeble volume through,
And deep transfixed her bosom too.
Some lines, more moving than the rest,
Stuck to the point that pierced her breast,
And, borne directly to her heart,
With pains unknown increased her smart.

Jonathan Swift, Cadenus and Vanessa

Books as Spokesmen

O! let my books be then the eloquence
And dumb presagers of my speaking breast.

William Shakespeare, Sonnet XXIII

To His Book: of His Lady

Happy, ye leaves, when as those lily hands,
Which hold my life in their dead doing might,
Shall handle you, and hold in love's soft bands,
Like captives trembling at the victor's sight.
And happy lines on which, with starry light,
Those lamping eyes will deign sometimes to look,
And read the sorrows of my dying spright,
Written with tears in heart's close bleeding book.
And happy rhymes bathed in the sacred brook
Of Helicon, whence she derivèd is,
When ye behold that Angel's blessèd look,
My soul's long-lackèd food, my heaven's bliss.
   Leaves, lines, and rhymes, seek her to please alone,
   Whom if ye please, I care for other none.

Edmund Spenser, Amoretti

To the Lady Lucy, Countess of Bedford

And this fair course of knowledge whereunto
   Your studies, learned Lady, are addressed,
   Is the only certain way that you can go
Unto true glory, to true happiness:
   All passages on earth besides, are so
   Incumbered with such vain disturbances;
As still we lose our rest in seeking it,
   Being but deluded with appearances;
   And no key had you else that was so fit
To unlock that prison of your sex, as this;
   To let you out of weakness, and admit
   Your powers into the freedom of that bliss
That sets you there where you may oversee
   This rolling world, and view it as it is;
   And apprehend how the outsides do agree
With the inward being of the things we deem
   And hold in our ill-cast accounts, to be
   Of highest value and of best esteem;
Since all the good we have rests in the mind,
   By whose proportions only we redeem
   Our thoughts from out confusion, and do find
The measure of our selves, and of our powers.
   ...

And though books, madam, cannot make this mind,
   Which we must bring apt to be set aright;
   Yet do they rectify it in that kind,
And touch it so, as that it turns that way
   Where judgement lies: and though we cannot find
   The certain place of truth, yet do they stay
And entertain us near about the same;
   And give the soul the best delight that may
   Encheer it most, and most our spirits inflame
To thoughts of glory, and to worthy ends.

Samuel Daniel

A Book of Flesh and Blood

There's a lady for my humour!
A pretty book of flesh and blood, and well
Bound up, in a fair letter, too. Would I
Had her, with all the Errata.

First I would marry her, that's a verb material,
Then I would print her with an *index*
Expurgatorius; a table drawn
Of her court heresies; and when she's read,
Cum privilegio, who dares call her wanton?

James Shirley, The Cardinal

Women's Eyes

From women's eyes this doctrine I derive:
They sparkle still the right Promethean fire;
They are the books, the arts, the academes,
That show, contain, and nourish all the world.

William Shakespeare, Love's Labour's Lost

  My only books
  Were woman's looks,—
And folly's all they've taught me.

Thomas Moore

Of a New Married Student that Played Fast and Loose

A student, at his book so placed
   That wealth he might have won,
From book to wife did flit in haste,
   From wealth to woe to run.
Now, who hath played a feater cast,
   Since juggling first begun?
In *knitting* of himself so *fast*,
   Himself he hath *undone*.

Sir Thomas More (?)

Marriage and Books

I understand with a deep sense of sorrow of the indisposition
of your Son: I fear he hath too much *mind* for his *body*, and
that superabounds with fancy, which brings him to these fits
of distemper, proceeding from the black humour of melancholy: moreover, I have observed that he is too much given
to his study and self-society, 'specially to converse with dead
men, I mean Books: you know anything in excess is naught.
Now, sir, were I worthy to give you advice, I could wish he
were well married, and it may wean him from that bookish
and thoughtful humour.

James Howell, *Familiar Letters*

Marriage! My Years are Young

Marriage, uncle! alas! my years are young,
And fitter is my study and my books
Than wanton dalliance with a paramour.

William Shakespeare, *First Part of King Henry the Sixth*

Love and the Library

I do not know that I am happiest when alone; but this I am
sure of, that I am never long even in the society of her I love
without a yearning for the company of my lamp and my
utterly confused and tumbled-over library.

George Gordon, Lord Byron

A Counter Attraction

So have I known a hopeful youth
Sit down in quest of lore and truth,
With tomes sufficient to confound him,
Like Tohu Bohu, heaped around him,—
Mamurra stuck to Theophrastus,
And Galen tumbling o'er Bombastus.
When lo! while all that's learned and wise
Absorbs the boy, he lifts his eyes,
And through the window of his study
Beholds some damsel fair and ruddy,
With eyes, as brightly turned upon him as
The angel's were on Hieronymus.
Quick fly the folios, widely scattered,
Old Homer's laurelled brow is battered,
And Sappho, headlong sent, flies just in
The reverend eye of St. Augustin.
Raptured he quits each dozing sage,
Oh woman, for thy lovelier page:
Sweet book!—unlike the books of art,—
Whose errors are thy fairest part:
In whom the dear errata column
Is the best page in all the volume!

Thomas Moore, The Devil among the Scholars

To Cosmelia

Some Verses, written in September, 1676, on presenting a Book.

Go, humble gift, go to that matchless saint,
Of whom thou only wast a copy meant:
And all, that's read in thee, more richly find
Comprised in the fair volume of her mind;
That living system, where are fully writ
All those high morals, which in books we meet:
Easy, as in soft air, there writ they are,
Yet firm, as if in brass they graven were.

John Oldham

On a Prayer Book Sent to Mrs M.R.

Lo, here a little volume, but great book!
A nest of new-born sweets,
Whose native fires disdaining
To be thus folded, and complaining
Of these ignoble sheets,
Affect more comely bands,
Fair one, from thy kind hands,
And confidently look
To find the rest
Of a rich binding in your breast!

It is in one choice handful, heaven; and all
Heaven's royal host; encamped thus small
To prove that true, schools use to tell,
A thousand angels in one point can dwell.

It is love's great artillery,
Which here contracts itself, and comes to lie
Close couched in your white bosom; and from thence,
As from a snowy fortress of defence,
Against your ghostly foes to take your part,
And fortify the hold of your chaste heart.

It is an armoury of light;
Let constant use but keep it bright,
    You'll find it yields
To holy hands and humble hearts
    More swords and shields
Than sin hath snares, or hell hath darts.
    Only be sure
    The hands be pure
That hold these weapons, and the eyes
Those of turtles, chaste and true,
    Wakeful, and wise;
Here is a friend shall fight for you;
Hold but this book before your heart,
Let prayer alone to play his part.

Richard Crashaw

On George Herbert's 'The Temple' Sent to a Gentlewoman

Know you, fair, on what you look?
Divinest love lies in this book:
Expecting fire from your fair eyes,
To kindle this his sacrifice.
When your hands untie these strings,
Think, you've an angel by the wings;
One that gladly would be nigh,
To wait upon each morning sigh;
To flutter in the balmy air

Of your well-perfumèd prayer;
These white plumes of his he'll lend you,
Which every day to heaven will send you:
To take acquaintance of each sphere,
And all your smooth-faced kindred there.
And though Herbert's name do owe

These devotions, fairest, know
While I thus lay them on the shrine
Of your white hand, they are mine.

Richard Crashaw

To Helen

Written in the first leaf of Keble's Christian Year,
a birthday Present.

My Helen, for its golden fraught
Of prayer and praise, of dream and thought,
Where Poesy finds fitting voice
For all who hope, fear, grieve, rejoice,
Long have I loved, and studied long,
The pious minstrel's varied song.

Whence is the volume dearer now?
There gleams a smile upon your brow,
Wherein, methinks, I read how well
You guess the reason, ere I tell,
Which makes to me the single rhymes
More prized, more conned, a hundred times.

Ere vanished quite the dread and doubt
Affection ne'er was born without,
Found we not here a magic key
Opening thy secret soul to me?
Found we not here a mystic sign
Interpreting thy heart to mine?

What sympathies up-springing fast
Through all the future, all the past,
In tenderest links began to bind
Spirit to spirit, mind to mind,
As we, together wandering o'er
The little volume's precious store,

Mused, with alternate smile and tear,
On the high themes awakened here
Of fervent hope, of calm belief,
Of cheering joy, of chastening grief,
The trials borne, the sins forgiven,
The task on earth, the meed in heaven.

My Own! oh surely from above
Was shed that confidence of love,
Which in such happy moments nurst
When soul with soul had converse first,
Now through the snares and storms of life
Blesses the husband and the wife!

W.M. Praed

Sent with Poems

Little volume, warm with wishes,
Fear not brows that never frown!
After Byron's peppery dishes
Matho's mild skim-milk goes down.

Change she wants not, self-concentered,
She whom Attic graces please,
She whose Genius never entered
Literature's gin-palaces.

Walter Savage Landor

A Cheap and Lasting Pleasure

I yet retain, and carefully cherish, my love of reading. If relays
of eyes were to be hired like post-horses, I would never admit
any but silent companions: they afford a constant variety of
entertainment, which is almost the only one pleasing in the
enjoyment, and inoffensive in the consequence.... Every
woman endeavours to breed her daughter a fine lady, qualify-
ing her for a station in which she never will appear: and at

the same time incapacitating her for that retirement to which she is destined. Learning, if she has a real taste for it, will not only make her contented, but happy in it. No entertainment is so cheap as reading, nor any pleasure so lasting. She will not want new fashions, nor regret the loss of expensive diversions, or variety of company, if she can be amused with an author in her closet.... Daughter! daughter! don't call names; you are always abusing my pleasures, which is what no mortal will bear. Trash, lumber, sad stuff, are the titles you give to my favourite amusement. If I called a white staff a stick of wood, a gold key gilded brass, and the ensigns of illustrious orders coloured strings, this may be philosophically true, but would be very ill received. We have all our playthings; happy are they that can be contented with those they can obtain: those hours are spent in the wisest manner that can easiest shade the ills of life, and are least productive of ill consequences. I think my time better employed in reading the adventures of imaginary people, than the Duchess of Marlborough's, who passed the latter years of her life in paddling with her will, and contriving schemes of plaguing some, and extracting praise from others to no purpose; eternally disappointed and eternally fretting. The active scenes are over at my age. I indulge, with all the art I can, my taste for reading. If I would confine it to valuable books, they are almost as rare as valuable men. I must be content with what I can find. As I approach a second childhood, I endeavour to enter into the pleasures of it. Your youngest son is, perhaps, at this very moment riding on a poker with great delight, not at all regretting that it is not a gold one, and much less wishing it an Arabian horse, which he would not know how to manage; I am reading an idle tale, not expecting wit or truth in it, and am very glad it is not metaphysics to puzzle my judgement, or history to mislead my opinion: he fortifies his health by exercise; I calm my cares by oblivion. The methods may appear low to busy people; but if he improves his strength, and I forget my infirmities, we both attain very desirable ends.

Lady Mary Wortley Montagu, Letters

The Poets

There, obedient to her praying, did I read aloud the poems
Made to Tuscan flutes, or instruments more various of our
      own;
Read the pastoral parts of Spenser—or the subtle
      interflowings
Found in Petrarch's sonnets—here's the book—the leaf is
      folded down!

Or at times a modern volume,—Wordsworth's
      solemn-thoughted idyl,
Howitt's ballad-verse, or Tennyson's enchanted reverie,—
Or from Browning some 'Pomegranate', which, if cut deep
      down the middle,
Shows a heart within blood-tinctured, of a veined humanity.

Elizabeth Barrett Browning, *Lady Geraldine's Courtship*

The World of Books

I sate on in my chamber green,
And lived my life, and thought my thoughts, and prayed
My prayers without the vicar; read my books,
Without considering whether they were fit
To do me good. Mark, there. We get no good
By being ungenerous, even to a book,
And calculating profits,—so much help
By so much reading. It is rather when
We gloriously forget ourselves and plunge
Soul-forward, headlong, into a book's profound,
Impassioned for its beauty and salt of truth—
'Tis then we get the right good from a book.

I read much. What my father taught before
From many a volume, Love re-emphasized

Upon the self-same pages: Theophrast
Grew tender with the memory of his eyes,
And Aelian made mine wet. The trick of Greek
And Latin, he had taught me, as he would
Have taught me wrestling or the game of fives
If such he had known,—most like a shipwrecked man
Who heaps his single platter with goats' cheese
And scarlet berries; or like any man
Who loves but one, and so gives all at once,
Because he has it, rather than because
He counts it worthy. Thus, my father gave;
And thus, as did the women formerly
By young Achilles, when they pinned the veil
Across the boy's audacious front, and swept
With tuneful laughs the silver-fretted rocks,
He wrapt his little daughter in his large
Man's doublet, careless did it fit or no....

I read books bad and good—some bad and good
At once (good aims not always make good books:
Well-tempered spades turn up ill-smelling soils
In digging vineyards even); books that prove
God's being so definitely, that man's doubt
Grows self-defined the other side the line,
Made atheist by suggestion; moral books,
Exasperating to licence; genial books,
Discounting from the human dignity;
And merry books, which set you weeping when
The sun shines,—ay, and melancholy books,
Which make you laugh that any one should weep
In this disjointed life for one wrong more.

The world of books is still the world, I write,
And both worlds have God's providence, thank God,
To keep and hearten.

Elizabeth Barrett Browning, Aurora Leigh

The Classical Education of Women

We have often heard men who wish, as almost all men of
sense wish, that women should be highly educated, speak
with rapture of the English ladies of the sixteenth century,
and lament that they can find no modern damsel resembling
those fair pupils of Ascham and Aylmer who compared, over
their embroidery, the styles of Isocrates and Lysias, and who,
while the horns were sounding and the dogs in full cry, sat
in the lonely oriel, with eyes riveted to that immortal page
which tells how meekly and bravely the first great martyr
of intellectual liberty took the cup from his weeping gaoler.
But surely these complaints have very little foundation. We
would by no means disparage the ladies of the sixteenth
century or their pursuits. But we conceive that those who
extol them at the expense of the women of our time forget
one very obvious and very important circumstance. In the
time of Henry the Eighth and Edward the Sixth, a person
who did not read Greek and Latin could read nothing, or
next to nothing. The Italian was the only modern language
which possessed anything that could be called a literature. All
the valuable books then extant in all the vernacular dialects
of Europe would hardly have filled a single shelf. England did
not yet possess Shakespeare's plays and the *Faery Queene*, nor
France Montaigne's *Essays*, nor Spain *Don Quixote*. In looking
round a well-furnished library, how many English or French
books can we find which were extant when Lady Jane Grey
and Queen Elizabeth received their education? Chaucer,
Gower, Froissart, Comines, Rabelais, nearly complete the
list. It was therefore absolutely necessary that a woman should
be uneducated or classically educated.

Thomas Macaulay, *Lord Bacon*

Girls' Reading

Whether novels, or poetry, or history be read, they should be chosen, not for what is *out* of them, but for what is *in* them. The chance and scattered evil that may here and there haunt, or hide itself in, a powerful book, never does any harm to a noble girl; but the emptiness of an author oppresses her, and his amiable folly degrades her. And if she can have access to a good library of old and classical books, there need be no choosing at all. Keep the modern magazine and novel out of your girl's way: turn her loose into the old library every wet day, and let her alone. She will find what is good for her; you cannot: for there is just this difference between the making of a girl's character and a boy's—you may chisel a boy into shape, as you would a rock, or hammer him into it, if he be of a better kind, as you would a piece of bronze. But you cannot hammer a girl into anything. She grows as a flower does,— she will wither without sun; she will decay in her sheath, as the narcissus does, if you do not give her air enough; she may fall, and defile her head in dust, if you leave her without help at some moments of her life; but you cannot fetter her; she must take her own fair form and way, if she take any, and in mind as in body, must have always

> Her household motions light and free
> And steps of virgin liberty.

Let her loose in the library, I say, as you do a fawn in a field. It knows the bad weeds twenty times better than you; and the good ones too, and will eat some bitter and prickly ones, good for it, which you had not the slightest thought were good.

John Ruskin, *Sesame and Lilies*

'Twere well with most, if books, that could engage
Their childhood, pleased them at a riper age.

William Cowper, *Tirocinium*

Poetry and Piety

Flavia buys all books of wit and humour, and has made an
expensive collection of all our English poets. For, she says,
one cannot have a true taste of any of them without being
very conversant with them all.

   She will sometimes read a book of piety, if it is a short one,
if it is much commended for style and language, and she can
tell where to borrow it.

William Law, *A Serious Call to a Devout and Holy Life*

A Lady's Library

Non illa colo calathisve Minervae
Focmineas assueta manus.—VIRGIL

Some months ago, my friend Sir Roger, being in the country,
enclosed a letter to me, directed to a certain lady whom I
shall here call by the name of Leonora, and as it contained
matters of consequence, desired me to deliver it to her with
my own hand. Accordingly I waited upon her ladyship pretty
early in the morning, and was desired by her woman to walk
into her lady's library, till such time as she was in readiness
to receive me. The very sound of a lady's library gave me
a great curiosity to see it; and, as it was some time before
the lady came to me, I had an opportunity of turning over
a great many of her books, which were ranged together in
a very beautiful order. At the end of the folios (which were
finely bound and gilt) were great jars of china placed one
above another in a very noble piece of architecture. The
quartos were separated from the octavos by a pile of smaller

vessels, which rose in a delightful pyramid. The octavos were bounded by tea-dishes of all shapes, colours, and sizes, which were so disposed on a wooden frame, that they looked like one continued pillar indented with the finest strokes of sculpture, and stained with the greatest variety of dyes. That part of the library which was designed for the reception of plays and pamphlets, and other loose papers, was enclosed in a kind of square, consisting of one of the prettiest grotesque works that I ever saw, and made up of scaramouches, lions, monkeys, mandarins, trees, shells, and a thousand other odd figures in china ware. In the midst of the room was a little japan table, with a quire of gilt paper upon it, and upon the paper a silver snuff-box made in the shape of a little book. I found there were several other counterfeit books upon the upper shelves, which were carved in wood, and served only to fill up the number, like faggots in the muster of a regiment. I was wonderfully pleased with such a mixed kind of furniture as seemed very suitable both to the lady and the scholar, and did not know at first whether I should fancy myself in a grotto or in a library.

Upon my looking into the books I found there were some few which the lady had bought for her own use, but that most of them had been got together, either because she had heard them praised, or because she had seen the authors of them. Among several that I examined, I very well remember these that follow:

Ogilby's *Virgil*. Dryden's *Juvenal*. *Cassandra*. *Cleopatra*. *Astraea*. Sir Isaac Newton's works. *The Grand Cyrus*, with a pin stuck in one of the middle leaves. Pembroke's *Arcadia*. Locke of *Human Understanding*; with a paper of patches in it. A spelling-book. A dictionary for the explanation of hard words. Sherlock upon Death. *The Fifteen Comforts of Matrimony*. Sir William Temple's Essays. Father Malebranche's *Search after Truth*, translated into English. A book of Novels. *The Academy of Compliments*. Culpepper's *Midwifery*. *The Ladies 'Calling*. Tales in Verse by Dr. D'Urfey: bound in red leather, gilt on the back, and doubled down in several places. All the Classic authors, in wood. A set of Elzevirs by the same hand. *Clelia*: which opened of itself in the place that describes two lovers in a bower. Baker's *Chronicle*. *Advice to a Daughter*. *The New Atlantis*, with a key to it. Mr. Steele's *Christian Hero*. A Prayer-book: with a bottle of Hungary water by the side of it. Dr. Sacheverell's Speech. Fielding's Trial. Seneca's *Morals*. Taylor's *Holy Living and Dying*. La Ferte's *Instructions for Country-dances*.

I was taking a catalogue in my pocket-book of these and several other authors, when Leonora entered.

Joseph Addison, *Spectator*, 37

Women's Want

Except some professed scholars, I have often observed that women in general read much more than men; but, for want of a plan, a method, a fixed object, their reading is of little benefit to themselves, or others.

Edward Gibbon, *Autobiography*

Books for a Lady's Library

Convivae prope dissentire videntur,
Poscentes vario multum diversa palato.
Quid dem? quid non dem?—HORACE

Since I have called out for help in my catalogue of a lady's library, I have received many letters upon that head, some of which I shall give an account of. In the first class I shall take notice of those which come to me from eminent booksellers, who every one of them mention with respect the authors they have printed, and consequently have an eye to their own advantage more than to that of the ladies. One tells me, that he thinks it absolutely necessary for women to have true notions of right and equity, and that therefore they cannot peruse a better book than Dalton's *Country Justice*: another thinks they cannot be without *The Compleat Jockey*. A third, observing the curiosity and desire of prying into secrets, which he tells me is natural to the fair sex, is of opinion this female inclination, if well directed, might turn very much to their advantage, and therefore recommends to me *Mr. Mede upon the Revelations*. A fourth lays it down as an unquestioned truth, that a lady cannot be thoroughly accomplished who has not read the *Secret Treaties and Negotiations of Marshal d'Estrades*. Mr. Jacob Tonson, junior, is of opinion, that *Bayle's Dictionary* might be of very great use to the ladies, in order to make them general scholars. Another, whose name I have forgotten, thinks it highly proper that every woman with child should read Mr. Wall's *History of Infant Baptism*: as another is very importunate with me to recommend to all my female readers *The Finishing Stroke: Being a Vindication of the Patriarchal Scheme*, &c.

In the second class I shall mention books which are recommended by husbands, if I may believe the writers of them. Whether or no they are real husbands or personated ones I cannot tell, but the books they recommend are as follow. *A Paraphrase on the History of Susanna. Rules to keep Lent. The Christian's Overthrow prevented. A Dissuasive from the Playhouse. The Virtues of Camphire, with Directions to make Camphire Tea. The pleasures of a Country Life. The Government of the Tongue.* A letter dated from Cheapside desires me that I would advise all young wives to make themselves mistresses of Wingate's *Arithmetic*, and concludes with a postscript, that he hopes I will not forget *The Countess of Kent's Receipts*.

I may reckon the ladies themselves as a third class among these my correspondents and privy-councillors. In a letter from one of them, I am advised to place *Pharamond* at the head of my catalogue, and, if I think proper, to give the second place to *Cassandra*. Coquetilla begs me not to think of nailing women upon their knees with manuals of devotion, nor of scorching their faces with books of housewifery. Florella desires to know if there are any books written against prudes, and entreats me, if there are, to give them a place in my library. Plays of all sorts have their several advocates: *All for Love* is mentioned in above fifteen letters; *Sophonisba, or Hannibal's Overthrow,* in a dozen; *The Innocent Adultery* is likewise highly approved of: *Mithridates, King of Pontus* has many friends; *Alexander the Great* and *Aurengzebe* have the same number of voices; but *Theodosius,* or *The Force of Love,* carries it from all the rest.

Joseph Addison, *Spectator*, 92

Lydia Languish and the Circulating Library

LUCY Indeed, ma'am, I traversed half the town in search of it: I don't believe there's a circulating library in Bath I ha'n't been at.

LYDIA LANGUISH And could not you get *The Reward of Constancy?*

LUCY No, indeed, ma'am.

LYDIA Nor *The Fatal Connexion?*

LUCY No, indeed, ma'am.

LYDIA Nor *The Mistakes of the Heart?*

LUCY Ma'am, as ill luck would have it, Mr. Bull said Miss Sukey Saunter had just fetched it away.

LYDIA Heigh-ho!—Did you inquire for *The Delicate Distress?*

LUCY —Or, *The Memoirs of Lady Woodford?* Yes, indeed, ma'am. I asked everywhere for it; and I might have brought it from Mr. Frederick's, but Lady Slattern Lounger, who had just sent it home, had so soiled and dog's-eared it, it wa'n't fit for a Christian to read.

LYDIA Heigh-ho!—Yes, I always know when Lady Slattern has been before me. She has a most observing thumb; and I believe cherishes her nails for the convenience of making marginal notes.—Well, child, what *have* you brought me?

LUCY Oh! here, ma'am.

[*Taking books from under her cloak, and from her pockets.*]
This is *The Gordian Knot*, and this *Peregrine Pickle*.
Here are *The Tears of Sensibility*, and *Humphrey Clinker*.
This is *The Memoirs of a Lady of Quality, written by herself,*
and here the second volume of *The Sentimental Journey.*

LYDIA Heigh-ho!—What are those books by the glass?

LUCY The great one is only *The Whole Duty of Man*, where I
press a few blonds, ma'am.

...

... O Lud! ma'am, they are both coming upstairs....

LYDIA Here, my dear Lucy, hide these books. Quick, quick.
Fling *Peregrine Pickle* under the toilet—throw *Roderick
Random* into the closet—put *The Innocent Adultery* into
The Whole Duty of Man—thrust *Lord Aimworth* under
the sofa—cram *Ovid* behind the bolster—there—put
The Man of Feeling into your pocket—so, so, now lay
Mrs. Chapone in sight, and leave *Fordyce's Sermons* open on
the table.

LUCY Oh, burn it, ma'am, the hairdresser has torn away as
far as *Proper Pride*.

LYDIA Never mind—open at *Sobriety*. Fling me *Lord
Chesterfield's Letters.*—Now for 'em.
[*Mrs. Malaprop and Sir Anthony Absolute enter
and after Lydia has been ordered to her room—*]

MRS. MALAPROP There's a little intricate hussy for you!

SIR ANTHONY It is not to be wondered at, ma'am—all this is
the natural consequence of teaching girls to read. Had I
a thousand daughters, by Heaven! I'd as soon have them
taught the black art as their alphabet!

MRS. MALAPROP Nay, nay, Sir Anthony, you are an absolute
misanthropy.

SIR ANTHONY In my way hither, Mrs. Malaprop, I observed
your niece's maid coming forth from a circulating
library! She had a book in each hand—they were half-
bound volumes, with marble covers! From that moment
I guessed how full of duty I should see her mistress!

MRS. MALAPROP Those are vile places, indeed!

SIR ANTHONY Madam, a circulating library in a town is as
an evergreen tree of diabolical knowledge! It blossoms
through the year! And depend on it, Mrs. Malaprop, that
they who are so fond of handling the leaves, will long for
the fruit at last.

Richard Sheridan, *The Rivals*

The Old Bachelor's Books

My books were changed; I now preferred the truth
To the light reading of unsettled youth;
Novels grew tedious, but by choice or chance,
I still had interest in the wild romance:
There is an age, we know, when tales of love
Form the sweet pabulum our hearts approve;
Then as we read we feel, and are indeed,
We judge, the heroic men of whom we read;
But in our after life these fancies fail,
We cannot be the heroes of the tale;
The parts that Cliffords, Mordaunts, Bevilles play
We cannot,—cannot be so smart and gay.
But all the mighty deeds and matchless powers
Of errant knights we never fancied ours,
And thus the prowess of each gifted knight
Must at all times create the same delight;
Lovelace a forward youth might hope to seem,
But Lancelot never,—that he could not dream;
Nothing reminds us in the magic page
Of old romance, of our declining age:
If once our fancy mighty dragons slew,
This is no more than fancy now can do;
But when the heroes of a novel come,
Conquered and conquering, to a drawing-room,
We no more feel the vanity that sees

Within ourselves what we admire in these,
And so we leave the modern tale, to fly
From realm to realm with Tristram or Sir Guy.
    Not quite a Quixote, I could not suppose
That queens would call me to subdue their foes;
But, by a voluntary weakness swayed,
When fancy called, I willingly obeyed.

George Crabbe, *Tales of the Hall*

    The state, whereon I studied,
Is like a good thing, being often read,
Grown feared and tedious.

William Shakespeare, *Measure for Measure*

The Oxford Scholar and His Books

A clerk ther was of Oxenford also
That un-to logik hadde long y-go.
As lene was his hors as is a rake,
And he was nat right fat, I undertake;
But loked holwe, and ther-to soberly.
Ful thredbar was his overest courtepy;
For he had geten him yet no benefyce,
Ne was so worldly for to have offyce.
For him was lever have at his beddes heed
Twenty bokes, clad in blak or reed,
Of Aristotle and his philosophye,
Than robes riche, or fithele, or gay sautrye:
But al be that he was a philosophre,
Yet hadde he but litel gold in cofre;
But al that he mighte of his freendes hente,
On bokes and on lerninge he it spente,
And bisily gan for the soules preye
Of hem that yaf him wher-with to scoleye.

Of studie took he most cure and most hede.
Noght o word spak he more than was nede.
And that was seyd in forme and reverence,
And short and quik, and ful of hy sentence.
Souninge in moral vertu was his speche,
And gladly wolde he lerne, and gladly teche.

Geoffrey Chaucer, The Canterbury Tales

The Envoy of Alexander Barclay, Translator

Exhorting the fooles accloyed with this vice to amend their folly

Say worthy doctors and clerks curious:
What moveth you of books to have such number,
Since divers doctrines through ways contrarious
Doth man's mind distract and sore encumber;
Alas, blind men awake, out of your slumber,
And if ye will needs your books multiply
With diligence endeavour you some to occupy.

Alexander Barclay

Letter-Ferrets

Dionysius scoffeth at those grammarians who ploddingly
labour to know the miseries of Ulysses, and are ignorant
of their own.... Except our mind be the better, unless our
judgement be the sounder, I had rather my scholar had employed his time in playing at tennis; I am sure his body would
be the nimbler. See but one of these our university men or
bookish scholars return from school, after he hath there spent
ten or twelve years under a pedant's charge: who is so inapt
for any matter? who so unfit for any company? who so to seek
if he come into the world? all the advantage you discover in
him is that his Latin and Greek have made him more sottish,

more stupid, and more presumptuous, than before he went
from home.... My vulgar Perigordian speech doth very pleasantly term such self-conceited wizards, letter-ferrets, as if
they would say letter-stricken men, to whom (as the common
saying is) letters have given a blow with a mallet.

Michel de Montaigne

Dainties that are Bred of a Book

Sir, he hath not fed of the dainties that are bred of a book;
he hath not eat paper, as it were; he hath not drunk ink: his
intellect is not replenished; he is only an animal, only sensible
in the duller parts.

William Shakespeare, Love's Labour's Lost

An Antiquary

He loves no library, but where there are more spiders'
volumes than authors', and looks with great admiration on
the antique work of cobwebs. Printed books he contemns,
as a novelty of this latter age; but a manuscript he pores on
everlastingly, especially if the cover be all moth-eaten, and
the dust make a parenthesis between every syllable. He would
give all the books in his study (which are rarities all) for one
of the old Roman binding, or six lines of Tully in his own
hand.

John Earle, Microcosmographie

Bibliosophia

I will begin, by designating the high and dignified passion
in question by its true name—BIBLIOSOPHIA,—which I
would define—*an appetite for* COLLECTING *Books*—carefully
distinguished from, wholly unconnected with, nay, absolutely
repugnant to, all idea of READING them.

Observe, then, with merited admiration, the several points
of superiority, which distinguish the *Collector*, when brought
into fair and close comparison with the *Student*. As

First; the said *Collector* proceeds straight forward to his
object, and (with one only exception which will hereafter be
shown) under the most rational hopes of accomplishing it.
There is but a certain, and limited, number of books to which
he and his inquisitive fraternity have agreed to consecrate
the epithet 'curious'; and all of these—with the requisite
allowance of cash, cunning, luck, patience, and time—he is
within the 'potentiality' of drawing, sooner or later, within
his clutches:—whereas the *Student*, granting him the wealth
of a brewer, the cunning of a horse-dealer, the luck of a fool,
the patience of Jerry Sneak, and the longevity of the Wandering Jew, can never hope even to *taste* an hundredth part of the
volumes which he meditates to devour.

In the next place, the treasures of the *Collector*, when once
he has submitted to the pleasing toil of procuring them, are
his own;—his own, I mean, in the single sense in which he
is desirous so to call them; for he leaves them in the safe
custody of his shelves, until the arrival of that proud moment,
when he shall be dared by an envious rival, to prove that
the title-page of some forgotten (and thence remembered)
volume, is perfect—or properly imperfect; or that it enjoys
the reputation of having been printed, long before the Art had
approached towards any tolerable degree of improvement; or,
that it possesses some one, or more, of those curious advantages, upon which a fitter occasion for expatiating will present
itself by and by:—and now, how stands the point of *possession*,

with the *Student?*—unprosperously indeed!—for besides that,
as already observed, he can never possibly possess, in *his* sense
of that expression, more than a wretched modicum of his
coveted treasures, he is doomed to a very precarious property
even in those which he may have actually hoarded; inasmuch
as they are entrusted to the care of that most treacherous of
all librarians, *Memory*,—which, at all times, and of necessity,
treats the Student's collections, as the professed Collector,
occasionally, and by choice only, is tempted to treat *his*,—by
casting out a great part of them for want of room.... 'Let us
now be told no more,' of the superiority of the *Student* over
the *Collector*.

James Beresford, Bibliosophia

Golden Volumes! Richest Treasures!

> Golden volumes! richest treasures!
> Objects of delicious pleasures!
> You my eyes rejoicing please,
> You my hands in rapture seize!
> Brilliant wits and moving sages,
> Lights who beamed through many ages,
> Left to your conscious leaves their story,
> And dared to trust you with their glory;
> And now their hope of fame achieved,
> Dear volumes!—you have not deceived!

This passion for the acquisition and enjoyment of *books* has
been the occasion of their lovers embellishing their outsides
with costly ornaments: a rage which ostentation may have
abused; but when these volumes belong to the real man of
letters, the most fanciful bindings are often the emblems
of his taste and feelings. The great Thuanus was eager to
procure the finest copies for his library, and his volumes are

still eagerly purchased, bearing his autograph on the last page.
A celebrated amateur was Grollier, whose library was opulent
in these luxuries; the Muses themselves could not more
ingeniously have ornamented their favourite works. I have
seen several in the libraries of our own curious collectors. He
embellished their outside with taste and ingenuity. They are
gilded and stamped with peculiar neatness, the compartments
on the binding are drawn, and painted, with different inventions of subjects, analogous to the works themselves; and they
are further adorned by that amiable inscription, *Jo. Grollierii
et amicorum!*—purporting that these literary treasures were
collected for himself and for his friends.

Isaac D'Israeli, Curiosities of Literature: Libraries

A Malady of Weak Minds

The Bibliomania, or the collecting an enormous heap of books
without intelligent curiosity, has, since libraries have existed,
infected weak minds, who imagine that they themselves
acquire knowledge when they keep it on their shelves. Their
motley libraries have been called the *madhouses of the human
mind*; and again, the *tomb of books*, when the possessor will not
communicate them, and coffins them up in the cases of his
library—and as it was facetiously observed, these collections
are not without a *Lock on the Human Understanding*.

Isaac D'Israeli, Curiosities of Literature

An Unworthy Professor

'I will frankly confess,' rejoined Lysander, 'that I am an arrant bibliomaniac—that I love books dearly—that the very sight, touch, and mere perusal—'

'Hold, my friend,' again exclaimed Philemon; 'you have renounced your profession—you talk of *reading* books—do bibliomaniacs ever *read* books?'

T.F. Dibdin, *Bibliomania*

A Bibliomaniac

You observe, my friends, said I, softly, yonder active and keen-visaged gentleman? 'Tis Lepidus. Like Magliabechi, content with frugal fare and frugal clothing and preferring the riches of a library to those of house-furniture, he is insatiable in his bibliomaniacal appetites. 'Long experience has made him sage:' and it is not therefore without just reason that his opinions are courted and considered as almost oracular. You will find that he will take his old station, commanding the right or left wing of the auctioneer; and that he will enliven, by the gaiety and shrewdness of his remarks, the circle that more immediately surrounds him. Some there are who will not bid till Lepidus bids; and who surrender all discretion and opinion of their own to his universal book-knowledge. The consequence is that Lepidus can, with difficulty, make purchases for his own library, and a thousand dexterous and happy manœuvres are of necessity obliged to be practised by him, whenever a rare or curious book turns up.... Justly respectable as are his scholarship and good sense, he is not what you may call a *fashionable* collector; for old chronicles and romances are most rigidly discarded from his library. Talk to him of Hoffman, Schoettgenius, Rosenmuller, and Michaelis, and he will listen courteously to your conversation; but when you expatiate, however learnedly and rapturously,

upon Froissart and Prince Arthur, he will tell you that he
has a heart of stone upon the subject; and that even a clean
uncut copy of an original impression of each, by Verard or by
Caxton, would not bring a single tear of sympathetic transport to his eyes.

T.F. Dibdin, Bibliomania

The Enviable Bookworm

The character of a scholar not unfrequently dwindles down
into the shadow of a shade, till nothing is left of it but the
mere bookworm. There is often something amiable as well
as enviable in this last character. I know one such instance, at
least. The person I mean has an admiration for learning, if he
is only dazzled by its light. He lives among old authors, if he
does not enter much into their spirit. He handles the covers,
and turns over the page, and is familiar with the names and
dates. He is busy and self-involved. He hangs like a film and
cobweb upon letters, or is like the dust upon the outside of
knowledge, which should not be rudely brushed aside. He
follows learning as its shadow; but as such, he is respectable.
He browses on the husk and leaves of books, as the young
fawn browses on the bark and leaves of trees. Such a one lives
all his life in a dream of learning, and has never once had his
sleep broken by a real sense of things. He believes implicitly
in genius, truth, virtue, liberty, because he finds the names of
these things in books. He thinks that love and friendship are
the finest things imaginable, both in practice and theory. The
legend of good women is to him no fiction. When he steals
from the twilight of his cell, the scene breaks upon him like
an illuminated missal, and all the people he sees are but so
many figures in a *camera obscura*. He reads the world, like a
favourite volume, only to find beauties in it, or like an edition
of some old work which he is preparing for the press, only

to make emendations in it, and correct the errors that have inadvertently slipt in. He and his dog Tray are much the same honest, simple-hearted, faithful, affectionate creatures—if Tray could but read! His mind cannot take the impression of vice: but the gentleness of his nature turns gall to milk. He would not hurt a fly. He draws the picture of mankind from the guileless simplicity of his own heart: and when he dies, his spirit will take its smiling leave, without having ever had an ill thought of others, or the consciousness of one in itself.

William Hazlitt, *On the Conversation of Authors*

Ears Nailed to Books

A mere scholar, who knows nothing but books, must be ignorant even of them. 'Books do not teach the use of books.' How should he know anything of a work who knows nothing of the subject of it? The learned pedant is conversant with books only as they are made of other books, and those again of others, without end. He parrots those who have parroted others. He can translate the same word into ten different languages, but he knows nothing of the *thing* which it means in any one of them. He stuffs his head with authorities built on authorities, with quotations quoted from quotations, while he locks up his senses, his understanding, and his heart. He is unacquainted with the maxims and manners of the world; he is to seek in the characters of individuals. He sees no beauty in the face of nature or of art. To him 'the mighty world of eye and ear' is hid; and 'knowledge', except at one entrance, 'quite shut out.' His pride takes part with his ignorance; and his self-importance rises with the number of things of which he does not know the value, and which he therefore despises as unworthy of his notice. He knows nothing of pictures,—'of the colouring of Titian, the grace of Raphael, the purity of Domenichino, the *corregioscity* of Correggio, the learning of Poussin, the airs of Guido, the taste of the Caracci, or the grand contour of Michael Angelo',—of all those glories of the Italian and miracles of the Flemish school, which have filled the eyes of mankind with delight, and to the study and imitation of which thousands have in vain devoted their lives. These are to him as if they had never been, a mere dead letter, a byword; and no wonder, for he neither sees nor understands their prototypes in nature. A print of Rubens' Watering-place, or Claude's Enchanted Castle may be hanging on the walls of his room for months without his once perceiving them; and if you point them out to him he will turn away from them. The language of nature, or of art (which is another nature), is one that he does not understand. He repeats indeed the names of Apelles and Phidias, because they are to be found in classic authors, and boasts of their works as prodigies, because they no longer exist; or when he sees the finest remains of Grecian art actually before him in the Elgin Marbles, takes no other interest in them than as they lead to a learned dispute, and (which is the same thing) a quarrel about the meaning of a Greek particle. He is equally ignorant of music; he 'knows no touch of it,' from the strains of the all-accomplished Mozart to the shepherd's pipe upon the mountain. His ears are nailed to his books; and deadened with the sound of the Greek and Latin tongues, and the din and smithery of school-learning.

William Hazlitt, *On the Ignorance of the Learned*

The Antiquary's Treasures

The collection was indeed a curious one, and might well be envied by an amateur. Yet it was not collected at the enormous prices of modern times, which are sufficient to have appalled the most determined as well as earliest bibliomaniac upon record, whom we take to have been none else than the renowned Don Quixote de la Mancha, as, among other slight indications of an infirm understanding, he is stated, by his veracious historian, Cid Hamet Benengeli, to have exchanged fields and farms for folios and quartos of chivalry.... Mr. Oldbuck did not follow these collectors in such excess of expenditure; but, taking a pleasure in the personal labour of forming his library, saved his purse at the expense of his time and toil.... 'Davy Wilson,' he said, 'commonly called Snuffy Davy, from his inveterate addiction to black rappee, was the very prince of scouts for searching blind alleys, cellars, and stalls, for rare volumes. He had the scent of a slow-hound, sir, and the snap of a bull-dog. He would detect you an old black-letter ballad among the leaves of a law-paper, and find an *editio princeps* under the mask of a school Corderius.' ... 'Even I, sir, 'he went on,' though far inferior in industry and discernment and presence of mind to that great man, can show you a few—a very few things, which I have collected, not by force of money, as any wealthy man might,—although, as my friend Lucian says, he might chance to throw away his coin only to illustrate his ignorance,—but gained in a manner that shows I know something of the matter. See this bundle of ballads, not one of them later than 1700, and some of them a hundred years older. I wheedled an old woman out of these, who loved them better than her psalm-book. Tobacco, sir, snuff, and the *Complete Syren*, were the equivalent! For that mutilated copy of the *Complaynt of Scotland*, I sat out the drinking of two dozen bottles of strong ale with the late learned proprietor, who, in gratitude, bequeathed it to me by his last will. These little Elzevirs are the memoranda and trophies of many a walk by night and morning through the Cowgate, the Canongate, the Bow, Saint Mary's Wynd,— wherever, in fine, there were to be found brokers and traders, those miscellaneous dealers in things rare and curious. How often have I stood haggling on a halfpenny, lest, by a too ready acquiescence in the dealer's first price, he should be led to suspect the value I set upon the article!—how have I trembled, lest some passing stranger should chop in between me and the prize, and regarded each poor student of divinity that stopped to turn over the books at the stall, as a rival amateur, or prowling bookseller in disguise!—And then, Mr. Lovel, the sly satisfaction with which one pays the consideration, and pockets the article, affecting a cold indifference, while the hand is trembling with pleasure!—Then to dazzle the eyes of our wealthier and emulous rivals by showing them such a treasure as this—(displaying a little black smoked book about the size of a primer)—'to enjoy their surprise and envy, shrouding meanwhile, under a veil of mysterious consciousness, our own superior knowledge and dexterity;—these, my young friend, these are the white moments of life, that repay the toil, and pains, and sedulous attention, which our profession, above all others, so peculiarly demands!' ...

Here were editions esteemed as being the first, and there stood those scarcely less regarded as being the last and best; here was a book valued because it had the author's final improvements, and there another which (strange to tell!) was in request because it had them not. One was precious because it was a folio, another because it was a duodecimo; some because they were tall, some because they were short; the merit of this lay in the title-page—of that in the arrangement of the letters in the word Finis. There was, it seemed, no peculiar distinction, however trifling or minute, which might not give value to a volume, providing the indispensable quality of scarcity, or rare occurrence, was attached to it.

Sir Walter Scott, The Antiquary

I would rather be a poor man in a garret with plenty of books than a king who did not love reading.

Thomas Macaulay

Kissing a Folio

Sitting, last winter, among my books, and walled round with
all the comfort and protection which they and my fireside
could afford me; to wit, a table of high-piled books at my
back, my writing-desk on one side of me, some shelves on
the other, and the feeling of the warm fire at my feet; I began
to consider how I loved the authors of those books: how I
loved them, too, not only for the imaginative pleasures they
afforded me, but for their making me love the very books
themselves, and delight to be in contact with them. I looked
sideways at my Spenser, my Theocritus, and my *Arabian
Nights*; then above them at my Italian poets; then behind me
at my Dryden and Pope, my romances, and my Boccaccio;
then on my left side at my Chaucer, who lay on a writing-
desk; and thought how natural it was in C[harles] L[amb] to
give a kiss to an old folio, as I once saw him do to Chapman's
Homer.... I entrench myself in my books equally against
sorrow and the weather. If the wind comes through a passage
I look about to see how I can fence it off by a better disposition of my movables; if a melancholy thought is importunate,
I give another glance at my Spenser. When I speak of being in
contact with my books, I mean it literally. I like to lean my
head against them.

J.H. Leigh Hunt, My Books

The Literary Harem

I must have my literary *harem*, my *parc aux cerfs*, where my
favourites await my moments of leisure and pleasure,—my
scarce and precious editions, my luxurious typographical
masterpieces; my Delilahs, that take my head in their lap; the
pleasant story-tellers and the like; the books I love because
they are fair to look upon, prized by collectors, endeared
by old associations, secret treasures that nobody else knows

anything about; books, in short, that I like for insufficient reasons it may be, but peremptorily, and mean to like and to love and to cherish till death us do part.... The bookcase of Delilahs, that you have paid wicked prices for, that you love without pretending to be reasonable about it, and would bag in case of fire before all the rest.

Oliver Wendell Holmes, *The Poet at the Breakfast-Table*

Definitions

To afford the reader an opportunity of noting at a glance the appropriate learned terms applicable to the different sets of persons who meddle with books, I subjoin the following definitions, as rendered in d'Israeli's *Curiosities* from the *Chasse aux Bibliographes et Antiquaires mal advisés* of Jean-Joseph Rive:

'A bibliognoste, from the Greek, is one knowing in title-pages and colophons, and in editions; the place and year when printed; the presses whence issued; and all the minutiae of a book.'

'A bibliographe is a describer of books and other literary arrangements.'

'A bibliomane is an indiscriminate accumulator, who blunders faster than he buys, cock-brained and purse-heavy.'

'A bibliophile, the lover of books, is the only one in the class who appears to read them for his own pleasure.'

'A bibliotaphe buries his books, by keeping them under lock, or framing them in glass cases.'

The accurate Peignot, after accepting of this classification with high admiration of its simplicity and exhaustiveness, is seized in his supplementary volume with a misgiving in the matter of the bibliotaphe, explaining that it ought to be translated as a grave of books, and that the proper technical expression for the performer referred to by Rive is bibliotapht. He adds to the nomenclature bibliolyte, as a destroyer of books; bibliologue, one who discourses about books; bibliotacte, a classifier of books; and bibliopée 'l'art d'écrire ou de composer des livres', or, as the unlearned would say, the function of an author.

J.H. Burton, *The Book Hunter*

The Last Editions the Best

Buy good books, and read them; the best books are the commonest, and the last editions are always the best, if the editors are not blockheads; for they may profit of the former. But take care not to understand editions and title-pages too well. It always smells of pedantry, and not always of learning.

Lord Chesterfield, *Letters to His Son*

Sibrandus Schafnaburgensis

Plague take all your pedants, say I!
   He who wrote what I hold in my hand,
Centuries back was so good as to die,
   Leaving this rubbish to cumber the land;
This, that was a book in its time,
   Printed on paper and bound in leather,
Last month in the white of a matin-prime
   Just when the birds sang all together.

Into the garden I brought it to read,
   And under the arbute and laurustine
Read it, so help me grace in my need,
   From title-page to closing line.
Chapter on chapter did I count,
   As a curious traveller counts Stonehenge;
Added up the mortal amount;
   And then proceeded to my revenge.

Yonder's a plum-tree with a crevice
    An owl would build in, were he but sage;
For a lap of moss, like a fine pont-levis
    In a castle of the middle age,
Joins to a lip of gum, pure amber;
    When he'd be private, there might he spend
Hours alone in his lady's chamber:
    Into this crevice I dropped our friend.

Splash, went he, as under he ducked,
    —I knew at the bottom rain-drippings stagnate;
Next a handful of blossoms I plucked
    To bury him with, my bookshelf's magnate;
Then I went indoors, brought out a loaf,
    Half a cheese, and a bottle of Chablis;
Lay on the grass and forgot the oaf
    Over a jolly chapter of Rabelais.

Now, this morning, betwixt the moss
    And gum that locked our friend in limbo,
A spider had spun his web across,
    And sat in the midst with arms akimbo:
So, I took pity, for learning's sake,
    And, *de profundis, accentibus laetis,*
Cantate! quoth I, as I got a rake,
    And up I fished his delectable treatise.

Here you have it, dry in the sun,
    With all the binding all of a blister,
And great blue spots where the ink has run,
    And reddish streaks that wink and glister
O'er the page so beautifully yellow:
    Oh, well have the droppings played their tricks!
Did he guess how toadstools grow, this fellow?
    Here's one stuck in his chapter six!

How did he like it when the live creatures
    Tickled and toused and browsed him all over,
And worm, slug, eft, with serious features,
    Came in, each one, for his right of trover?
—When the water-beetle with great blind deaf face
    Made of her eggs the stately deposit,
And the newt borrowed just so much of the preface
    As tiled in the top of his black wife's closet?

All that life and fun and romping,
    All that frisking and twisting and coupling,
While slowly our poor friend's leaves were swamping
    And clasps were cracking and covers suppling!
As if you had carried sour John Knox
    To the play-house at Paris, Vienna or Munich,
Fastened him into a front-row box,
    And danced off the ballet with trousers and tunic.

Come, old martyr! What, torment enough is it?
    Back to my room shall you take your sweet self!
Good-bye, mother-beetle; husband-eft, *sufficit*!
    See the snug niche I have made on my shelf.
A.'s book shall prop you up, B.'s shall cover you,
    Here's C. to be grave with, or D. to be gay,
And with E. on each side, and F. right over you,
    Dry-rot at ease till the Judgement-day!

                    Robert Browning, *Garden Fancies*

A Student

Over an ancient scroll I bent,
Steeping my soul in wise content,
Nor paused a moment, save to chide
A low voice whispering at my side.

I wove beneath the stars' pale shine
A dream, half human, half divine;
And shook off (not to break the charm)
A little hand laid on my arm.

I read until my heart would glow,
With the great deeds of long ago;
Nor heard, while with those mighty dead,
Pass to and fro a faltering tread.

On the old theme I pondered long—
The struggle between right and wrong;
I could not check such visions high,
To soothe a little quivering sigh.

I tried to solve the problem—Life;
Dreaming of that mysterious strife,
How could I leave such reasonings wise,
To answer two blue pleading eyes?

I strove how best to give, and when,
My blood to save my fellow-men—
How could I turn aside, to look
At snowdrops laid upon my book?

Now Time has fled—the world is strange,
Something there is of pain and change;
My books lie closed upon the shelf;
I miss the old heart in myself.

I miss the sunbeams in my room—
It was not always wrapped in gloom:
I miss my dreams—they fade so fast,
Or flit unto some trivial past.

The great stream of the world goes by;
None care, or heed, or question, why
I, the lone student, cannot raise
My voice or hand as in old days.

No echo seems to wake again
My heart to anything but pain,
Save when a dream of twilight brings
The fluttering of an angel's wings!

Adelaide Anne Procter

Of Handling Books

We not only set before ourselves a service to God in preparing volumes of new books, but we exercise the duties of a
holy piety if we just handle so as not to injure them, then
return them to their proper places, and commend them to
undefiling custody that they may rejoice in their purity while
held in the hand, and repose in security when laid up in their
repositories....

In the first place, then, let there be a mature decorum
in opening and closing of volumes, that they may neither
be unclasped with precipitous haste, nor thrown aside after
inspection without being duly closed; for it is necessary that a
book should be much more carefully preserved than a shoe....

A stiff-necked youth, lounging sluggishly in his study
... distributes innumerable straws in various places, with
the ends in sight, that he may recall by the mark what his
memory cannot retain.... He is not ashamed to eat fruit and
cheese over an open book, and to transfer his empty cup from

side to side upon it: and because he has not his alms-bag at hand, he leaves the rest of the fragments in his books.... He next reclines with his elbows on the book, and by a short study invites a long nap; and by way of repairing the wrinkles, he twists back the margins of the leaves, to the no small detriment of the volume....

But impudent boys are to be specially restrained from meddling with books, who, when they are learning to draw the forms of letters, if copies of the most beautiful books are allowed them, begin to become incongruous annotators, and wherever they perceive the broadest margin about the text, they furnish it with a monstrous alphabet, or their unchastened pen immediately presumes to draw any other frivolous thing whatever, that occurs to their imagination.... There are also certain thieves who enormously dismember books by cutting off the side margins for letter paper, leaving only the letters or text, or the fly-leaves put in for the preservation of the book, which they take away for various uses and abuses, which sort of sacrilege ought to be prohibited under a threat of anathema.

But it is altogether befitting the decency of a scholar that washing should without fail precede reading, as often as he returns from his meals to study, before his fingers, besmeared with grease, loosen a clasp or turn over the leaf of a book.

Richard de Bury, *Philobiblon*

An Edition De Luxe

With that of the book loosened were the clasps—
The margin was illumined all with golden rails
And bees, enpictured with grasshops and wasps,
With butterflies and fresh peacock tails,
Engloried with flowers and slimy snails;
Ennyield pictures well touched and quickly;
It would have made a man whole that had be right sickly

To behold how it was garnished and bound,
Encovered over with gold of tissue fine;
The clasps and bullions were worth a thousand pound;
With belassis and carbuncles the borders did shine;
With aurum mosaicum every other line
Was written.

John Skelton, *A Replycacion agaynst
certayne yong Scolers*, &c.

Care as to Bindings

Have a care of keeping your books handsome, and well
bound, not casting away overmuch in their gilding or string-
ing for ostentation sake, like the prayer-books of girls and
gallants, which are carried to church but for their outsides.
Yet for your own use spare them not for noting or interlin-
ing (if they be printed), for it is not likely you mean to be
a gainer by them, when you have done with them: neither
suffer them through negligence to mould and be moth-eaten
or want their strings and covers. King Alphonsus, about to lay
the foundation of a castle at Naples, called for Vitruvius his
book of architecture; the book was brought in very bad case,
all dusty and without covers; which the king observing said,
'He that must cover us all, must not go uncovered himself';
then commanded the book to be fairly bound and brought
unto him. So say I, suffer them not to lie neglected, who must
make you regarded; and go in torn coats, who must apparel
your mind with the ornaments of knowledge, above the robes
and riches of the most magnificent princes.

Henry Peacham, *The Compleat Gentleman*

Gold Clasps and a Golden Story

This precious book of love, this unbound lover,
To beautify him, only lacks a cover:
The fish lives in the sea, and 'tis much pride
For fair without the fair within to hide:
That book in many eyes doth share the glory,
That in gold clasps locks in the golden story.

William Shakespeare, *Romeo and Juliet*

Nobler than Contents

A book? O rare one!
Be not, as is our fangled world, a garment
Nobler than that it covers: let thy effects
So follow, to be most unlike our courtiers,
As good as promise.

William Shakespeare, *Cymbeline*

Lines Have their Linings, and Books their Buckram

As in our clothes, so likewise he who looks
Shall find much forcing buckram in our books.

Robert Herrick

Bookbindings

Embodied thought enjoys a splendid rest
On guardian shelves, in emblem costume dressed;
Like gems that sparkle in the parent mine,
Through crystal mediums the rich coverings shine;
Morocco flames in scarlet, blue and green,
Impressed with burnished gold, of dazzling sheen;
Arms deep embossed the owner's state declare,
Test of their worth—their age—and his kind care.
Embalmed in russia stands a valued pile,
That time impairs not, nor vile worms defile;
Russia, exhaling from its scented pores
Its saving power to these thrice-valued stores,
In order fair arranged in volumes stand,
Gay with the skill of many a modern hand;
At the expense of sinew and of bone,
The fine papyrian leaves are firm as stone:
Here all is square as by masonic rule,
And bright the impression of the burnished tool.
On some the tawny calf a coat bestows,
Where flowers and fillets beauteous forms compose:
Others in pride the virgin vellum wear,
Beaded with gold—as breast of Venus fair;
On either end the silken head-bands twine,
Wrought by some maid with skilful fingers fine—
The yielding back falls loose, the hinges play,
And the rich page lies open to the day.
Where science traces the unerring line,
In brilliant tints the forms of beauty shine;
These, in our works, as in a casket laid,
Increase the splendour by their powerful aid.

John Maccreery

Hark you, sir; I'll have them very fairly bound:
All books of love, see that at any hand.

William Shakespeare, *The Taming of the Shrew*

Discrimination in Bindings

To be strong-backed and neat-bound is the desideratum
of a volume. Magnificence comes after. This, when it can
be afforded, is not to be lavished upon all kinds of books
indiscriminately. I would not dress a set of Magazines, for
instance, in full suit. The dishabille, or half-binding (with
Russia backs ever) is *our* costume. A Shakespeare, or a Milton
(unless the first editions), it were mere foppery to trick out
in gay apparel. The possession of them confers no distinction. The exterior of them (the things themselves being
so common), strange to say, raises no sweet emotions, no
tickling sense of property in the owner. Thomson's *Seasons*,
again, looks best (I maintain it) a little torn, and dog's-eared.
How beautiful to a genuine lover of reading are the sullied
leaves, and worn out appearance, nay, the very odour (beyond
Russia), if we would not forget kind feelings in fastidiousness,
of an old 'Circulating Library' *Tom Jones*, or *Vicar of Wakefield*!
How they speak of the thousand thumbs, that have turned
over their pages with delight!—of the lone sempstress,
whom they may have cheered (milliner, or harder-working
mantua-maker) after her long day's needle-toil, running far
into midnight, when she has snatched an hour, ill spared from
sleep, to steep her cares, as in some Lethean cup, in spelling
out their enchanting contents! Who would have them a whit
less soiled? What better condition could we desire to see
them in?

In some respects the better a book is, the less it demands
from binding. Fielding, Smollett, Sterne, and all that class
of perpetually self-reproductive volumes—Great Nature's
Stereotypes—we see them individually perish with less

regret, because we know the copies of them to be 'eterne'. But where a book is at once both good and rare—where the individual is almost the species, and when *that* perishes,

> We know not where is that Promethean torch
> That can its light relumine—

such a book, for instance, as the *Life of the Duke of Newcastle*, by his Duchess—no casket is rich enough, no casing sufficiently durable, to honour and keep safe such a jewel.

Not only rare volumes of this description, which seem hopeless ever to be reprinted; but old editions of writers, such as Sir Philip Sidney, Bishop Taylor, Milton in his prose works, Fuller—of whom we *have* reprints, yet the books themselves, though they go about, and are talked of here and there, we know, have not endenizened themselves (nor possibly ever will) in the national heart, so as to become stock books—it is good to possess these in durable and costly covers. I do not care for a First Folio of Shakespeare. I rather prefer the common editions of Rowe and Tonson, without notes, and with *plates*, which, being so execrably bad, serve as maps, or modest remembrancers to the text; and without pretending to any supposable emulation with it, are so much better than the Shakespeare gallery *engravings*, which *did*. I have a community of feeling with my countrymen about his Plays, and I like those editions of him best, which have been oftenest tumbled about and handled.—On the contrary, I cannot read Beaumont and Fletcher but in Folio. The Octavo editions are painful to look at. I have no sympathy with them. If they were as much read as the current editions of the other poet, I should prefer them in that shape to the older one. I do not know a more heartless sight than the reprint of the *Anatomy of Melancholy*. What need was there of unearthing the bones of that fantastic old great man, to expose them in a winding-sheet of the newest fashion to modern censure? what hapless stationer could dream of Burton ever becoming popular?—The wretched Malone could not do worse, when he bribed the sexton of Stratford Church to let him white-wash the painted effigy of old Shakespeare, which stood there, in rude but lively fashion depicted, to the very colour of the cheek, the eye, the eyebrow, hair, the very dress he used to wear—the only authentic testimony we had, however imperfect, of these curious parts and parcels of him. They covered him over with a coat of white paint. By——, if I had been a justice of peace for Warwickshire, I would have clapt both commentator and sexton fast in the stocks, for a pair of meddling sacrilegious varlets.

I think I see them at their work—these sapient trouble-tombs.

Charles Lamb, Detached Thoughts on Books and Reading

Suitable Bindings

Books, no less than their authors, are liable to get ragged, and to experience that neglect and contempt which generally follows the outward and visible signs of poverty. We do therefore most heartily commend the man, who bestows on a tattered and shivering volume such decent and comely apparel as may protect it from the insults of the vulgar, and the more cutting slights of the fair. But if it be a rare book, 'the lone survivor of a numerous race,' the one of its family that has escaped the trunk-makers and pastry-cooks, we would counsel a little extravagance in arranging it. Let no book perish, unless it be such an one as it is your duty to throw into the fire. There is no such thing as a worthless book, though there are some far worse than worthless; no book which is not worth preserving, if its existence may be tolerated; as there are some men whom it may be proper to hang, but none who should be suffered to starve.

The binding of a book should always suit its complexion. Pages, venerably yellow, should not be cased in military morocco, but in sober brown russia. Glossy hot-pressed paper looks best in vellum. We have sometimes seen a collection of old whitey-brown black-letter ballads, &c., so gorgeously tricked out, that they remind us of the pious liberality of the Catholics, who dress in silk and gold the images of saints, part of whose saintship consisted in wearing rags and hair-cloth. The costume of a volume should also be in keeping with its subject, and with the character of its author. How absurd to see the works of William Penn in flaming scarlet, and George Fox's Journal in Bishop's purple! Theology should be solemnly gorgeous. History should be ornamented after the antique or Gothic fashion. Works of science, as plain as is consistent with dignity. Poetry, *simplex munditiis.*

Hartley Coleridge, *Biographia Borealis*

'Tis Folly to be Wise

Due attention to the inside of books, and due contempt for the outside, is the proper relation between a man of sense and his books.

Lord Chesterfield, *Letters to his Son*

The Outside of a Book

As great philosophers hold that the *esse* of things is *percipi*, so a gentleman's furniture exists to be looked at. Nevertheless, sir, there are some things more fit to be looked at than others; for instance, there is nothing more fit to be looked at than the outside of a book. It is, as I may say, from repeated experience, a pure and unmixed pleasure to have a goodly volume lying before you, and to know that you may open it if you please, and need not open it unless you please. It is a resource against *ennui*, if *ennui* should come upon you. To have the resource and not to feel the *ennui*, to enjoy your bottle in the present, and your book in the indefinite future, is a delightful condition of human existence. There is no place, in which a man can move or sit, in which the outside of a book can be otherwise than an innocent and becoming spectacle.

Thomas Love Peacock, *Crotchet Castle*

Books You May Hold in Your Hand

Johnson used to say that no man read long together with a folio on his table. 'Books,' said he, 'that you may carry to the fire, and hold readily in your hand, are the most useful after all.'

James Boswell, *Life of Johnson*

Book Illustrations and Nightmare

Of the great passion of Henry the Seventh for fine books, even before he ascended the throne of England, there can be no doubt. I will not, however, take upon me to say that the slumbers of this monarch were disturbed in consequence of the extraordinary and frightful passages, which, accompanied with bizarre cuts, were now introduced into almost every work, both of ascetic divinity, and also of plain practical morality. His predecessor, Richard, had in all probability been alarmed by the images which the reading of these books had created; and I guess that it was from such frightful objects, rather than from the ghosts of his murdered brethren, that he was compelled to pass a sleepless night before the memorable battle of Bosworth Field. If one of those artists who used to design the horrible pictures which are engraved in many old didactic volumes of the period, had ventured to take a peep into Richard's tent, I question whether he would not have seen, lying upon an oaken table, an early edition of some of those fearful works of which he had himself aided in the embellishment, and of which Heinecken has given us such curious facsimiles: and this, in my humble apprehension, is quite sufficient to account for all the terrible workings in Richard which Shakespeare has so vividly described.

T.F. Dibdin, *Bibliomania*

A Neat Rivulet of Text

LADY SNEERWELL I wonder, Sir Benjamin, you never publish anything.

SIR BENJAMIN BACKBITE To say truth, ma'am, 'tis very vulgar to print; and as my little productions are mostly satires and lampoons on particular people, I find they circulate more by giving copies in confidence to the friends of the parties. However, I have some love elegies, which, when favoured with this lady's smiles, I mean to give to the public.

CRABTREE 'Fore Heaven, ma'am, they'll immortalize you!— you will be handed down to posterity, like Petrarch's Laura, or Waller's Sacharissa.

SIR BENJAMIN Yes, madam, I think you will like them, when you shall see them on a beautiful quarto page, where a neat rivulet of text shall meander through a meadow of margin.

Richard Sheridan, *The School for Scandal*

The Bookworms

Through and through the inspired leaves,
　Ye maggots, make your windings;
But, oh! respect his lordship's taste,
　And pare his golden bindings.

Robert Burns

The Cure for Bookworms

There is a sort of busy worm
That will the fairest books deform,
By gnawning holes throughout them;
Alike through every leaf they go,
Yet of its merits naught they know,
Nor care they aught about them.
Their tasteless tooth will tear and taint
The poet, patriot, sage, or saint,
Nor sparing wit nor learning:
Now, if you'd know the reason why,
The best of reasons I'll supply—
'Tis bread to the poor vermin.
Of pepper, snuff, or 'bacca smoke,
And russia-calf they make a joke.
Yet why should sons of science
These puny, rankling reptiles dread?
'Tis but to let their books be read,
And bid the worms defiance.

J.F.M. Dovaston

Royal Patronage of Books

Queen Charlotte, when discussing books with Fanny Burney
and Mrs. Delany, during the former's residence at Court at
Windsor, praised the work of a writer who had translated a
German book into English, saying 'I wish I knew the translator,' to which Miss Burney replied, 'I wish the translator
knew that!'

'Oh,' said the Queen,—'it is not—I should not like to give
my name, for fear I have judged ill: I picked it up on a stall.
Oh, it is amazing what good books there are on stalls.'

'It is amazing to me,' said Mrs. Delany, 'to hear that.'

'Why, I don't pick them up myself; but I have a servant very clever; and if they are not to be had at the bookseller's, they are not for me any more than for another.'

Madame d'Arblay, Diary

The Treasure

Do you remember the brown suit, which you made to hang upon you, till all your friends cried shame upon you, it grew so thread-bare—and all because of that folio Beaumont and Fletcher, which you dragged home late at night from Barker's in Covent-garden? Do you remember how we eyed it for weeks before we could make up our minds to the purchase, and had not come to a determination till it was near ten o'clock of the Saturday night, when you set off from Islington, fearing you should be too late—and when the old bookseller with some grumbling opened his shop, and by the twinkling taper (for he was setting bedwards) lighted out the relic from his dusty treasures—and when you lugged it home, wishing it were twice as cumbersome—and when you presented it to me— and when we were exploring the perfectness of it (*collating* you called it)—and while I was repairing some of the loose leaves with paste, which your impatience would not suffer to be left till daybreak—was there no pleasure in being a poor man? or can those neat black clothes, which you wear now, and are so careful to keep brushed, since we have become rich and finical, give you half the honest vanity, with which you flaunted it about in that over-worn suit—your old corbeau—for four or five weeks longer than you should have done, to pacify your conscience for the mighty sum of fifteen—or sixteen shillings was it?—a great affair we thought it then—which you had lavished on the old folio. Now you can afford to buy any book that pleases you, but I do not see that you ever bring me home any nice old purchases now.

Charles Lamb, Old China

The Most Valuable Book

We ought not to get books too cheaply. No book, I believe, is ever worth half so much to its reader as one that has been coveted for a year at a bookstall, and bought out of saved halfpence; and perhaps a day or two's fasting. That's the way to get at the cream of a book.

John Ruskin, *Political Economy of Art* (*A Joy for Ever*)

The Readers at the Bookstall

There is a class of street-readers, whom I can never contemplate without affection—the poor gentry, who, not having wherewithal to buy or hire a book, filch a little learning at the open stalls—the owner, with his hard eye, casting envious looks at them all the while, and thinking when they will have done. Venturing tenderly, page after page, expecting every moment when he shall interpose his interdict, and yet unable to deny themselves the gratification, they 'snatch a fearful joy'. Martin B——, in this way, by daily fragments, got through two volumes of Clarissa, when the stall-keeper damped his laudable ambition, by asking him (it was in his younger days) whether he meant to purchase the work. M. declares that under no circumstances of his life did he ever peruse a book with half the satisfaction which he took in those uneasy snatches. A quaint poetess of our day has moralized upon this subject in two very touching but homely stanzas:

I saw a boy with eager eye
Open a book upon a stall,
And read, as he'd devour it all;
Which when the stall-man did espy,
Soon to the boy I heard him call,
'You, Sir, you never buy a book,

Therefore in one you shall not look.'
The boy passed slowly on and with a sigh
He wished he never had been taught to read,
Then of the old churl's books he should have had no need.

Of sufferings the poor have many,
Which never can the rich annoy:
I soon perceived another boy,
Who looked as if he'd not had any
Food, for that day at least—enjoy
The sight of cold meat in a tavern larder.
This boy's case, then thought I, is surely harder,
Thus hungry, longing, thus without a penny,
Beholding choice of dainty-dressèd meat:
No wonder if he wish he ne'er had learned to eat.

Charles Lamb, Detached Thoughts on Books and Reading

Tetrachordon

A book was writ of late called Tetrachordon;
   And woven close, both matter, form and style;
   The subject new: it walked the town a while,
   Numbering good intellects; now seldom pored on.
Cries the stall-reader, bless us! what a word on
   A title-page is this! and some in file
   Stand spelling false, while one might walk to Mile-
   End Green. Why is it harder, Sirs, than Gordon,
Colkitto, or Macdonnel, or Galasp?
   Those rugged names to our like mouths grow sleek
   That would have made Quintilian stare and gasp.
Thy age, like ours, O soul of Sir John Cheek,
   Hated not learning worse than toad or asp;
   When thou taught'st Cambridge, and King Edward Greek.

John Milton

The Second-Hand Catalogue

A Second-hand Bookseller's Catalogue is not a mere catalogue
or list of saleables, as the uninitiated may fancy. Even a
common auctioneer's catalogue of goods and chattels suggests
a thousand reflections to a peruser of any knowledge; judge
then what the case must be with a catalogue of Books; the
very titles of which run the rounds of the whole world, visible
and invisible; geographies—biographies—histories—loves—
hates—joys—sorrows—cookeries—sciences—fashion—and
eternity! We speak on this subject from the most literal
experience; for often and often have we cut open a new
catalogue of old books, with all the fervour and ivory folder
of a first love; often read one at tea; nay, at dinner; and have
put crosses against dozens of volumes in the list, out of the
pure imagination of buying them, the possibility being *out of
the question!*—

Nothing delights us more than to overhaul some dingy
tome, and read a chapter gratuitously. Occasionally when we
have opened some very attractive old book, we have stood
reading for hours at the stall, lost in a brown study and
worldly forgetfulness, and should probably have read on to
the end of the last chapter, had not the vendor of published
wisdom offered, in a satirically polite way, to bring us out a
chair—'Take a chair, sir; you must be tired.'

J.H. Leigh Hunt, *Retrospective Review*

The Find

Do you see this square old yellow Book, I toss
I' the air, and catch again, and twirl about
By the crumpled vellum covers,—pure crude fact
Secreted from man's life when hearts beat hard,
And brains, high-blooded, ticked two centuries since?
Examine it yourselves! I found this book,

Gave a *lira* for it, eightpence English just,
(Mark the predestination!) when a Hand,
Always above my shoulder, pushed me once,
One day still fierce 'mid many a day struck calm,
Across a Square in Florence, crammed with booths,
Buzzing and blaze, noontide and market-time;
Toward Baccio's marble,—ay, the basement-ledge
O' the pedestal where sits and menaces
John of the Black Bands with the upright spear,
'Twixt palace and church.—Riccardi where they lived,
His race, and San Lorenzo where they lie.
This book,—precisely on that palace-step
Which, meant for lounging knaves o' the Medici,
Now serves re-venders to display their ware,—
'Mongst odds and ends of ravage, picture-frames
White through the worn gilt, mirror-sconces chipped,
Bronze angel-heads once knobs attached to chests,
(Handled when ancient dames chose forth brocade)
Modern chalk drawings, studies from the nude,
Samples of stone, jet, breccia, porphyry
Polished and rough, sundry amazing busts
In baked earth, (broken, Providence be praised!)
A wreck of tapestry, proudly-purposed web
When reds and blues were indeed red and blue,
Now offered as a mat to save bare feet
(Since carpets constitute a cruel cost)
Treading the chill scagliola bedward: then
A pile of brown-etched prints, two *crazie* each,
Stopped by a conch a-top from fluttering forth
— Sowing the Square with works of one and the same
Master, the imaginative Sienese
Great in the scenic backgrounds—(name and fame
None of you know, nor does he fare the worse:)
From these ... Oh, with a Lionard going cheap
If it should prove, as promised, that Joconde
Whereof a copy contents the Louvre!—these

I picked this book from. Five compeers in flank
Stood left and right of it as tempting more—
A dogseared Spicilegium, the fond talc
O' the Frail One of the Flower, by young Dumas,
Vulgarized Horace for the use of schools,
The Life, Death, Miracles of Saint Somebody,
Saint Somebody Else, his Miracles, Death, and Life,—
With this, one glance at the lettered back of which,
And 'Stall!' cried I: a *lira* made it mine.

Here it is, this I toss and take again;
Small-quarto size, part print part manuscript:
A book in shape but, really, pure crude fact
Secreted from man's life when hearts beat hard,
And brains, high-blooded, ticked two centuries since.
Give it me back! The thing's restorative
I' the touch and sight.

Robert Browning, *The Ring and the Book*

Purchasing an Act of Piety

When Providence throws a good book in my way, I bow to
its decree and purchase it as an act of piety, if it is reasonably
or unreasonably cheap. I *adopt* a certain number of books
every year, out of a love for the foundlings and stray children
of other people's brains that nobody seems to care for. Look
here.

He took down a Greek Lexicon finely bound in calf, and
spread it open.

Do you see that Hedericus? I had Greek dictionaries
enough and to spare, but I saw that noble quarto lying in
the midst of an ignoble crowd of cheap books, and marked
with a price which I felt to be an insult to scholarship, to the
memory of Homer, sir, and the awful shade of Aeschylus. I

paid the mean price asked for it, and I wanted to double it, but I suppose it would have been a foolish sacrifice of coin to sentiment. I love that book for its looks and behaviour. None of your 'half-calf' economies in that volume, sir! And see how it lies open anywhere! There isn't a book in my library that has such a generous way of laying its treasures before you. From Alpha to Omega, calm, assured rest at any page that your choice or accident may light on. No lifting of a rebellious leaf like an upstart servant that does not know his place and can never be taught manners, but tranquil, well-bred repose. A book may be a perfect gentleman in its aspect and demeanour, and this book would be good company for personages like Roger Ascham and his pupils the Lady Elizabeth and the Lady Jane Grey.

Oliver Wendell Holmes, *The Poet at the Breakfast-Table*

A Forced Sale

I fear that I must sell this residue
Of my father's books; although the Elzevirs
Have fly-leaves over-written by his hand,
In faded notes as thick and fine and brown
As cobwebs on a tawny monument
Of the old Greeks—*conferenda haec cum his*—
Corruptè citat—lege potiùs,
And so on, in the scholar's regal way
Of giving judgement on the parts of speech,
As if he sate on all twelve thrones up-piled,
Arraigning Israel. Ay, but books and notes
Must go together. And this Proclus too,
In quaintly dear contracted Grecian types,
Fantastically crumpled, like his thoughts
Which would not seem too plain; you go round twice
For one step forward, then you take it back,
Because you're somewhat giddy! there's the rule

For Proclus. Ah, I stained this middle leaf
With pressing in't my Florence iris-bell,
Long stalk and all: my father chided me
For that stain of blue blood,—I recollect
The peevish turn his voice took,—'Silly girls,
Who plant their flowers in our philosophy
To make it fine, and only spoil the book!
No more of it, Aurora.' Yes—no more!
Ah, blame of love, that's sweeter than all praise
Of those who love not! 'tis so lost to me,
I cannot, in such beggared life, afford
To lose my Proclus....

The kissing Judas, Wolff, shall go instead,
Who builds us such a royal book as this
To honour a chief-poet, folio-built,
And writes above, 'The house of Nobody':
Who floats in cream, as rich as any sucked
From Juno's breasts, the broad Homeric lines,
And, while with their spondaic prodigious mouths
They lap the lucent margins as babe-gods,
Proclaims them bastards. Wolff's an atheist;
And if the Iliad fell out, as he says,
By mere fortuitous concourse of old songs,
We'll guess as much, too, for the universe.

Elizabeth Barrett Browning, *Aurora Leigh*

The Vocation

One of the shop-windows he paused before was that of a
second-hand book-shop, where, on a narrow table outside,
the literature of the ages was represented in judicious
mixture, from the immortal verse of Homer to the mortal
prose of the railway novel. That the mixture was judicious
was apparent from Deronda's finding in it something that he

wanted—namely, that wonderful bit of autobiography, the life of the Polish Jew, Salomon Maimon; which, as he could easily slip it into his pocket, he took from its place, and entered the shop to pay for, expecting to see behind the counter a grimy personage showing that nonchalance about sales which seems to belong universally to the second-hand book-business. In most other trades you find generous men who are anxious to sell you their wares for your own welfare; but even a Jew will not urge Simson's Euclid on you with an affectionate assurance that you will have pleasure in reading it, and that he wishes he had twenty more of the article, so much is it in request. One is led to fear that a second-hand bookseller may belong to that unhappy class of men who have no belief in the good of what they get their living by, yet keep conscience enough to be morose rather than unctuous in their vocation.

George Eliot, *Daniel Deronda*

To My Bookseller

Thou that makst gain thy end, and, wisely well,
    Callst a book good, or bad, as it doth sell,
Use mine so too: I give thee leave; but crave
    For the luck's sake it thus much favour have
To lie upon thy stall, till it be sought;
    Not offered, as it made suit to be bought;
Nor have my title-leaf on posts or walls,
    Or in cleft sticks, advanced to make calls
For termers, or some clerk-like servingman,
    Who scarce can spell the hard names: whose knight
      less can.
If without these vile arts it will not sell,
    Send it to Bucklersbury, there 'twill well.

Ben Jonson

The Writer to His Book

Whither thus hastes my little book so fast?
To Paul's Churchyard. What? in those cells to stand,
With one leaf like a rider's cloak put up
To catch a termer? or lie musty there
With rhymes a term set out, or two, before?
Some will redeem me. Few. Yes, read me too.
Fewer. Nay, love me. Now thou dot'st, I see.
Will not our English Athens art defend?
Perhaps. Will lofty courtly wits not aim
Still at perfection? If I grant? I fly.
Whither? To Paul's. Alas, poor book, I rue
Thy rash self-love; go, spread thy papery wings:
Thy lightness cannot help or hurt my fame.

                                        Thomas Campion

Ad Bibliopolam

Printer or stationer or whate'er thou prove
Shalt me record to Time's posterity:
I'll not enjoin thee, but request in love,
Thou so much deign my Book to dignify,
As, first, it be not with your ballads mixed
Next, not at play-houses 'mongst pippins sold:
Then that on posts by the ears it stand not fixt,
For every dull mechanic to behold.
Last, that it come not brought in pedler's packs,
To common fairs, of country, town, or city:
Sold at a booth 'mongst pins and almanacks;
Yet on thy hands to lie, thou'lt say 'twere pity;
    Let it be rather for tobacco rent,
    Or butchers-wives, next Cleansing-week in Lent.

Henry Parrot, *The Mastive, or Young-Whelpe of the Olde-Dogge*

In Bondage to the Bookseller

Nevertheless conceive me not, I pray you, that I go about to lay a general imputation upon all stationers. For to disparage the whole profession were an act neither becoming an honest man to do, nor a prudent auditory to suffer. Their mystery, as they not untruly term it, consists of divers trades incorporated together: as printers, bookbinders, clasp-makers, booksellers, &c. And of all these be some honest men, who to my knowledge are so grieved, being overborne by the notorious oppressions and proceedings of the rest, that they have wished themselves of some other calling. The printers' mystery is ingenious, painful, and profitable: the book-binders' necessary; the clasp-makers' useful. And indeed, the retailer of books, commonly called a bookseller, is a trade, which, being well governed and limited within certain bounds, might become somewhat serviceable to the rest. But as it is now, for the most part abused, the bookseller hath not only made the printer, the binder, and the clasp-maker a slave to him: but hath brought authors, yea, the whole Commonwealth, and all the liberal sciences into bondage. For he makes all professors of Art labour for his profit, at his own price, and utters it to the Commonwealth in such fashion, and at those rates, which please himself. Insomuch, that I wonder so insupportable and so impertinent a thing as a mere bookseller, considering what the profession is become now, was ever permitted to grow up in the Commonwealth.

George Wither, *The Schollers Purgatory*

No furniture so charming as books, even if you never open them or read a single word.

Sydney Smith, *Memoirs*

In Paternoster Row

Methinks, oh vain, ill-judging book!
I see thee cast a wistful look,
Where reputations won and lost are
In famous row called *Paternoster*.
Incensed to find your precious olio
Buried in unexplored port-folio,
You scorn the prudent lock and key;
And pant, well-bound and gilt, to see
Your volume in the window set
Of Stockdale, Hookham, and Debrett.
Go then, and pass that dangerous bourne
Whence never book can back return;
And when you find—condemned, despised,
Neglected, blamed, and criticized—
Abuse from all who read you fall
(If haply you be read at all),
Sorely will you for folly sigh at,
And wish for me, and home, and quiet.

Assuming now a conjurer's office, I
Thus on your future fortune prophesy:—
Soon as your novelty is o'er,
And you are young and new no more,
In some dark dirty corner thrown,
Mouldy with damps, with cobwebs strown,
Your leaves shall be the bookworm's prey;
Or sent to chandler's shop away,
And doomed to suffer public scandal,
Shall line the trunk, or wrap the candle.

Matthew Lewis, *The Monk*

The Elephant and the Bookseller

The Bookseller, who heard him speak,
And saw him turn a page of Greek,
Thought, what a genius have I found!
Then thus addressed with bow profound:
   Learned Sir, if you'd employ your pen
Against the senseless sons of men,
Or write the history of Siam,
No man is better pay than I am.
Or, since you're learned in Greek, let's see
Something against the Trinity.'
   When, wrinkling with a sneer his trunk,
'Friend', quoth the Elephant, 'you're drunk:
E'en keep your money, and be wise;
Leave man on man to criticize:
For that you ne'er can want a pen
Among the senseless sons of men.
They unprovoked will court the fray;
Envy's a sharper spur than pay.
No author ever spared a brother;
Wits are gamecocks to one another.'

John Gay, Fables

Literary Upholsterers

Our booksellers here at London disgrace literature by the
trash they bespeak to be written, and at the same time prevent
everything else from being sold. They are little more or less
than upholsterers, who sell *sets* or *bodies* of arts and sciences for
furniture; and the purchasers, for I am very sure they are not
readers, buy only in that view. I never thought there was much
merit in reading: but yet it is too good a thing to be put upon
no better footing than damask and mahogany.

Horace Walpole, letter to Sir David Dalrymple

On a Miscellany of Poems

TO BERNARD LINTOTT

Ipsa varietate tentamus efficere ut alia aliis, quaedam fortasse omnibus placeant.—PLINY, *Epistulae*

As when some skilful cook, to please each guest,
Would in one mixture comprehend a feast,
With due proportion and judicious care
He fills his dish with different sorts of fare,
Fishes and fowls deliciously unite,
To feast at once the taste, the smell, and sight.
   So, Bernard, must a Miscellany be
Compounded of all kinds of poetry;
The Muses' olio, which all tastes may fit,
And treat each reader with his darling wit.
   Wouldst thou for Miscellanies raise thy fame,
And bravely rival Jacob's mighty name,
Let all the Muses in the piece conspire;
The lyric bard must strike the harmonious lyre;
Heroic strains must here and there be found;
And nervous sense be sung in lofty sound;
Let elegy in moving numbers flow,
And fill some pages with melodious woe;
Let not your amorous songs too numerous prove,
Nor glut thy reader with abundant love;
Satire must interfere, whose pointed rage
May lash the madness of a vicious age;
Satire! the Muse that never fails to hit,
For if there's scandal, to be sure there's wit.
Tire not our patience with Pindaric lays,
Those swell the piece, but very rarely please;
Let short-breathed epigram its force confine,
And strike at follies in a single line.
Translations should throughout the work be sown,
And Homer's godlike Muse be made our own;
Horace in useful numbers should be sung,

And Virgil's thoughts adorn the British tongue.
Let Ovid tell Corinna's hard disdain,
And at her door in melting notes complain;
His tender accents pitying virgins move,
And charm the listening ear with tales of love
Let every classic in the volume shine,
And each contribute to thy great design;
Through various subjects let the reader range,
And raise his fancy with a grateful change.
Variety's the source of joy below,
From whence still fresh revolving pleasures flow.
In books and love, the mind one end pursues,
And only *change* the expiring flame renews.

Where Buckingham will condescend to give,
That honoured piece to distant times must live;
When noble Sheffield strikes the trembling strings,
The little Loves rejoice, and clap their wings;
Anacreon lives, they cry, the harmonious swain
Retunes the lyre, and tries his wonted strain,
'Tis he—our lost Anacreon lives again.
But, when the illustrious poet soars above
The sportive revels of the God of Love,
Like Mars's Muse, he takes a loftier flight,
And towers beyond the wondering Cupid's sight.

If thou wouldst have thy volume stand the test,
And of all others be reputed best,
Let Congreve teach the listening groves to mourn,
As when he wept o'er fair Pastora's urn.

Let Prior's Muse with softening accents move,
Soft as the strains of constant Emma's love:
Or let his fancy choose some jovial theme,
As when he told Hans Carvel's jealous dream;
Prior the admiring reader entertains
With Chaucer's humour, and with Spenser's strains.

Waller in Granville lives; when Mira sings,
With Waller's hand he strikes the sounding strings,

With sprightly turns his noble genius shines,
And manly sense adorns his easy lines.
　On Addison's sweet lays attention waits,
And silence guards the place while he repeats;
His Muse alike on every subject charms,
Whether she paints the god of love, or arms;
In him pathetic Ovid sings again,
And Homer's *Iliad* shines in his *Campaign*.
　Whenever Garth shall raise his sprightly song,
Sense flows in easy numbers from his tongue;
Great Phoebus in his learned son we see,
Alike in physic, as in poetry.
　When Pope's harmonious Muse with pleasure roves
Amidst the plains, the murmuring streams, and groves,
Attentive Echo, pleased to hear his songs,
Through the glad shade each warbling note prolongs;
His various numbers charm our ravished ears,
His steady judgement far out-shoots his years,
And early in the youth the god appears.
　From these successful bards collect thy strains;
And praise with profit shall reward thy pains:
Then, while calf's-leather-binding bears the sway,
And sheepskin to its sleeker gloss gives way;
While neat old Elzevir is reckoned better
Than Pirate Hill's brown sheets and scurvy letter;
While print-admirers careful Aldous choose,
Before John Morphew, or the Weekly News;
So long shall live thy praise in books of fame,
And Tonson yield to Lintott's lofty name.

John Gay

Verses to be Prefixed before
Bernard Lintott's New Miscellany

Some Colinaeus praise, some Bleau,
Others account them but so so;
Some Plantin to the rest prefer,
And some esteem old Elzevir;
Others with Aldous would besot us;
I, for my part, admire Lintotus.—
His character's beyond compare,
Like his own person, large and fair.
They print their names in letters small,
But LINTOTT stands in capital:
Author and he with equal grace
Appear, and stare you in the face.
Stephens prints Heathen Greek, 'tis said,
Which some can't construe, some can't read;
But all that comes from Lintott's hand,
Even Rawlinson might understand.
Oft in an Aldous, or a Plantin,
A page is blotted, or leaf wanting:
Of Lintott's books this can't be said,
All fair, and not so much as read.
Their copy cost 'em not a penny
To Homer, Virgil, or to any;
They ne'er gave sixpence for two lines
To them, their heirs, or their assigns:
But Lintott is at vast expense,
And pays prodigious dear for—sense.
Their books are useful but to few,
A scholar or a wit or two;
Lintott's for general use are fit.

Alexander Pope

To Mr Murray

Strahan, Tonson, Lintott of the times,
Patron and publisher of rhymes,
For thee the bard up Pindus climbs,
        My Murray.

To thee, with hope and terror dumb,
The unpledged MS. authors come;
Thou printest all—and sellest some—
        My Murray.

Upon thy table's baize so green
The last new *Quarterly* is seen,—
But where is thy new Magazine,
        My Murray?

Along thy sprucest bookshelves shine
The works thou deemest most divine—
The 'Art of Cookery', and mine,
        My Murray.

Tours, Travels, Essays, too, I wist,
And Sermons, to thy mill bring grist;
And then thou hast the 'Navy List',
        My Murray.

And heaven forbid I should conclude
Without 'the Board of Longitude',
Although this narrow paper would,
        My Murray.

George Gordon, Lord Byron

What a Heart-breaking Shop

But what were even gold and silver, precious stones and
clockwork, to the bookshops, whence a pleasant smell of
paper freshly pressed came issuing forth, awakening instant
recollections of some new grammar had at school, long time
ago, with 'Master Pinch, Grove House Academy', inscribed in
faultless writing on the fly-leaf! That whiff of russia leather,
too, and all those rows on rows of volumes, neatly ranged
within: what happiness did they suggest! And in the window
were the spick-and-span new works from London, with the
title-pages, and sometimes even the first page of the first
chapter, laid wide open: tempting unwary men to begin
to read the book, and then, in the impossibility of turning
over, to rush blindly in, and buy it! Here too were the dainty
frontispiece and trim vignette, pointing like handposts on
the outskirts of great cities, to the rich stock of incident
beyond; and store of books, with many a grave portrait and
time-honoured name, whose matter he knew well, and would
have given mines to have, in any form, upon the narrow shelf
beside his bed at Mr. Pecksniff's. What a heart-breaking shop
it was!

Charles Dickens, *Martin Chuzzlewit*

Genteel Ornaments

If people bought no more books than they intended to read,
and no more swords than they intended to use, the two worst
trades in Europe would be a bookseller's and a sword-cutler's;
but luckily for both they are reckoned genteel ornaments.

Lord Chesterfield

Mammon and Books

All who are affected by the love of books hold worldly affairs and money very cheap, as Jerome writes to Vigilantius (Epist. 54): 'It is not for the same man to ascertain the value of gold coins and of writings;' which somebody thus repeated in verse:

No tinker's hand shall dare a book to stain;
  No miser's heart can wish a book to gain;
The gold assayer cannot value books;
  On them the epicure disdainful looks.
One house at once, believe me, cannot hold
  Lovers of books and hoarders up of gold.

No man, therefore, can serve mammon and books.

Richard de Bury, *Philobiblon*

The Poor Student

In the depth of college shades, or in his lonely chamber, the poor student shrunk from observation. He found shelter among books, which insult not; and studies, that ask no questions of a youth's finances. He was lord of his library, and seldom cared for looking out beyond his domains.

Charles Lamb, *Poor Relations*

National Expenditure on Books

I say first we have despised literature. What do we, as a nation, care about books? How much do you think we spend altogether on our libraries, public or private, as compared with what we spend on our horses? If a man spends lavishly on his library, you call him mad—a bibliomaniac. But you never call any one a horse-maniac, though men ruin themselves every day by their horses, and you do not hear of people ruining themselves by their books. Or, to go lower still, how much do you think the contents of the book-shelves of the United Kingdom, public and private, would fetch, as compared with the contents of its wine-cellars? What position would its expenditure on literature take, as compared with its expenditure on luxurious eating? We talk of food for the mind, as of food for the body; now a good book contains such food inexhaustibly; it is a provision for life, and for the best part of us; yet how long most people would look at the best book before they would give the price of a large turbot for it! Though there have been men who have pinched their stomachs and bared their backs to buy a book, whose libraries were cheaper to them, I think, in the end, than most men's dinners are. We are few of us put to such trial, and more the pity; for, indeed, a precious thing is all the more precious to us if it has been won by work or economy; and if public libraries were half as costly as public dinners, or books cost the tenth part of what bracelets do, even foolish men and women might sometimes suspect there was good in reading, as well as in munching and sparkling; whereas the very cheap-ness of literature is making even wise people forget that if a book is worth reading, it is worth buying. No book is worth anything which is not worth *much*; nor is it serviceable until it has been read, and re-read, and loved, and loved again; and marked, so that you can refer to the passages you want in it, as a soldier can seize the weapon he needs in an armoury, or a housewife bring the spice she needs from her store. Bread of flour is good; but there is bread, sweet as honey, if we would eat it, in a good book; and the family must be poor indeed which, once in their lives, cannot, for such multipliable barley-loaves, pay their baker's bill. We call ourselves a rich nation, and we are filthy and foolish enough to thumb each other's books out of circulating libraries!

John Ruskin, *Sesame and Lilies*

The Value of Book Borrowing

I have sent you the Philosophy—books you writ to me for; anything that you want of this kind for the advancement of your studies, do but write, and I shall furnish you. When I was a student as you are, my practice was to borrow rather than buy, some sort of books, and to be always punctual in restoring them upon the day assigned, and in the interim to swallow of them as much as made for my turn. This obliged me to read them through with more haste to keep my word, whereas I had not been so careful to peruse them had they been my own books, which I knew were always ready at my dispose.

James Howell, *Familiar Letters*

Accidents to Books

Fortunate are those who only consider a book for the utility and pleasure they may derive from its possession. Those students who, though they know much, still thirst to know more, may require this vast sea of books; yet in that sea they may suffer many shipwrecks.

Great collections of books are subject to certain accidents besides the damp, the worms, and the rats; one not less common is that of the *borrowers*, not to say a word of the *purloiners*!

Isaac D'Israeli, *Curiosities of Literature*

Borrowing and Lending

I own I borrow books with as much facility as I lend. I
cannot see a work that interests me on another person's shelf,
without a wish to carry it off: but, I repeat, that I have been
much more sinned against than sinning in the article of non-
return; and am scrupulous in the article of intention.

J.H. Leigh Hunt, *My Books*

Wedded to Books

If people are to be wedded to their books, it is hard that,
under our present moral dispensations, they are not to be
allowed the usual exclusive privileges of marriage. A friend
thinks no more of borrowing a book nowadays, than a Roman
did of borrowing a man's wife; and what is worse, we are
so far gone in our immoral notions on this subject, that we
even lend it as easily as Cato did his spouse. Now what a
happy thing ought it not to be to have exclusive possession
of a book,—one's Shakespeare for instance; for the finer the
wedded work, the more anxious of course we should be, that
it should give nobody happiness but ourselves. Think of the
pleasure of not only being with it in general, of having by
far the greater part of its company, but of having it entirely
to oneself; of always saying internally, 'It is my property'; of
seeing it well-dressed in 'black or red', purely to please one's
own eyes; of wondering how any fellow could be so impudent
as to propose borrowing it for an evening; of being at once
proud of his admiration, and pretty certain that it was in
vain; of the excitement nevertheless of being a little uneasy
whenever we saw him approach it too nearly; of wishing that
it could give him a cuff of the cheek with one of its beautiful
boards, for presuming to like its beauties as well as ourselves;
of liking other people's books, but not at all thinking it

proper that they should like ours; of getting perhaps indifferent to it, and then comforting ourselves with the reflection
that others are not so, though to no purpose; in short, of all
the mixed transport and anxiety to which the exclusiveness
of the book-wedded state would be liable; not to mention the
impossibility of other people's having any literary offspring
from our fair unique, and consequently of the danger of
loving any compilations but our own. Really, if we could burn
all other copies of our originals, as the Roman Emperor once
thought of destroying Homer, this system would be worth
thinking of. If we had a good library, we should be in the
situation of the Turks with their seraglios, which are a great
improvement upon our petty exclusivenesses. Nobody could
then touch our Shakespeare, our Spenser, our Chaucer, our
Greek and Italian writers. People might say, 'Those are the
walls of the library!' and 'sigh, and look, and sigh again';
but they should never get in. No Retrospective rake should
anticipate our privileges of quotation. Our Mary Wollstone-
crafts and our Madame de Staëls—no one should know how
finely they were lettered,—what soul there was in their
disquisitions. We once had a glimpse of the feelings which
people would have on these occasions. It was in the library
of Trinity College, Cambridge. The keeper of it was from
home; and not being able to get a sight of the manuscript of
Milton's *Comus*, we were obliged to content ourselves with
looking through a wire-work, a kind of safe, towards the
shelf on which it reposed. How we winked, and yearned, and
imagined we saw a corner of the all-precious sheets, to no
purpose! The feelings were not very pleasant, it is true; but
then as long as they were confined to others, they would of
course only add to our satisfaction.

J.H. Leigh Hunt, *Wedded to Books*

The Art of Book-Keeping

How hard, when those who do not wish
 To lend, that's lose, their books,
Are snared by anglers—folks that fish
 With literary hooks;

Who call and take some favourite tome,
 But never read it through;—
They thus complete their set at home,
 By making one at you.

Behold the bookshelf of a dunce
 Who borrows—never lends;
Yon work, in twenty volumes, once
 Belonged to twenty friends.

New tales and novels you may shut
 From view—'tis all in vain;
They're gone—and though the leaves are 'cut'
 They never 'come again'.

For pamphlets lent I look around,
 For tracts my tears are spilt;
But when they take a book that's bound,
 'Tis surely extra-guilt.

A circulating library
 Is mine—my birds are flown;
There's one odd volume left to be
 Like all the rest, a-lone.

I, of my Spenser quite bereft,
 Last winter sore was shaken;
Of Lamb I've but a quarter left,
 Nor could I save my Bacon.

My Hall and Hill were levelled flat,
    But Moore was still the cry;
And then, although I threw them Sprat,
    They swallowed up my Pye.

O'er everything, however slight,
    They seized some airy trammel;
They snatched my Hogg and Fox one night,
    And pocketed my Campbell.

And then I saw my Crabbe at last,
    Like Hamlet's, backward go;
And as my tide was ebbing fast,
    Of course I lost my Rowe.

I wondered into what balloon
    My books their course had bent;
And yet, with all my marvelling, soon
    I found my Marvell went.

My Mallet served to knock me down,
    Which makes me thus a talker;
And once, while I was out of town,
    My Johnson proved a Walker.

While studying o'er the fire one day
    My Hobbes amidst the smoke,
They bore my Colman clean away,
    And carried off my Coke.

They picked my Locke, to me far more
    Than Bramah's patent's worth;
And now my losses I deplore
    Without a Home on earth.

If once a book you let them lift,
    Another they conceal;
For though I caught them stealing Swift,
    As swiftly went my Steele.

Hope is not now upon my shelf,
    Where late he stood elated;
But, what is strange, my Pope himself
    Is excommunicated.

My little Suckling in the grave
    Is sunk, to swell the ravage;
And what 'twas Crusoe's fate to save
    'Twas mine to lose—a Savage.

Even Glover's works I cannot put
    My frozen hands upon;
Though ever since I lost my Foote
    My Bunyan has been gone.

My Hoyle with Cotton went; oppressed,
    My Taylor too must sail;
To save my Goldsmith from arrest,
    In vain I offered Bayle.

I Prior sought, but could not see
    The Hood so late in front;
And when I turned to hunt for Lee,
    Oh! where was my Leigh Hunt?

I tried to laugh, old care to tickle,
    Yet could not Tickell touch,
And then, alas! I missed my Mickle,
    And surely mickle's much.

'Tis quite enough my griefs to feed,
    My sorrows to excuse,
To think I cannot read my Reid.
    Nor even use my Hughes.

To West, to South, I turn my head,
    Exposed alike to odd jeers;
For since my Roger Ascham's fled,
    I ask 'em for my Rogers.

They took my Horne—and Horne Tooke, too,
    And thus my treasures flit;
I feel when I would Hazlitt view,
    The flames that it has lit.

My word's worth little, Wordsworth gone,
    If I survive its doom;
How many a bard I doated on
    Was swept off—with my Broome.

My classics would not quiet lie,
    A thing so fondly hoped;
Like Dr. Primrose, I may cry,
    'My Livy has eloped!'

My life is wasting fast away—
    I suffer from these shocks;
And though I've fixed a lock on Gray,
    There's grey upon my locks.

I'm far from young—am growing pale—
    I see my Butter fly;
And when they ask about my *ail*,
    'Tis Burton! I reply.

They still have made me slight returns,
    And thus my griefs divide;
For oh! they've cured me of my Burns,
    And eased my Akenside.

But all I think I shall not say,
    Nor let my anger burn;
For as they never found me Gay,
    They have not left me Sterne.

Samuel Laman Blanchard

The Book of Life

That Life is a Comedy oft hath been shown,
By all who Mortality's changes have known;
But more like a Volume its actions appear,
Where each Day is a Page and each Chapter a year.
'Tis a Manuscript Time shall full surely unfold,
Though with Black-Letter shaded, or shining with gold;
The Initial, like youth, glitters bright on its Page,
But its text is as dark—as the gloom of old Age.
    Then Life's Counsels of Wisdom engrave on thy breast,
    And deep on thine Heart be her lessons impressed.

Though the Title stands first it can little declare
The Contents which the Pages ensuing shall bear;
As little the first day of Life can explain
The succeeding events which shall glide in its train.
The Book follows next, and, delighted, we trace
An Elzevir's beauty, a Gutenberg's grace;
Thus on pleasure we gaze with as raptured an eye,
Till, cut off like a Volume imperfect, we die!
    Then Life's Counsels of Wisdom engrave on thy breast,
    And deep on thine Heart be her lessons impressed.

Yet e'en thus imperfect, complete, or defaced,
The skill of the Printer is still to be traced;
And though death bend us early in life to his will,
The wise hand of our Author is visible still.
Like the Colophon lines is the Epitaph's lay,
Which tells of what age and what nation our day,
And, like the Device of the Printer, we bear
The form of the Founder, whose Image we wear.
   Then Life's Counsels of Wisdom engrave on thy breast,
   And deep on thine Heart be her lessons impressed.

The work thus completed its Boards shall enclose,
Till a Binding more bright and more beauteous it shows;
And who can deny, when Life's Vision hath passed,
That the dark Boards of Death shall surround us at last.
Yet our Volume illumed with fresh splendours shall rise,
To be gazed at by Angels, and read to the skies,
Reviewed by its Author, revised by his Pen,
In a fair new Edition to flourish again.
   Then Life's Counsels of Wisdom engrave on thy breast,
   And deep on thine Heart be her lessons impressed.

                                        Richard Thomson

A Great Necromancer

Alonso of Aragon was wont to say of himself that he was a
great Necromancer, for that he used to ask counsel of the
dead: meaning Books.

                                  Francis Bacon, *Apophthegmes*

The Secret of Strength

> 'Tis a custom with him
> I' the afternoon to sleep: there thou may'st brain him,
> Having first seized his books; or with a log
> Batter his skull, or paunch him with a stake.
> Or cut his wezand with thy knife. Remember
> First to possess his books; for without them
> He's but a sot, as I am, nor hath not
> One spirit to command: they all do hate him
> As rootedly as I. Burn but his books.

William Shakespeare, *The Tempest*

Red Letters and Conjuring

SMITH The clerk of Chatham: he can write and read
    and cast accompt.
CADE O monstrous!
SMITH We took him setting of boys' copies.
CADE Here's a villain!
SMITH Has a book in his pocket with red letters in't.
CADE Nay, then, he is a conjurer.

William Shakespeare, *Second Part of King Henry the Sixth*

Merlin's Book

You read the book, my pretty Vivien!
O aye, it is but twenty pages long,
But every page having an ample marge,
And every marge enclosing in the midst
A square of text that looks a little blot,
The text no larger than the limbs of fleas;
And every square of text an awful charm,
Writ in a language that has long gone by.

So long, that mountains have arisen since
With cities on their flanks—*you* read the book!
And every margin scribbled, crost, and crammed
With comment, densest condensation, hard.
To mind and eye; but the long sleepless nights
Of my long life have made it easy to me.
And none can read the text, not even I;
And none can read the comment but myself;
And in the comment did I find the charm.

Alfred, Lord Tennyson,
Idylls of the King

Fast and Loose

Fast bind, fast find: my Bible was well bound;
A Thief came fast, and loose my Bible found:
Was't bound and loose at once? how can that be?
'Twas loose for him, although 'twas bound for me.

John Taylor

To the Holy Bible

O Book! Life's guide! how shall we part,
And thou so long seized of my heart?
Take this last kiss; and let me weep
True thanks to thee before I sleep.

Thou wert the first put in my hand
When yet I could not understand,
And daily didst my young eyes lead
To letters, till I learnt to read.

But as rash youths, when once grown strong,
Fly from their nurses to the throng,
Where they new consorts choose, and stick
To those till either hurt or sick;

So with the first light gained from thee
Ran I in chase of vanity,
Cried dross for gold, and never thought
My first cheap book had all I sought.
Long reigned this vogue; and thou cast by,
With meek, dumb looks didst woo mine eye,
And oft left open would'st convey
A sudden and most searching ray
Into my soul, with whose quick touch
Refining still, I struggled much.
By this mild art of love at length
Thou overcam'st my sinful strength,
And having brought me home, didst there
Show me that pearl I sought elsewhere,—
Gladness, and peace, and hope, and love,
The secret favours of the Dove;
Her quickening kindness, smiles, and kisses,
Exalted pleasures, crowning blisses,
Fruition, union, glory, life,
Thou didst lead to, and still all strife.
Living, thou wert my soul's sure ease,
And dying mak'st me go in peace:—
Thy next effects no tongue can tell;
Farewell, O Book of God! farewell!

Henry Vaughan

On Buying the Bible

'Tis but a folly to rejoice or boast
How small a price thy well-bought Pen'worth cost:
Until thy death thou shalt not fully know
Whether thy purchase be good cheap, or no;
And at that day, believe't, it will appear
If not extremely cheap, extremely dear.

Francis Quarles, *Divine Fancies*

'I Read Only the Bible'

Read the most useful books, and that regularly, and constantly. Steadily spend all the morning in this employ, or, at least, five hours in four-and-twenty.

'But I read only the Bible.' Then you ought to teach others to read only the Bible, and, by parity of reason, to hear only the Bible. But if so, you need preach no more.

'Just so,' said George Bell. 'And what is the fruit? Why, now he neither reads the Bible, nor anything else. This is rank enthusiasm.' If you need no book but the Bible, you are got above St. Paul. He wanted others too. 'Bring the books,' says he, 'but especially the parchments,' those wrote on parchment. 'But I have no taste for reading.' Contract a taste for it by use, or return to your trade.

John Wesley, *Minutes of Some Late Conversations*

A Man of One Book

I want to know one thing,—the way to heaven; how to land safe on the happy shore. God himself has condescended to teach me the way. For this very end He came from heaven. He hath written it down in a book. O give me the book! At any price, give me the book of God. I have it: here is knowledge enough for me. Let me be *homo unius libri*. Here then I am, far from the busy ways of men. I sit down alone; only God is here. In His presence I open, I read His book.... And what I thus learn, that I teach.

John Wesley, Preface to *Sermons*

Homo Unius Libri

When St. Thomas Aquinas was asked in what manner a man might best become learned, he answered. 'By reading one book.' The *homo unius libri* is indeed proverbially formidable to all conversational figurantes.

Robert Southey, *The Doctor*

The Scriptures: What Are They?

I remember he alleged many a scripture, but those I valued not; the scriptures, thought I, what are they? A dead letter, a little ink and paper, of three or four shillings price. Alas! What is the scripture? Give me a ballad, a news-book, George on horseback, or Bevis of Southampton; give me some book that teaches curious arts, that tells of old fables; but for the holy scriptures I cared not.

John Bunyan, *Sighs from Hell*

The Pilgrim's Progress

I know of no book, the Bible excepted, as above all comparison, which I, according to my judgement and experience, could so safely recommend as teaching and enforcing the whole saving truth according to the mind that was in Christ Jesus, as the *Pilgrim's Progress*. It is, in my conviction, incomparably the best *summa theologiae evangelicae* ever produced by a writer not miraculously inspired.

This wonderful work is one of the few books which may be read repeatedly at different times, and each time with a new and different pleasure. I read it once as a theologian —and let me assure you that there is great theological acumen in the work—once with devotional feelings—and once as a poet. I could not have believed beforehand that Calvinism could be painted in such exquisitely delightful colours....

The *Pilgrim's Progress* is composed in the lowest style of
English, without slang or false grammar. If you were to
polish it, you would at once destroy the reality of the vision.
For works of imagination should be written in very plain
language; the more imaginative they are the more necessary it
is to be plain.

S.T. Coleridge, Table Talk

No Book Like the Bible

I would have you every morning read a portion of the Holy
Scriptures, till you have read the Bible from the beginning to
the end: observe it well, read it reverently and attentively, set
your heart upon it, and lay it up in your memory and make it
the direction of your life: it will make you a wise and a good
man. I have been acquainted somewhat with men and books,
and have had long experience in learning, and in the world:
there is no book like the Bible for excellent learning, wisdom,
and use; and it is want of understanding in them that think or
speak otherwise.

Sir Matthew Hale, A Letter to one of his Sons,
after his recovery from the Smallpox

The Book of Books

No man was a greater lover of books than he [Shelley]. He
was rarely to be seen, unless attending to other people's
affairs, without a volume of some sort, generally of Plato or
one of the Greek tragedians. Nor will those who understand
the real spirit of his scepticism, be surprised to hear that one
of his companions was the Bible. He valued it for the beauty
of some of its contents, for the dignity of others, and the

curiosity of all; though the philosophy of Solomon he thought too *Epicurean*, and the inconsistencies of other parts afflicted him. His favourite part was the book of Job, which he thought the grandest of tragedies. He projected founding one of his own upon it; and I will undertake to say, that Job would have sat in that tragedy with a patience and profundity of thought worthy of the original. Being asked on one occasion, what book he would save for himself if he could save no other? he answered, 'The oldest book, the Bible.'

J.H. Leigh Hunt, My Books

A Very Priceless Thing

Precious temporal things are growing [in these years of peace]; priceless spiritual things. We know the Shakespeare Dramaturgy; the Rare-Ben and Elder-Dramatist affair; which has now reached its culmination. Yes; and precisely when the Wit-combats at the Mermaid are waning somewhat, and our Shakespeare is about packing up for Stratford,—there comes out another very priceless thing; a correct Translation of the Bible; that which we still use. Priceless enough this latter; of importance unspeakable! Reynolds and Chadderton petitioned for it, at the Hampton-Court Conference, long since; and now, in 1611, by labour of Reynolds, Chadderton, Dr. Abbot, and other prodigiously learned and earnest persons, 'forty-seven in number,' it comes out beautifully printed; dedicated to the Dread Sovereign; really in part a benefit of his to us. And so we have it here to read, that Book of Books: 'barbarous enough to rouse, tender enough to assuage, and possessing how many other properties,' says Goethe;—possessing this property, inclusive of all, add we, That it is written under the eye of the Eternal; that it is of a Sincerity like very Death; the truest Utterance that ever came by Alphabetic Letters from the Soul of Man. Through which, as through a window divinely opened, all men could look, and can still look, beyond the visual Air-firmaments and mysterious Time-oceans, into the Light-sea of Infinitude, into the stillness of Eternity; and discern in glimpses, with such emotions and practical suggestions as there may be, their far-distant, longforgotten Home.

Thomas Carlyle, Historical Sketches

Sacred and Profane Writers

Let those who will, hang rapturously o'er
The flowing eloquence of Plato's page,
Repeat, with flashing eye, the sounds that pour
From Homer's verse as with a torrent's rage;
Let those who list, ask Tully to assuage
Wild hearts with high-wrought periods, and restore
The reign of rhetoric; or maxims sage
Winnow from Seneca's sententious lore.
Not these, but Judah's hallowed bards, to me
Are dear; Isaiah's noble energy;
The temperate grief of Job; the artless strain
Of Ruth and pastoral Amos; the high songs
Of David; and the tale of Joseph's wrongs,
Simply pathetic, eloquently plain.

Sir Aubrey de Vere

A Standard for Language

It is your lordship's observation, that if it were not for the Bible and Common Prayer Book in the vulgar tongue, we should hardly be able to understand anything that was written among us a hundred years ago; which is certainly true: for those books, being perpetually read in churches, have proved a kind of standard for language, especially to the common people... As to the greatest parts of our liturgy, compiled long before the translation of the Bible now in use, and little altered since, these seem to be in as great strains of true sublime eloquence as are anywhere to be found in our language.

Jonathan Swift, *A Proposal for Correcting, Improving and Ascertaining the English Tongue*

The Grand Mine of Diction

He [the translator of Homer] will find one English book and one only, where, as in the *Iliad* itself, perfect plainness of speech is allied with perfect nobleness; and that book is the Bible. No one could see this more clearly than Pope saw it: 'This pure and noble simplicity,' he says, 'is nowhere in such perfection as in the Scripture and Homer': yet even with Pope a woman is a 'fair', a father is a 'sire', and an old man a 'reverend sage', and so on through all the phrases of that pseudo-Augustan, and most unbiblical, vocabulary. The Bible, however, is undoubtedly the grand mine of diction, for the translator of Homer; and, if he knows how to discriminate truly between what will suit him and what will not, the Bible may afford him also invaluable lessons of style.

Matthew Arnold, *On Translating Homer*

The Bible and Burns

Search Scotland over, from the Pentland to the Solway, and
there is not a cottage-hut so poor and wretched as to be
without its Bible; and hardly one that, on the same shelf,
and next to it, does not treasure a Burns. Have the people
degenerated since their adoption of this new manual? Has
their attachment to the Book of Books declined? Are their
hearts less firmly bound, than were their fathers', to the old
faith and the old virtues? I believe he that knows the most
of the country will be the readiest to answer all these questions, as every lover of genius and virtue would desire to hear
them answered ... Extraordinary... has been the unanimity
of his critics. While differing widely in their estimates of his
character and *morale*, they have, without a single exception,
expressed a lofty idea of his powers of mind and of the excel-
lence of his poetry. Here, as on the subject of Shakespeare,
and on scarcely any other, have Whigs and Tories. Infidels
and Christians, bigoted Scotchmen and bigoted sons of John
Bull, the high and the low, the rich and the poor, the prosaic
and the enthusiastic lovers of poetry, the strait-laced and the
morally lax, met and embraced each other.

J.G. Lockhart, *Life of Burns*

The Big Ha'-Bible

The cheerfu' supper done, wi' serious face,
   They round the ingle form a circle wide;
The sire turns o'er, wi' patriarchal grace,
   The big ha'-bible, ance his father's pride:
   ...
The priest-like father reads the sacred page,
   How Abram was the friend of God on high;
Or Moses bade eternal warfare wage
   With Amalek's ungracious progeny;

Or how the royal Bard did groaning lie
Beneath the stroke of Heaven's avenging ire;
   Or Job's pathetic plaint, and wailing cry;
Or rapt Isaiah's wild, seraphic fire;
Or other holy seers that tune the sacred lyre.

Robert Burns, The Cotter's Saturday Night

Of the Imitation of Christ

She read on and on in the old book, devouring eagerly the
dialogues with the invisible Teacher, the pattern of sorrow,
the source of all strength; returning to it after she had been
called away, and reading till the sun went down behind the
willows. With all the hurry of an imagination that could
never rest in the present, she sat in the deepening twilight
forming plans of self-humiliation and entire devotedness; and,
in the ardour of first discovery, renunciation seemed to her
the entrance into that satisfaction which she had so long been
craving in vain. She had not perceived—how could she until
she had lived longer?—the inmost truth of the old monk's
outpourings, that renunciation remains sorrow, though a
sorrow borne willingly. Maggie was still panting for happiness, and was in ecstasy because she had found the key to it.
She knew nothing of doctrines and systems—of mysticism
or quietism; but this voice out of the far-off middle ages was
the direct communication of a human soul's belief and experience, and came to Maggie as an unquestioned message.

   I suppose that is the reason why the small old-fashioned
book, for which you need only pay sixpence at a bookstall,
works miracles to this day, turning bitter waters into sweetness; while expensive sermons and treatises, newly issued,
leave all things as they were before. It was written down by a
hand that waited for the heart's prompting; it is the chronicle
of a solitary, hidden anguish, struggle, trust and triumph—
not written on velvet cushions to teach endurance to those

who are treading with bleeding feet on the stones. And so it remains to all time a lasting record of human needs and human consolations: the voice of a brother who, ages ago, felt and suffered and renounced— in the cloister, perhaps, with serge gown and tonsured head, with much chanting and long fasts, and with a fashion of speech different from ours—but under the same silent far-off heavens, and with the same passionate desires, the same strivings, the same failures, the same weariness.

George Eliot, *The Mill on the Floss*

Literary Geography

SCOTLAND

The globe we inhabit is divisible into two worlds; one hardly less tangible, and far more known than the other,—the common geographical world, and the world of books; and the latter may be as geographically set forth. A man of letters, conversant with poetry and romance, might draw out a very curious map, in which this world of books should be delineated and filled up, to the delight of all genuine readers, as truly as that in Guthrie or Pinkerton. To give a specimen, and begin with Scotland,—Scotland would not be the mere territory it is, with a scale of so many miles to a degree, and such and such a population. Who (except a patriot or cosmopolite) cares for the miles or the men, or knows that they exist, in any degree of consciousness with which he cares for the never-dying population of books? How many generations of men have passed away, and will pass, in Ayrshire or Dumfries, and not all the myriads be as interesting to us as a single Burns? What have we known of them, or shall ever know, whether lairds, lords, or ladies, in comparison with the inspired ploughman? But we know of the bards and the lasses, and the places which he has recorded in song; we know the scene of 'Tam o' Shanter's' exploit; we know the pastoral landscapes... and the scenes immortalized in Walter Scott and the old ballads; and, therefore, the book-map of Scotland would present us with the most prominent of these. We should have the Border, with its banditti, towns, and woods; Tweedside, Melrose, and Roslin, 'Edina,' otherwise called Edinburgh and Auld Reekie, or the town of Hume, Robertson, and others; Woodhouselee, and other classical and haunted places; the bower built by the fair hands of 'Bessie Bell' and 'Mary Gray'; the farm-houses of Burns's friends; the scenes of his loves and sorrows; the land of 'Old Mortality', of the 'Gentle Shepherd', and of 'Ossian'. The Highlands, and the great blue billowy domains of heather, would be distinctly marked out, in their most poetical regions; and we should have the tracks of Ben Jonson to Hawthornden, of 'Rob Roy' to his hiding-places, and of 'Jeanie Deans' towards England. Abbotsford, be sure, would not be left out; nor the house of the 'Antiquary'—almost as real a man as his author. Nor is this all: for we should have older Scotland, the Scotland of James the First, and of 'Peeblis at the Play', and Gawin Douglas, and Bruce, and Wallace; we should have older Scotland still, the Scotland of Ariosto, with his tale of 'Ginevra', and the new 'Andromeda', delivered from the sea-monster at the Isle of Ebuda (the Hebrides); and there would be the residence of the famous 'Launcelot of the Lake', at Berwick, called the Joyeuse Garde, and other ancient sites of chivalry and romance; nor should the nightingale be left out in 'Ginevra's' bower, for Ariosto has put it there, and there, accordingly, it is and has been heard, let ornithology say what it will; for what ornithologist knows so much of the nightingale as a poet? We would have an inscription put on the spot—'Here the nightingale sings, contrary to what has been affirmed by White and others.' This is the Scotland of books, and a beautiful place it is. I will venture to affirm, Sir, even to yourself, that it is a more beautiful place than the other Scotland, always excepting to an exile or a lover.

ENGLAND

Book-England, on the map, would shine as the Albion of the old Giants; as the 'Logres' of the Knights of the Round Table; as the scene of Amadis of Gaul, with its *island* of Windsor; as the abode of fairies, of the Druids, of the divine Countess of Coventry, of Guy, Earl of Warwick, of 'Alfred' (whose reality was a romance), of the Fair Rosamond, of the *Arcades* and *Comus*, of Chaucer and Spenser, of the poets of the Globe and the Mermaid, the wits of Twickenham and Hampton Court. Fleet Street would be Johnson's Fleet Street; the Tower would belong to Julius Caesar; and Blackfriars to Suckling, Vandyke, and the *Dunciad*. Chronology and the mixture of truth and fiction, that is to say, of one sort of truth and another, would come to nothing in a work of this kind; for, as it has been before observed, things are real in proportion as they are impressive. And who has not as 'gross, open, and palpable' an idea of 'Falstaff' in Eastcheap, as of 'Captain Grose' himself, beating up his quarters? A map of fictitious, literary, and historical London, would, of itself, constitute a great curiosity.

IRELAND

Swift speaks of maps, in which they

Place elephants for want of towns.

Here would be towns and elephants too, the popular and the prodigious. How much would not Swift do for Ireland, in this geography of wit and talent! What a figure would not St. Patrick's Cathedral make! The other day, mention was made of a 'Dean of St. Patrick's' *now living*; as if there was, or ever could be, more than one Dean of St. Patrick's! In the Irish maps we should have the Saint himself driving out all venomous creatures (what a pity that the most venomous retain a property as absentees!); and there would be the old Irish kings, and O'Donoghue with his White Horse, and the lady of the 'gold wand' who made the miraculous virgin pilgrimage, and all the other marvels of lakes and ladies, and

the Round Towers still remaining to perplex the antiquary,
and Goldsmith's 'Deserted Village', and Goldsmith himself,
and the birthplaces of Steele and Sterne, and the brief hour
of poor Lord Edward Fitzgerald, and Carolan with his harp,
and the schools of the poor Latin boys under the hedges,
and Castle Rackrent, and Edgeworth's-town, and the Giant's
Causeway, and Ginleas and other classical poverties, and
Spenser's castle on the river Mulla, with the wood-gods
whom his pipe drew round him.

J.H. Leigh Hunt, *The World of Books*

On 'Coryat's Crudities'

Tom Coryat, I have seen thy Crudities,
And, methinks, very strangely brewed—it is
With piece and patch together glued—it is
And how, like thee, ill-favoured hued—it is
In many lines I see that lewd—it is
And therefore fit to be subdued—it is
Within thy broiling brain-pan stewed—it is
And 'twixt thy grinding jaws well chewed—it is
Within thy stomach closely mewed—it is
And last, in Court and Country spewed—it is
But now by wisdom's eye that viewed—it is
They all agree that very rude—it is
With foolery so full endued—it is

That wondrously by fools pursued—it is
As sweet as gall's amaritude—it is
And seeming full of pulchritude—it is
But more to write, but to intrude—it is
And therefore wisdom to conclude—it is.

John Taylor, *The World's Eighth Wonder*

Literature for Desolate Islands

I've thought very often 'twould be a good thing
In all public collections of books, if a wing
Were set off by itself, like the seas from the dry lands,
Marked *Literature suited to desolate islands*,
And filled with such books as could never be read
Save by readers of proofs, forced to do it for bread,—
Such books as one's wrecked on in small country taverns,
Such as hermits might mortify over in caverns,
Such as Satan, if printing had then been invented,
As a climax of woe, would to Job have presented,
Such as Crusoe might dip in, although there are few so
Outrageously cornered by fate as poor Crusoe;
...
I propose to shut up every doer of wrong
With these desperate books, for such term, short or long,
As by statute in such cases made and provided,
Shall be by you wise legislators decided.

J.R. Lowell, A Fable for Critics

I have sometimes heard of an Iliad in a nutshell; but it has
been my fortune to have much oftener seen a nutshell in an
Iliad.

Jonathan Swift, A Tale of a Tub

Books for the Salon

I am sure that if Madame de Sablé lived now, books would be
seen in her salon as part of its natural indispensable furniture;
not brought out, and strewed here and there when 'company
was coming', but as habitual presences in her room, wanting
which, she would want a sense of warmth and comfort and
companionship. Putting out books as a sort of preparation
for an evening, as a means for making it pass agreeably, is
running a great risk. In the first place, books are by such
people, and on such occasions, chosen more for their outside
than their inside. And in the next, they are the 'mere material with which wisdom (or wit) builds'; and if persons don't
know how to use the material, they will suggest nothing. I
imagine Madame de Sablé would have the volumes she herself
was reading, or those which, being new, contained any matter
of present interest, left about, as they would naturally be.
I could also fancy that her guests would not feel bound to
talk continually, whether they had anything to say or not,
but that there might be pauses of not unpleasant silence—a
quiet darkness out of which they might be certain that the
little stars would glimmer soon. I can believe that in such
pauses of repose, some one might open a book, and catch on
a suggestive sentence, might dash off again into a full flow of
conversation. But I cannot fancy any grand preparations for
what was to be said among people, each of whom brought the
best dish in bringing himself; and whose own store of living,
individual thought and feeling, and mother-wit, would be
infinitely better than any cut-and-dry determination to devote
the evening to mutual improvement. If people are really good
and wise, their goodness and their wisdom flow out uncon-
sciously, and benefit like sunlight. So, books for reference,
books for impromptu suggestion, but never books to serve for
texts to a lecture.

Elizabeth Gaskell, *Company Manners*

The Library and the Grave

TO SIR H.G.

Sir,—This letter hath more merits than one of more diligence, for I wrote it in bed, and with much pain. I have
occasion to sit late some nights in my study (which your
books make a pretty library) and now I find that that room
hath a wholesome emblematic use: for having under it a vault,
I make that promise me that I shall die reading; since my
book and a grave are so near.

John Donne, *Letters to Several Persons of Honour*

The Library a Glorious Court

That place, that does contain
My books, the best companions, is to me
A glorious court, where hourly I converse
With the old sages and philosophers.
And sometimes, for variety, I confer
With kings and emperors, and weigh their counsels;
Calling their victories, if unjustly got,
Unto a strict account: and in my fancy,
Deface their ill-planned statues. Can I then
Part with such constant pleasures, to embrace
Uncertain vanities? No: be it your care
To augment your heap of wealth; it shall be mine
To increase in knowledge. Lights there for my study!

John Fletcher, *The Elder Brother*

Far more seemly were it for thee to have thy study full of
books, than thy purse full of money.

John Lyly, *Euphues*

The Library as Study

I like a great library next my study; but for the study itself, give me a small snug place, almost entirely walled with books. There should be only one window in it, looking upon trees. Some prefer a place with few, or no books at all— nothing but a chair or a table, like Epictetus; but I should say that these were philosophers, not lovers of books, if I did not recollect that Montaigne was both. He had a study in a round tower, walled as aforesaid. It is true, one forgets one's books while writing—at least they say so. For my part, I think I have them in a sort of sidelong mind's eye; like a second thought, which is none— like a waterfall, or a whispering wind.

I dislike a grand library to study in. I mean an immense apartment, with books all in Museum order, especially wire-safed. I say nothing against the Museum itself, or public libraries. They are capital places to go to, but not to sit in; and talking of this, I hate to read in public, and in strange company. The jealous silence; the dissatisfied looks of the messengers; the inability to help yourself; the not knowing whether you really ought to trouble the messengers, much less the Gentleman in black, or brown, who is, perhaps, half a trustee; with a variety of other jarrings between privacy and publicity, prevent one's settling heartily to work.... A grand private library, which the master of the house also makes his study, never looks to me like a real place of books, much less of authorship. I cannot take kindly to it. It is certainly not out of envy; for three parts of the books are generally trash, and I can seldom think of the rest and the proprietor together. It reminds me of a fine gentleman, of a collector, of a patron, of Gil Blas and the Marquis of Marialva; of anything but genius and comfort. I have a particular hatred of a round table (not *the* Round Table, for that was a dining one) covered and irradiated with books, and never met with one in the house of a clever man but once. It is the reverse of Montaigne's Round

Tower. Instead of bringing the books around you, they all seem turning another way, and eluding your hands.

Conscious of my propriety and comfort in these matters, I take an interest in the bookcases as well as the books of my friends. I long to meddle and dispose them after my own notions.

J.H. Leigh Hunt, *My Books*

Come, and take choice of all my library.

William Shakespeare, *Titus Andronicus*

Libraries are the wardrobes of literature, whence men, properly informed, might bring forth something for ornament, much for curiosity, and more for use.

George Dyer

The Consulting Room of a Wise Man

The great consulting room of a wise man is a library. When I am in perplexity about life, I have but to come here, and, without fee or reward, I commune with the wisest souls that God has blessed the world with. If I want a discourse on immortality Plato comes to my help. If I want to know the human heart Shakespeare opens all its chambers. Whatever be my perplexity or doubt, I know exactly the great man to call to me, and he comes in the kindest way, he listens to my doubts and tells me his convictions. So that a library may be regarded as the solemn chamber in which a man can take counsel with all that have been wise and great and good and glorious amongst the men that have gone before him. If we come down for a moment and look at the bare and immediate utilities of a library we find that here a man gets himself ready for his calling, arms himself for his profession, finds out the facts that are to determine his trade, prepares himself for his examination. The utilities of it are endless and priceless. It is too a place of pastime; for man has no amusement more innocent, more sweet, more gracious, more elevating, and more fortifying than he can find in a library.

George Dawson, *Address at the opening of the Birmingham Free Reference Library,* 1866

The Library a Key to Character

The first thing, naturally, when one enters a scholar's study or library, is to look at his books. One gets a notion very speedily of his tastes and the range of his pursuits by a glance round his bookshelves.

Of course, you know there are many fine houses where a library is a part of the upholstery, so to speak. Books in handsome binding kept locked under plate-glass in showy dwarf bookcases are as important to stylish establishments as servants in livery, who sit with folded arms, are to stylish equipages. I suppose those wonderful statues with the folded arms do sometimes change their attitude, and I suppose those books with the gilded backs do sometimes get opened, but it is nobody's business whether they do or not, and it is best not to ask too many questions.

This sort of thing is common enough, but there is another case that may prove deceptive if you undertake to judge from appearances. Once in a while you will come on a house where you will find a family of readers and almost no library. Some of the most indefatigable devourers of literature have very few books. They belong to book clubs, they haunt the public libraries, they borrow of friends, and somehow or other get hold of everything they want, scoop out all it holds for them, and have done with it.

Oliver Wendell Holmes, *The Poet at the Breakfast-Table*

The Scent of Books

I know men who say they had as lief read any book in a library copy as in one from their own shelf. To me that is unintelligible. For one thing, I know every book of mine by its *scent*, and I have but to put my nose between the pages to be reminded of all sorts of things. My Gibbon, for example, my well-bound eight-volume Milman edition, which I have read and read and read again for more than thirty years— never do I open it but the scent of the noble pages restores to me all the exultant happiness of that moment when I received it as a prize. Or my Shakespeare, the great Cambridge Shakespeare—it has an odour which carries me yet further back in life; for these volumes belonged to my father, and before I was old enough to read them with understanding, it was often permitted me, as a treat, to take down one of them from the bookcase, and reverently to turn the leaves. The volumes smell exactly as they did in that old time, and what a strange tenderness comes upon me when I hold one of them in hand. For that reason I do not often read Shakespeare in this edition.

George Gissing, *The Private Papers*
of Henry Ryecroft

Of his gentleness,
Knowing I loved my books, he furnished me,
From mine own library with volumes that
I prize above my dukedom.

William Shakespeare, *The Tempest*

An Episcopal Library

Here, duly placed on consecrated ground,
The studied works of many an age are found,
The ancient Fathers' reverend remains;
The Roman Laws, which freed a world from chains;
Whate'er of law passed from immortal Greece
To Latin lands, and gained a rich increase;
All that blessed Israel drank in showers from heaven,
Or Afric sheds, soft as the dew of even.

Alcuin

Safe and Untouched

'In another century it may be impossible to find a collection
of the whole [Greek tragedies] unless some learned and rich
man, like Pericles, or some protecting King, like Hiero,
should preserve them in his library.' 'Prudently have you
considered how to preserve all valuable authors. The cedar
doors of a royal library fly open to receive them: aye, there
they will be safe... and untouched.'

Walter Savage Landor, Pericles and Aspasia

Cibber's Library

Next o'er his books his eyes began to roll,
In pleasing memory of all he stole,
How here he sipped, how there he plundered snug,
And sucked all o'er, like an industrious bug.
Here lay poor Fletcher's half-eat scenes, and here
The frippery of crucified Moliere;
There hapless Shakespeare, yet of Tibbald sore,
Wished he had blotted for himself before.
The rest on outside merit but presume,
Or serve (like other fools) to fill a room;

Such with their shelves as due proportion hold,
Or their fond parents dressed in red and gold;
Or where the pictures for the page atone
And Quarles is saved by beauties not his own.
Here swells the shelf with Ogilby the great;
There, stamped with arms, Newcastle shines complete:
Here all his suffering brotherhood retire,
And 'scape the martyrdom of jakes and fire:
A Gothic Library! of Greece and Rome
Well purged, and worthy Settle, Banks, and Broome.
But, high above, more solid learning shone,
The classics of an age that heard of none;
There Caxton slept, with Wynkyn at his side,
One clasped in wood, and one in strong cow-hide;
There saved by spice, like mummies, many a year,
Dry Bodies of Divinity appear;
De Lyra there a dreadful front extends,
And here the groaning shelves Philemon bends.
    Of these twelve volumes, twelve of amplest size,
Redeemed from tapers and defrauded pies,
Inspired he seizes; these an altar raise;
An hecatomb of pure unsullied lays
That altar crowns; a folio Commonplace
Founds the whole pile, of all his works the base;
Quartos, octavos, shape the lessening pyre;
A twisted birthday ode completes the spire.

Alexander Pope, The Dunciad

Mr. Shandy's Library

Few men of great genius had exercised their parts in writing
books upon the subject of great noses: by the trotting of my
lean horse, the thing is incredible! and I am quite lost in my
understanding, when I am considering what a treasure of precious time and talents together has been wasted upon worse

subjects—and how many millions of books in all languages, and in all possible types and bindings, have been fabricated upon points not half so much tending to the unity and peace-making of the world. What was to be had, however, he set the greater store by; and though my father would ofttimes sport with my uncle Toby's library—which, by the by, was ridiculous enough—yet at the very same time he did it, he collected every book and treatise which had been systematically wrote upon noses, with as much care as my honest uncle Toby had done those upon military architecture....

My father's collection was not great, but, to make amends, it was curious; and consequently he was some time in making it ... he got hold of Prignitz—purchased Scroderus, Andrea Paraeus, Bonchet's Evening Conferences, and above all, the great and learned Hafen Slawkenbergius.... To do justice to Slawkenbergius, he has entered the list with a stronger lance, and taken a much larger career in it than any one man who had ever entered it before him—and indeed, in many respects, deserves to be en-niched as a prototype for all writers, of voluminous works at least, to model their books by—for he has taken in, Sir, the whole subject—examined every part of it dialectically—then brought it into full day; dilucidating it with all the light which either the collision of his own natural parts could strike—or the profoundest knowledge of the sciences had empowered him to cast upon it—collating, collecting, and compiling—begging, borrowing, and stealing, as he went along, all that had been wrote or wrangled thereupon in the schools and porticoes of the learned: so that Slawkenbergius his book may properly be considered, not only as a model—but as a thorough-stitched digest and regular institute of noses, comprehending in it all that is or can be needful to be known about them.

For this cause it is that I forbear to speak of so many (otherwise) valuable books and treatises of my father's collecting, wrote either, plump upon noses—or collaterally touching them;—such for instance as Prignitz, now lying upon the table before me, who with infinite learning, and from the most candid and scholar-like examination of above four thousand different skulls, in upwards of twenty charnel-houses in Silesia, which he had rummaged—has informed us, that the mensuration and configuration of the osseous or bony parts of human noses, in any given tract of country, except Crim Tartary, where they are all crushed down by the thumb, so that no judgement can be formed upon them—are much nearer alike, than the world imagines.

Lawrence Sterne, *Tristram Shandy*

Dominie Sampson in the Library

Dominie Sampson was occupied, body and soul, in the arrangement of the late bishop's library, which had been sent from Liverpool by sea, and conveyed by thirty or forty carts from the seaport at which it was landed. Sampson's joy at beholding the ponderous contents of these chests arranged upon the floor of the large apartment, from whence he was to transfer them to the shelves, baffles all description. He grinned like an ogre, swung his arms like the sails of a wind-mill, shouted 'Prodigious' till the roof rung to his raptures. 'He had never,' he said, 'seen so many books together, except in the College Library;' and now his dignity and delight in being superintendent of the collection, raised him, in his own opinion, almost to the rank of the academical librarian, whom he had always regarded as the greatest and happiest man on earth. Neither were his transports diminished upon a hasty examination of the contents of these volumes. Some, indeed, of belles lettres, poems, plays, or memoirs, he tossed indignantly aside, with the implied censure of 'psha', or 'frivolous'; but the greater and bulkier part of the collection bore a very different character. The deceased prelate, a divine of the old and deeply-learned east, had loaded his shelves with volumes which displayed the antique and venerable attributes so happily described by a modern poet:

That weight of wood, with leathern coat o'erlaid;
Those ample clasps, of solid metal made;
The close-pressed leaves unoped for many an age;
The dull red edging of the well-filled page;
On the broad back the stubborn ridges rolled,
Where yet the title stands in tarnished gold.

Books of theology and controversial divinity, commentaries, and polyglots, sets of the Fathers, and sermons, which might each furnish forth ten brief discourses of modern date, books of science, ancient and modern, classical authors in their best and rarest forms; such formed the late bishop's venerable library, and over such the eye of Dominie Sampson gloated with rapture. He entered them in the catalogue in his best running hand, forming each letter with the accuracy of a lover writing a valentine, and placed each individually on the destined shelf with all the reverence which I have seen a lady pay to a jar of old china. With all this zeal his labours advanced slowly. He often opened a volume when half-way up the library-steps, fell upon some interesting passage, and, without shifting his inconvenient posture, continued immersed in the fascinating perusal until the servant pulled him by the skirts to assure him that dinner waited. He then repaired to the parlour, bolted his food down his capacious throat in squares of three inches, answered aye or no at random to whatever question was asked at him, and again hurried back to the library as soon as his napkin was removed, and sometimes with it hanging round his neck like a pinafore—

How happily the days
Of Thalaba went by!

Sir Walter Scott, *Guy Mannering*

Me, poor man,—my library
Was dukedom large enough.

William Shakespeare, The Tempest

The Library in the Garret

Books, books, books!
I had found the secret of a garret-room
Piled high with cases in my father's name;
Piled high, packed large,—where, creeping in and out
Among the giant fossils of my past,
Like some small nimble mouse between the ribs
Of a mastodon, I nibbled here and there
At this or that box, pulling through the gap,
In heats of terror, haste, victorious joy,
The first book first. And how I felt it beat
Under my pillow, in the morning's dark,
An hour before the sun would let me read!
My books!

Elizabeth Barrett Browning, Aurora Leigh

Every library should try to be complete on something, if it
were only on the history of pin-heads.

Oliver Wendell Holmes, The Poet at the Breakfast-Table

Montaigne's Library

At home I betake me somewhat the oftener to my library,
whence all at once I command and survey all my household.
It is seated in the chief entry of my house, thence I behold
under me my garden, my base court, my yard, and look even
into most rooms of my house. There without order, without

method, and by piece-meals I turn over and ransack, now
one book and now another. Sometimes I muse and rave;
and walking up and down I indite and en-register these my
humours, these my conceits. It is placed on the third story of
a tower. The lowermost is my chapel; the second a chamber
with other lodgings, where I often lie, because I would be
alone. Above it is a great wardrobe. It was in times past the
most unprofitable place of all my house. There I pass the
greatest part of my life's days, and wear out most hours of
the day. I am never there a nights. Next unto it is a handsome
neat cabinet, able and large enough to receive fire in winter,
and very pleasantly windowen. And if I feared not care more
than cost (care which drives and diverts me from all business), I might easily join a convenient gallery of a hundred
paces long and twelve broad on each side of it, and upon
one floor; having already, for some other purpose, found all
the walls raised unto a convenient height. Each retired place
requireth a walk. My thoughts are prone to sleep if I sit long.
My mind goes not alone, as if ledges did move it. Those that
study without books are all in the same case. The form of it
is round, and hath no flat side, but what serveth for my table
and chair: in which bending or circling manner, at one look
it offereth me the full sight of all my books, set round about
upon shelves or desks, five ranks one upon another. It hath
three bay-windows, of a far-extending, rich and unresisted
prospect, and is in diameter sixteen paces void. In winter
I am less continually there: for my house (as the name of it
importeth) is perched upon an over-peering hillock; and hath
no part more subject to all weathers than this: which pleaseth
me the more, both because the access unto it is somewhat
troublesome and remote, and for the benefit of the exercise
which is to be respected; and that I may the better seclude
myself from company, and keep encroachers from me: There
is my seat, that is my throne. I endeavour to make my rule
therein absolute, and to sequester that only corner from
the community of wife, of children, and of acquaintance.

Elsewhere I have but a verbal authority, of confused essence.
Miserable in my mind is he who in his own home hath
nowhere to be to himself; where he may particularly court,
and at his pleasure hide or withdraw self.

Michel de Montaigne

Charles Lamb's Library

His library, though not abounding in Greek or Latin (which
are the only things to help some persons to an idea of literature), is anything but superficial. The depths of philosophy
and poetry are there, the innermost passages of the human
heart. It has some Latin too. It has also a handsome contempt
for appearance. It looks like what it is, a selection made
at precious intervals from the bookstalls; now a Chaucer
at nine and twopence; now a Montaigne or a Sir Thomas
Browne at two shillings; now a Jeremy Taylor; a Spinoza; an
old English Dramatist, Prior, and Sir Philip Sidney; and the
books are 'neat as imported'. The very perusal of the backs is
a 'discipline of humanity'. There Mr. Southey takes his place
again with an old Radical friend: there Jeremy Collier is at
peace with Dryden: there the lion, Martin Luther, lies down
with the Quaker lamb, Sewell: there Guzman d'Alfarache
thinks himself fit company for Sir Charles Grandison, and has
his claims admitted. Even the 'high fantastical' Duchess of
Newcastle, with her laurel on her head, is received with grave
honours, and not the less for declining to trouble herself with
the constitutions of her maids.

J.H. Leigh Hunt, My Books

The Shrines of the Ancient Saints

The works or acts of merit towards learning are conversant
about three objects; the places of learning, the books of learning, and the persons of the learned.... The works touching
books are two: first, libraries which are as the shrines where
all the relies of the ancient saints, full of true virtue, and that
without delusion or imposture, are preserved and reposed;
secondly, new editions of authors, with more correct impressions, more faithful translations, more profitable glosses, more
diligent annotations, and the like.

Francis Bacon, *Of the Advancement of Learning*

A Most Horrible Infamy

Never had we been offended for the loss of our libraries,
being so many in number, and in so desolate places for the
most part, if the chief monuments and most notable works of
our excellent writers had been reserved. If there had been in
every shire of England but one Solempne Library, to the preservation of those noble works, and preferment of good learning in our posterity, it had been yet somewhat. But to destroy
all without consideration is, and will be, unto England for
ever, a most horrible infamy among the grave seniors of other
nations. A great number of them which purchased those
superstitious mansions, reserved of those library-books, some
to serve the jakes, some to scour their candlesticks, and some
to rub their boots. Some they sold to the grocers and soap-
sellers; some they sent over sea to the bookbinders, not in
small number, but at times whole ships full, to the wondering
of the foreign nations. Yea, the universities of this realm are
not all clear of this detestable fact. But, cursed is that belly
which seeketh to be fed with such ungodly gains, and shameth
his natural country. I know a merchantman, which shall at
this time be nameless, that bought the contents of two noble

libraries for forty shillings price; a shame it is to be spoken!
This stuff hath he occupied in the stead of gray paper, by the
space of more than ten years, and yet he hath store enough for
as many years to come!

John Bale, *Preface to the Laboryouse Journey of Leland*

Libraries for Every City

I hope it will not be long before royal or national libraries will
be founded in every considerable city, with a royal series of
books in them; the same series in every one of them, chosen
books, the best in every kind, prepared for that national
series in the most perfect way possible; their text printed
all on leaves of equal size, broad of margin, and divided into
pleasant volumes, light in the hand, beautiful, and strong, and
thorough as examples of binders' work; and that these great
libraries will be accessible to all clean and orderly persons at
all times of the day and evening; strict law being enforced for
this cleanliness and quietness.

John Ruskin, *Sesame and Lilies*

The Reference Library

One of the great offices of a Reference Library is to keep
at the service of everybody what everybody cannot keep at
home for his own service. It is not convenient to every man to
have a very large telescope; I may wish to study the skeleton
of a whale but my house is not large enough to hold one; I
may be curious in microscopes but I may have no money to
buy one of my own. But provide an institution like this and
here is the telescope, here is the microscope, and here the
skeleton of the whale. Here are the great picture, the mighty
book, the ponderous atlas, the great histories of the world.
They are here always ready for the use of every man without

his being put to the cost of purchase or the discomfort of giving them houseroom. Here are books that we only want to consult occasionally and which are very costly. These are the books proper for a Library like this—mighty cyclopaedias, prodigious charts, books that only Governments can publish. It is almost the only place where I would avoid cheapness as a plague and run away from mean printing and petty pages with disgust.

George Dawson, *Address at the opening of the Birmingham Free Reference Library,* 1866

In the British Museum Library

The shade deepens as I turn from the portico to the hall and vast domed house of books. The half-hearted light under the dome is stagnant and dead. For it is the nature of light to beat and throb; it has a pulse and undulation like the swing of the sea. Under the trees in the woodlands it vibrates and lives; on the hills there is a resonance of light.... It is renewed and fresh every moment, and never twice do you see the same ray. Stayed and checked by the dome and book-built walls, the beams lose their elasticity, and the ripple ceases in the motionless pool. The eyes, responding, forget to turn quickly, and only partially see. Deeper thought and inspiration quit the heart, for they can only exist where the light vibrates and communicates its tone to the soul. If any imagine they shall find thought in many books, certainly they will be disappointed. Thought dwells by the stream and sea, by the hill and in the woodland, in the sunlight and free wind, where the wild dove haunts. Walls and roof shut it off as they shut off the undulation of light. The very lightning cannot penetrate here. A murkiness marks the coming of the cloud, and the dome becomes vague, but the fierce flash is shorn to a pale reflection, and the thunder is no more than the rolling of a heavier truck loaded with tomes. But in closing out the sky, with it is cut off all that the sky can tell you with its light, or in its passion of storm.

Sitting at these long desks and trying to read, I soon find that I have made a mistake; it is not here I shall find that which I seek. Yet the magic of books draws me here time after time, to be as often disappointed. Something in a book tempts the mind as pictures tempt the eye; the eye grows weary of pictures, but looks again. The mind wearies of books, yet cannot forget that once when they were first opened in youth they gave it hope of knowledge. Those first books exhausted, there is nothing left but words and covers. It seems as if all the books in the world—really books—can be bought for £10. Man's whole thought is purchaseable at that small price, for the value of a watch, of a good dog. For the rest it is repetition and paraphrase.

Richard Jefferies, *The Life of the Fields:*
The Pigeons at the British Museum

The Library an Heraclea

Now behold us, ... settled in all the state and grandeur of our own house in Russell Street, Bloomsbury: the library of the Museum close at hand. My father spends his mornings in those *lata silentia*, as Virgil calls the world beyond the grave. And a world beyond the grave we may well call that land of the ghosts, a book collection.

'Pisistratus,' said my father, one evening as he arranged his notes before him, and rubbed his spectacles. 'Pisistratus, a great library is an *awful* place! There, are interred all the remains of men since the Flood.'

'It is a burial-place!' quoth my Uncle Roland, who had that day found us out.

'It is an Heraclea!' said my father.

'Please, not such hard words,' said the Captain, shaking his head.

'Heraclea was the city of necromancers, in which they raised the dead. Do I want to speak to Cicero?—I invoke him. Do I want to chat in the Athenian market-place, and hear news two thousand years old?—I write down my charm on a slip of paper, and a grave magician calls me up Aristophanes.... But it is not *that* which is awful. It is the presuming to vie with these "spirits elect": to say to them, " Make way—I too claim place with the chosen. I too would confer with the living, centuries after the death that consumes my dust." '

Edward Bulwer-Lytton, The Caxtons

Books in a New Light

I should explain that I cannot write unless I have a sloping desk, and the reading-room of the British Museum, where alone I can compose freely, is unprovided with sloping desks. Like every other organism, if I cannot get exactly what I want, I make shift with the next thing to it; true, there are no desks in the reading-room, but, as I once heard a visitor from the country say, 'it contains a large number of very interesting works.' I know it was not right, and hope the Museum authorities will not be severe upon me if any one of them reads this confession; but I wanted a desk, and set myself to consider which of the many very interesting works which a grateful nation places at the disposal of its would-be authors was best suited for my purpose.

For mere reading I suppose one book is pretty much as good as another: but the choice of a desk-book is a more serious matter. It must be neither too thick nor too thin; it must be large enough to make a substantial support; it must be strongly bound so as not to yield or give; it must not be too troublesome to carry backwards and forwards; and it must live on shelf C, D, or E, so that there need be no stooping or reaching too high.... For weeks I made experiments upon sundry poetical and philosophical works, whose names I have forgotten, but could not succeed in finding my ideal desk, until at length, more by luck than cunning, I happened to light upon Frost's 'Lives of Eminent Christians', which I had no sooner tried than I discovered it to be the very perfection and *ne plus ultra* of everything that a book should be.... On finding myself asked for a contribution to the *Universal Review*, I went, as I have explained, to the Museum, and presently repaired to bookcase No. 2008 to get my favourite volume. Alas! it was in the room no longer. It was not in use, for its place was filled up already; besides, no one ever used it but myself.... Till I have found a substitute I can write no more, and I do not know how to find even a tolerable one. I should try a volume of Migne's *Complete Course of Patrology*, but I do not like books in more than one volume, for the volumes vary in thickness, and one never can remember which one took; the four volumes, however, of Bede in Giles's *Anglican Fathers* are not open to this objection, and I have reserved them for favourable consideration. Mather's *Magnalia* might do, but the binding does not please me; Cureton's *Corpus Ignatianum* might also do if it were not too thin. I do not like taking Norton's *Genuineness of the Gospels*, as it is just possible some one may be wanting to know whether the Gospels are genuine or not, and be unable to find out because I have got Mr. Norton's book. Baxter's *Church History of England*, Lingard's *Anglo-Saxon Church*, and Cardwell's *Documentary Annals*, though none of them as good as Frost, are works of considerable merit; but on the whole I think Arvine's *Cyclopaedia of Moral and Religious Anecdote* is perhaps the one book in the room which comes within measurable distance of Frost.... Some successor I must find, or I must give up writing altogether, and this I should be sorry to do.

Samuel Butler, *Essays on Life, Art, and Science*

Reflections in a Library

There are more ways to derive instruction from books than the direct and chief one of applying the attention to what they contain. Things connected with them, by natural or casual association, will sometimes suggest themselves to a reflective and imaginative reader, and divert him into secondary trains of ideas. In these, the mind may, indeed, float along in perfect indolence and acquire no good; but a serious disposition might regulate them to a profitable result. . . .

Even in the most cursory notice of them, when the attention is engaged by no one in particular, ideas may be started of a tendency not wholly foreign to instruction. A reflective person, in his library, in some hour of intermittent application, when the mind is surrendered to vagrant musing, may glance along the ranges of volumes with a slight recognition of the authors, in long miscellaneous array of ancients and moderns. And that musing may become shaped into ideas like these:—What a number of our busy race have deemed themselves capable of informing and directing the rest of mankind! What a vast amount is collected here of the results of the most strenuous and protracted exertions of so many minds! What were in each of these claimants that the world should think as they did, the most prevailing motives? How many of them sincerely loved truth, honestly sought it, and faithfully, to the best of their knowledge, declared it? What might be the circumstances and influences which determined in the case of that one author, and the next, and the next again, their own modes of opinion?

And how much have they actually done for truth and righteousness in the world? Do not the contents of these accumulated volumes constitute a chaos of all discordant and contradictory principles, theories, representations of facts, and figurings of imaginations? Could I not instantly place beside each other the works of two noted authors, who maintain for truth directly opposite doctrines, or systems of doctrine; and then add a third book which explodes them both? I can take some one book in which the prime spirits of the world, through all time, are brought together, announcing the speculations which they, respectively, proclaimed to be the essence of all wisdom, protesting, with solemn censure or sneering contempt, against the dogmas and theories of one another, and conflicting in a huge Babel of all imaginable opinions and vagaries....

Thus far the instructive reflections which even the mere exterior of an accumulation of books may suggest are supposed to occur in the way of thinking of the *authors*. But the same books may also excite some interesting ideas through their less obvious but not altogether fanciful association with the persons who may have been their *readers* or *possessors*. The mind of a thoughtful looker over a range of volumes of many dates, and a considerable portion of them old, will sometimes be led into a train of conjectural questions:—Who were they that, in various times and places, have had these in their possession? Perhaps many hands have turned over the leaves, many eyes have passed along the lines. With what measure of intelligence, and of approval or dissent, did those persons respectively follow the train of thoughts? How many of them were honestly intent on becoming wise by what they read? How many sincere prayers were addressed by them to the Eternal Wisdom during the perusal? How many have been determined, in their judgement or their actions, by these books? What emotions, temptations, or painful occurrences, may have interrupted the reading of this book, or of that?

John Foster, *Introductory Essay to Doddridge's Rise and Progress of Religion in the Soul*

Thoughts in a Library

A great library! What a mass of human misery is here com-
memorated!—how many buried hopes surround us!

The author of that work was the greatest natural philosopher that ever enlightened mankind. His biographers are
now disputing whether at one period of his life he was not of
unsound mind—but all agree that he was afterwards able to
understand his own writings.

The author of those numerous volumes was logician,
metaphysician, natural historian, philosopher; his sanity was
never doubted, and with his last breath he regretted his birth,
mourned over his life, expressed his fear of death, and called
upon the Cause of causes to pity him. His slightest thoughts
continued to domineer over the world for ages, until they
were in some measure silenced by those works which contain
the unfettered meditations of a very great man, who, being
more careless than corrupt in the administration of his high
office, has gone down to posterity, as

The wisest, brightest, meanest, of mankind.

For his wisdom has embalmed his meanness.

Those volumes contain the weighty, if not wise opinions of
one who, amidst penury and wretchedness, first learnt to mor-
alize with companions as poor and wretched as himself. Even
in his latter years, when sought by a monarch, and listened
to with submission by all who approached him, his life can
scarcely be called a happy one; yet he must have enjoyed some
moments of triumph, if not of happiness, in contemplating the
severe but well-merited rebuke which he inflicted upon that
courtier, who could behold his difficulties with all the indifference that belongs to good breeding, and then thought fit, in the
hour of his success, to encumber him with paltry praises.

Those poems were the burning words of one

... Cradled into poetry by wrong,
Who learnt in suffering what he taught in song.

The slightest foibles of this unhappy man have been brought into odious prominence, for he was the favourite author of his age, and therefore the property of the public.

That boyish book absolved its author from a father's cares; and he was one to whom those cares would have been dearest joys, who loved to look upon a poor man's child. Listen to the music of his sadness—

> I see the deep's untrampled floor
>   With green and purple seaweeds strown;
> I see the waves upon the shore,
>   Like light dissolv'd in star-showers, thrown;
> I sit upon the sands alone.
>   The lightning of the noon-tide ocean
> Is flashing round me, and a tone
>   Arises from its measured motion.
> How sweet! did any heart now share in my emotion!

The sharp arrows of criticism were successfully directed against that next volume, and are said to have been the means of hurrying its author to that world of dreams and shadows, for which, in the critic's opinion, he was so preeminently fitted.

> Where is the youth, for deeds immortal born.
> Who loved to whisper to the embattled corn,
> And clustered woodbines, breathing o'er the stream
> Endymion's beauteous passion for a dream?

You already smile, my friend; but to know the heights and the depths, you must turn your attention to those numberless, unread, unheard-of volumes. Their authors did not suffer from the severity of the critic or the judge, but were only neglected. If Mephistopheles ever requires rest and seclusion—But, hark! is there not a laugh? and that grotesque face in the carved woodwork, how scoffingly it is looking down upon us!

Sir Arthur Helps, *Thoughts in a Cloister*

The Library

Here, e'en the sturdy democrat may find,
Nor scorn their rank, the nobles of the mind;
While kings may learn, nor blush at being shown
How Learning's patents abrogate their own.
A goodly company and fair to see;
Royal plebeians; earls of low degree;
Beggars whose wealth enriches every clime;
Princes who scarce can boast a mental dime;
Crowd here together like the quaint array
Of jostling neighbours on a market day.
Homer and Milton,—can we call them blind?—
Of godlike sight, the vision of the mind;
Shakespeare, who calmly looked creation through,
'Exhausted worlds, and then imagined new';
Plato the sage, so thoughtful and serene,
He seems a prophet by his heavenly mien;
Shrewd Socrates, whose philosophic power
Xantippe proved in many a trying hour;
And Aristophanes, whose humour run
In vain endeavour to be 'cloud' the sun;
Majestic Aeschylus, whose glowing page
Holds half the grandeur of the Athenian stage;
Pindar, whose odes, replete with heavenly fire,
Proclaim the master of the Grecian lyre;
Anacreon, famed for many a luscious line,
Devote to Venus and the god of wine.
I love vast libraries; yet there is a doubt
If one be better with them or without—
Unless he use them wisely, and, indeed,
Knows the high art of what and how to read.
At Learning's fountain it is sweet to drink,
But 'tis a nobler privilege to think;
And oft, from books apart, the thirsting mind
May make the nectar which it cannot find.

'Tis well to borrow from the good and great;
'Tis wise to learn; 'tis godlike to create!

J.G. Saxe

Of Libraries: the Bodleian

What oweth Oxford, nay this Isle, to the most worthy
Bodley, whose Library, perhaps, containeth more excellent
books than the ancients by all their curious search could find?
... To such a worthy work all the lovers of learning should
conspire and contribute; and of small beginnings who is
ignorant what great effects may follow? If, perhaps, we will
consider the beginnings of the greatest libraries of Europe (as
Democritus said of the world, that it was made up of atoms),
we shall find them but small; for how great soever in their
present perfection they are now, these Carthages were once
Magalia. Libraries are as forests, in which not only tall cedars
and oaks are to be found, but bushes too and dwarfish shrubs;
and as in apothecaries' shops all sorts of drugs are permitted
to be, so may all sorts of books be in a library. And as they
out of vipers and scorpions, and poisoning vegetables, extract
often wholesome medicaments, for the life of mankind; so out
of whatsoever book, good instructions and examples may be
acquired.

William Drummond, Of Libraries

On the Death of Sir Thomas Bodley

One Homer was enough to blazon forth
In a full lofty style Ulysses' praise,
Caesar had Lucan to enrol his worth
Unto the memory of endless days.
Of thy deeds, Bodley, from thine own pure spring
A thousand Homers and sweet Lucans sing.

One volume was a monument to bound
The large extent of their deserving pains,
In learning's commonwealth was never found
So large a decade to express thy strains,
Which who desires to character aright,
Must read more books than they had lines to write.
Yet give this little river leave to run,
Into the boundless ocean of thy fame;
Had they first ended I had not begun,
Sith each is a Protogenes to frame
So curiously the picture of thy worth
That when all's done, art wants to set it forth.

Peter Prideaux (Exeter College, 1613)

To be Chained with Good Authors

King James, 1605, when he came to see our University of
Oxford, and amongst other edifices now went to view that
famous library, renewed by Sir Thomas Bodley in imitation of
Alexander at his departure, brake out into that noble speech,
'If I were not a king, I would be a University man: and if it
were so that I must be a prisoner, if I might have my wish, I
would desire to have no other prison than that library, and
to be chained together with so many good authors, *et mortuis
magistris*.' So sweet is the delight of study, the more learning
they have (as he that hath a dropsy, the more he drinks the
thirstier he is) the more they covet to learn, and the last day
is *prioris discipulus*; harsh at first learning is, *radices amarae*,
but *fructus dulces*, according to that of Isocrates, pleasant at
last; the longer they live, the more they are enamoured with
the Muses. Heinsius, the keeper of the library at Leyden, in
Holland, was mewed up in it all the year long; and that which
to thy thinking should have bred a loathing, caused in him a
greater liking. 'I no sooner (saith he) come into, but I bolt the
door to me, excluding lust, ambition, avarice, and all such

vices, whose nurse is Idleness, the mother of Ignorance, and Melancholy herself, and in the very lap of eternity, amongst so many divine souls, I take my seat with so lofty a spirit and sweet content, that I pity all our great ones, and rich men that know not this happiness.'

I am not ignorant in the meantime (notwithstanding this which I have said) how barbarously and basely, for the most part, our ruder gentry esteem of libraries and books, how they neglect and contemn so great a treasure, so inestimable a benefit, as Aesop's cock did the jewel he found in the dung-hill; and all through error, ignorance, and want of education.

Robert Burton, *The Anatomy of Melancholy*

An Ode Addressed to Mr. John Rouse, Librarian of the University of Oxford

On a lost volume of my poems, which he desired me to replace, that he might add them to my other works deposited in the library.

STROPHE

My two-fold book! single in show,
    But double in contents,
Neat, but not curiously adorned,
    Which, in his early youth,
A poet gave, no lofty one in truth,
Although an earnest wooer of the Muse—
Say while in cool Ausonian shades
    Or British wilds he roamed,
Striking by turns his native lyre,
    By turns the Daunian lute,
    And stepped almost in air,—

ANTISTROPHE

Say, little book, what furtive hand
Thee from thy fellow-books conveyed,

What time, at the repeated suit
        Of my most learnèd friend,
I sent thee forth, an honoured traveller,
From our great city to the source of Thames,
        Caerulian sire!
Where rise the fountains, and the raptures ring,
        Of the Aonian choir,
Durable as yonder spheres,
And through the endless lapse of years
        Secure to be admired?

STROPHE II
    Now what God, or Demigod
For Britain's ancient Genius moved,
        (If our afflicted land
Have expiated at length the guilty sloth
        Of her degenerate sons)
        Shall terminate our impious feuds,
And discipline, with hallowed voice, recall?
        Recall the Muses too,
        Driven from their ancient seats
In Albion, and well nigh from Albion's shore,
        And with keen Phoebean shafts,
        Piercing the unseemly birds,
            Whose talons menace us,
Shall drive the Harpy race from Helicon afar?

ANTISTROPHE
But thou, my book, though thou hast strayed,
        Whether by treachery lost
Or indolent neglect, thy bearer's fault,
        From all thy kindred books,
To some dark cell or cave forlorn,
        Where thou endurest, perhaps
The chafing of some hard untutored hand,
        Be comforted—

For lo! again the splendid hope appears
    That thou mayest yet escape,
The gulfs of Lethe, and on oary wings
Mount to the everlasting courts of Jove!

STROPHE III
Since Rouse desires thee, and complains
    That, though by promise his,
    Thou yet appear'st not in thy place
Among the literary noble stores,
        Given to his care,
But, absent, leavest his numbers incomplete:
    He, therefore, guardian vigilant
    Of that unperishing wealth,
Calls thee to the interior shrine, his charge,
Where he intends a richer treasure far
Than Iön kept (Ion, Erectheus' son
Illustrious, of the fair Creüsa born)
In the resplendent temple of his God,
Tripods of gold, and Delphic gifts divine.

ANTISTROPHE
    Haste, then, to the pleasant groves,
        The Muses' favourite haunt;
Resume thy station in Apollo's dome,
            Dearer to him
Than Delos, or the forked Parnassian hill!
        Exulting go,
Since now a splendid lot is also thine,
And thou art sought by my propitious friend;
        For there thou shalt be read
        With authors of exalted note,
The ancient glorious lights of Greece and Rome.

EPODE

Ye, then, my works, no longer vain,
  And worthless deemed by me!
Whate'er this sterile genius has produced
Expect, at last, the rage of envy spent,
    An unmolested happy home,
Gift of kind Hermes, and my watchful friend,
    Where never flippant tongue profane
      Shall entrance find,
And whence the coarse unlettered multitude
      Shall babble far remote.
    Perhaps some future distant age,
Less tinged with prejudice, and better taught,
    Shall furnish minds of power
    To judge more equally.
  Then, malice silenced in the tomb,
    Cooler heads and sounder hearts,
    Thanks to Rouse, if aught of praise
I merit, shall with candour weigh the claim.

William Cowper, *Translated from Milton*

Pindaric Ode

Hail! Learning's Pantheon! Hail, the sacred Ark,
Where all the world of science does embark!
Which ever shall withstand, and hast so long withstood,
Insatiate time's devouring flood!
Hail, Tree of Knowledge! thy leaves fruit! which well
Dost in the midst of Paradise arise,
  Oxford, the Muses' Paradise!
From which may never Sword the blest expel.
Hail, Bank of all past ages, where they lie
To enrich with interest posterity!

Hail, Wit's illustrious Galaxy,
Where thousand lights into one brightness spread,
Hail, living University of the Dead!

Unconfused Babel of all Tongues, which e'er
The mighty linguist, Fame, or Time, the mighty traveller,
That could speak or this could hear!
Majestic Monument and Pyramid,
Where still the shapes of parted souls abide
Embalmed in verse! exalted souls, which now,
Enjoy those Arts they wooed so well below!
Which now all wonders printed plainly see
    That have been, are, or are to be,
    In the mysterious Library,
The Beatific Bodley of the Dead!

Will ye into your sacred throng admit
    The meanest British wit?
Ye General Council of the Priests of Fame,
Will ye not murmur and disdain
    That I a place amongst ye claim
    The humblest Deacon of her train?
Will ye allow me the honourable chain?
    The chain of ornament, which here
    Your noble prisoners proudly wear?
A chain which will more pleasant seem to me
Than all my own Pindaric liberty.
Will ye to bind me with these mighty names submit
    Like an Apocrypha with Holy Writ?
Whatever happy Book is chainèd here,
No other place or people needs to fear;
His chain's a passport to go everywhere.

    As when a seat in Heaven
Is to an unmalicious sinner given,
    Who casting round his wondering Eye

Does none but Patriarchs and Apostles there espy,
　　Martyrs who did their lives bestow
　　And Saints who Martyrs lived below,
With trembling and amazement he begins
To recollect his frailties past and sins,
　　He doubts almost his station there,
His soul says to itself, 'How came I here?'
　　It fares no otherwise with me
When I myself with conscious wonder see
Amidst this purified elected company;
　　With hardship they and pain
　　Did to their happiness attain.
No labours I or merits can pretend;
I think, Predestination only was my friend.
Ah! if my author had been tied like me,
To such a place and such a company,
Instead of several countries, several men,
　　And business, which the Muses hate!
He might have then improved that small estate
Which Nature sparingly did to him give,
　　He might perhaps have thriven then,
And settled upon me, his child, somewhat to live;
It had happier been for him, as well as me.
　　For when all, alas, is done,
We Books, I mean you Books, will prove to be
The best and noblest conversation.
　　For though some errors will get in,
　　Like tinctures of original sin,
　　Yet sure we from our Father's wit
　　Draw all the strength and spirits of it,
Leaving the grosser parts for conversation,
As the best blood of man's employed on generation.

Abraham Cowley

On Sir Thomas Bodley's Library, the Author Being then in Oxford

Boast not, proud Golgotha, that thou canst show
The ruins of mankind and let us know
How frail a thing is flesh! though we see there
But empty skulls, the Rabbins still live here.
They are not dead, but full of blood again,
I mean the sense, and every line a vein.
Triumph not o'er their dust; whoever looks
In here, shall find their brains all in their books.
    Nor is't old Palestine alone survives,
Athens lives here, more than in Plutarch's Lives.
The stones which sometimes danced unto the strain
Of Orpheus, here do lodge his muse again.
And you the Roman spirits, Learning has
Made your lives longer than your empire was.
Caesar had perished from the world of men,
Had not his sword been rescued by his pen.
Rare Seneca! how lasting is thy breath!
Though Nero did, thou could'st not bleed to death.
How dull the expert tyrant was, to look
For that in thee, which lived in thy book!
Afflictions turn our blood to ink, and we
Commence, when writing, our eternity.
Lucilius here I can behold, and see
His counsels and his life proceed from thee.
But what care I to whom thy Letters be?
I change the name, and thou dost write to me;
And in this age, as sad almost as thine,
Thy stately Consolations are mine.
Poor earth! what though thy viler dust enrolls
The frail enclosures of these mighty souls?
Their graves are all upon record; not one
But is as bright and open as the sun,
And though some part of them obscurely fell

And perished in an unknown, private cell,
Yet in their books they found a glorious way
To live unto the Resurrection-day!
Most noble Bodley! we are bound to thee
For no small part of our eternity.
Thy treasure was not spent on horse and hound,
Nor that new mode, which doth old States confound.
Thy legacies another way did go,
Nor were they left to those would spend them so.
Thy safe, discreet expense on us did flow;
Walsam is in the midst of Oxford now.
Thou hast made us all thine heirs; whatever we
Hereafter write, 'tis thy posterity.
This is thy monument! here thou shalt stand
Till the times fail in their last grain of sand.
And wheresoe'er thy silent relics keep,
This tomb will never let thine honour sleep.
Still we shall think upon thee; all our fame
Meets here to speak one letter of thy name.
Thou canst not die! Here thou art more than safe,
Where every book is thy large epitaph.

Henry Vaughan

The Bodleians of Oxford

Above all thy rarities, old Oxenford, what do most arride and
solace me, are thy repositories of mouldering learning, thy
shelves—

What a place to be in is an old library! It seems as though
all the souls of all the writers, that have bequeathed their
labours to these Bodleians, were reposing here, as in some
dormitory, or middle state. I do not want to handle, to
profane the leaves, their winding-sheets. I could as soon dis-
lodge a shade. I seem to inhale learning, walking amid their

foliage; and the odour of their old moth-scented coverings
is fragrant as the first bloom of those sciential apples which
grew amid the happy orchard.

Charles Lamb, *Oxford in the Vacation*

The Bodleian: a Dead Sea of Books

Few places affected me more than the Libraries, and especially the Bodleian Library, reputed to have half a million printed
books and manuscripts. I walked solemnly and reverently
among the alcoves and through the halls, as if in the pyramid
of embalmed souls. It was their life, their heart, their mind,
that they treasured in these book-urns. Silent as they are,
should all the emotions that went to their creation have utterance, could the world itself contain the various sound? They
longed for fame? Here it is—to stand silently for ages, moved
only to be dusted and catalogued, valued only as units in the
ambitious total, and gazed at, occasionally, by men as ignorant
as I am, of their name, their place, their language, and their
worth. Indeed, unless a man can link his written thoughts
with the everlasting wants of men, so that they shall draw
from them as from wells, there is no more immortality to the
thoughts and feelings of the soul than to the muscles and the
bones. A library is but the soul's burial-ground. It is the land
of shadows.

Yet one is impressed with the thought, the labour, and the
struggle, represented in this vast catacomb of books. Who
could dream, by the placid waters that issue from the level
mouths of brooks into the lake, all the plunges, the whirls,
the divisions, and foaming rushes that had brought them
down to the tranquil exit? And who can guess through what
channels of disturbance, and experiences of sorrow, the heart
passed that has emptied into this Dead Sea of books?

Henry Ward Beecher, *Star Papers*

A College Library

A churchyard with a cloister running round
And quaint old effigies in act of prayer,
And painted banners mouldering strangely there
Where mitred prelates and grave doctors sleep,
Memorials of a consecrated ground!
Such is this antique room, a haunted place
Where dead men's spirits come, and angels keep
Long hours of watch with wings in silence furled.
Early and late have I kept vigil here;
And I have seen the moonlight shadows trace
Dim glories on the missal's blue and gold,
The work of my scholastic sires, that told
Of quiet ages men call dark and drear,
For Faith's soft light is darkness to the world.

Frederick William Faber

Merton Library

Quaint gloomy chamber, oldest relic left
Of monkish quiet, like a ship thy form,
Stranded keel upward by some sudden storm;
Now that a safe and polished age hath cleft
Locks, bars and chains, that saved thy tomes from theft,
May Time, a surer robber, spare thine age,
And reverence each huge black-lettered page,
Of real boards and gilt-stamped leather reft.
Long may ambitious students here unseal
The secret mysteries of classic lore;
Though urged not by that blind and aimless zeal
With which the Scot within these walls of yore
Transcribed the Bible without breaking fast,
Toiled through each word and perished at the last.

John Bruce Norton

Oxford Nights

About the august and ancient *Square*,
Cries the wild wind; and through the air,
The blue night air, blows keen and chill:
Else, all the night sleeps, all is still.
Now, the lone *Square* is blind with gloom:
Now, on that clustering chestnut bloom,
A cloudy moonlight plays, and falls
In glory upon *Bodley's* walls:
Now, wildlier yet, while moonlight pales,
Storm the tumultuary gales.
O rare divinity of Night!
Season of undisturbed delight:
Glad interspace of day and day!
Without, a world of winds at play:
Within, I hear what dead friends say.
Blow, winds! and round that perfect *Dome*,
Wail as you will, and sweep, and roam:
Above *Saint Mary's* carven home,
Struggle, and smite to your desire
The sainted watchers on her spire:
Or in the distance vex your power
Upon mine own *New College* tower:
You hurt not these! On me and mine,
Clear candlelights in quiet shine:
My fire lives yet! nor have I done
With *Smollett*, nor with *Richardson*:
With, gentlest of the martyrs! *Lamb*,
Whose lover I, long lover, am:
With *Gray*, whose gracious spirit knew
The sorrows of art's lonely few:
With *Fielding*, great, and strong, and tall;
Sterne, exquisite, equivocal;
Goldsmith, the dearest of them all:
While *Addison's* demure delights

Turn *Oxford*, into *Attic*, nights.
Still *Trim* and *Parson Adams* keep
Me better company, than sleep:
Dark sleep, who loves not me; nor I
Love well her nightly death to die,
And in her haunted chapels lie.
Sleep wins me not: but from his shelf
Brings me each wit his very self:
Beside my chair the great ghosts throng,
Each tells his story, sings his song:
And in the ruddy fire I trace
The curves of each *Augustan* face.
I sit at *Doctor Primrose'* board:
I hear *Beau Tibbs* discuss a lord.
Mine, *Matthew Bramble's* pleasant wrath;
Mine, all the humours of the *Bath*.
Sir Roger and the *Man in Black*
Bring me the *Golden Ages* back.
Now white *Clarissa* meets her fate,
With virgin will inviolate:
Now *Lovelace* wins me with a smile,
Lovelace, adorable and vile.
I taste, in slow alternate way,
Letters of *Lamb*, letters of *Gray*:
Nor lives there, beneath Oxford towers,
More joy, than in my silent hours.
Dream, who love dreams! forget all grief:
Find, in sleep's nothingness, relief:
Better my dreams! Dear, human books,
With kindly voices, winning looks!
Enchaunt me with your spells of art,
And draw me homeward to your heart:
Till weariness and things unkind
Seem but a vain and passing wind:
Till the grey morning slowly creep
Upward, and rouse the birds from sleep:

Till *Oxford* bells the silence break,
And find me happier, for your sake.
Then, with the dawn of common day,
Rest you! But I, upon my way,
What the fates bring, will cheerlier do,
In days not yours, through thoughts of you!

                                        Lionel Johnson

On the Library at Cambridge

In that great maze of books I sighed, and said,—
   'It is a grave-yard, and each tome a tomb;
Shrouded in hempen rags, behold the dead,
   Coffined and ranged in crypts of dismal gloom,—
Food for the worm and redolent of mould,
Traced with brief epitaph in tarnished gold.'—
   Ah, golden-lettered hope!—Ah, dolorous doom!
Yet, mid the common death, when all is cold,
   And mildewed pride in desolation dwells,
A few great Immortalities of old
   Stand brightly forth;—not tombs but living shrines,
Where from high saint or martyr virtue wells,
Which on the living yet works miracles,
   Spreading a relic wealth, richer than golden mines.

                                        J.M.

The Soul's Viaticum

Books looked on as to their readers or authors do at the
very first mention challenge pre-eminence above the world's
admired fine things. Books are the glass of council to dress
ourselves by. They are life's best business: vocation to these
hath more emolument coming in than all the other busy
terms of life. They are fee-less councillors, no delaying

patrons, of easy access, and kind expedition, never sending away empty any client or petitioner. They are for company the best friends; in doubts, counsellors; in damp, comforters; Time's perspective; the home traveller's ship, or horse, the busy man's best recreation; the opiate of idle weariness; the mind's best ordinary; Nature's garden and seed-plot of Immortality. Time spent, needlessly, from them is consumed, but with them twice gained. Time captivated and snatched from thee by incursions of business, thefts of visitants, or by thy own carelessness lost, is by these redeemed in life; they are the soul's viaticum; and against death its cordial. In a true verdict, no such treasure as a library.

Bulstrode Whitelocke

Notes

1   LAMB. The extracts from the works of Charles Lamb are from the Oxford edition, edited by T. Hutchinson. Not content with 'grace' before Milton and Shakespeare, Lamb suggests elsewhere (see p. 121) a solemn service.

1   PETRARCH. When the love-sick Petrarch retired from Avignon to Vaucluse, in 1338, his only companions were his books; for his friends rarely visited him, alleging that his mode of life was unnatural. Petrarch replied as in the text, which is quoted from Mrs. S. Dodson's *Life*. On another occasion, however, Petrarch wrote: 'Many have found the multitude of their books a hindrance to learning, and abundance has bred want, as sometimes happens. But if the many books are at hand, they are not to be east aside, but to be gleaned, and the best used; and care should be taken that those which might have proved seasonable auxiliaries do not become hindrances out of season. See Leigh Hunt's reference on page 20 to Petrarch as 'the god of the Bibliomaniacs'.

3   CHESTERFIELD. Folio, a book whose sheets are folded into two leaves; quarto, sheets folded into four leaves, abbreviated into 4to; octavo, sheets folded into eight leaves, 8vo; duodecimo, sheets folded into twelve leaves, 12mo. The first three words come to us from the Italian, through the French; the last is from the Latin *duodecim*.

5   SOUTHEY. Castanheda died in 1559, Barros in 1570, Osorio (da Fonseca) in 1580. They were Portuguese historians.

6   EMERSON.
> There comes Emerson first, whose rich words, every one,
> Are like gold nails in temples to hang trophies on.
> —J.R. Lowell.

7   WHITTIER. The poet explains that the 'lettered magnate' was his friend Fields (James Thomas, 1817–81), who edited the *Atlantic Monthly*. Among Fields's friends were Leigh Hunt, Barry Cornwall, Miss Mitford, and Dickens. Longfellow's 'Auf Wiedersehen' was written 'in memory of J.T.F.', and Whittier himself wrote some elegiac verse after his death.

It may be noted that Elzevir was the name of a famous family of Dutch printers, whose books were chiefly issued between 1592 and 1681. Louis Elzevir (?1540–1617) was the first to make the name famous.

9   IRVING. The sale of Roscoe's library, necessary on account of financial failure, took place in August and September 1816. This Roscoe is the historian of the Medici. Washington Irving quotes Roscoe's sonnet in his reference to the incident.

9   LONGFELLOW. These valedictory lines were written in December 1881. In the following year Longfellow died.

10   JONSON. Goodyer or Goodier (spelt Goodyere by Herrick) was the

friend of Donne and of many other literary men, and he wrote verses on his own account. His father, Sir Henry Goodyer, was the patron of Michael Drayton.

10 SHERIDAN. Written to Dean Swift, then in London.

12 DE BURY. Richard de Bury was born near Bury St. Edmunds in 1287, his father being Sir Richard Aungervile. He had a distinguished career at Oxford, and was the tutor of Edward III. Sent as ambassador to the papal court at Avignon, he formed a friendship with Petrarch (see pp. 1 and 316). While Bishop of Durham, he was for a short time Lord Chancellor and also Treasurer of England. He finished the *Philobiblon* less than three months before he died, in 1345. Thomas Fuller says that he had more books than all the other English bishops in that age put together. He had a library at each of his residences, and Mr. E.C. Thomas tells us, on the authority of William de Chambre, that wherever he was residing so many books lay about his bedchamber that it was hardly possible to stand or move without treading upon them. All the time he could spare from business was devoted either to religious offices or to books, and daily at table he would have a book read to him. The *Philobiblon* was printed first at Cologne in 1473, then ten years later at Spires, and in 1500 at Paris. The first edition printed in England appeared in 1598, and it was a product of the Oxford Press. It was not until 1832 that any English translation was published. This, although the name was not divulged in the book, was the work of John Bellingham Inglis. More than half a century passed before another translation was made—that of Mr. Thomas, who personally examined or collated twenty-eight MSS. Inglis's translation, according to his successor, is a work of more spirit than accuracy, but it is the spirit that quickeneth, and it is the 1832 volume which has been used.

14 ADDISON. Ovid, *Met.* xv. 871:
—which nor dreads the rage
Of tempests, fire, or war, or wasting age.
—Welsted.
Fielding says in *Tom Jones*:—'I question not but the ingenious author of the *Spectator* was principally induced to prefix Greek and Latin mottoes to every paper, from the same consideration of guarding against the pursuit of those scribblers who, having no talents of a writer but what is taught by the writing-master, are yet not more afraid nor ashamed to assume the same titles with the greatest genius, than their good brother in the fable was of braying in the lion's skin. By the device, therefore, of his motto, it became impracticable for any man to presume to imitate the *Spectators*, without understanding at least one sentence in the learned languages.'
'No praise of Addison's style,' Lord Lytton declares, 'can exaggerate its merits. Its art is perfectly marvellous. No change of time can render the workmanship obsolete. His manner has that nameless urbanity in which we recognize the perfection of manner— courteous, but not courtier-like; so dignified, yet so kindly; so easy, yet so high-bred. Its form of English is fixed—a safe and eternal model, of which all imitation pleases—to which all approach is scholarship—like the Latin of the Augustan age.'

So much for style. For the rest Hazlitt remarks that 'it is the extremely moral and didactic tone of the *Spectator* which makes us apt to think of Addison (according to Mandeville's sarcasm) as "a parson in a tie-wig" '. How often history repeats itself.

15 DODD. His *Beauties of Shakespeare*, published in 1752, is still well known. Dodd was hanged for forgery, despite many efforts, including those of Dr. Johnson, on his behalf.

15 HUNT. The periods referred to by Leigh Hunt are 'the dark ages, as they are called', and 'the gay town days of Charles II, or a little afterwards'. In the first the essayist imagines 'an age of iron warfare and energy, with solitary retreats, in which the monk or the hooded scholar walks forth to meditate, his precious volume under his arm. The other is a triumphant example of the power of books and wit to contest the victory with sensual pleasure:——Rochester staggering home to pen a satire in the style of Monsieur Boileau; Butler, cramming his jolly duodecimo with all the learning that he laughed at; and a new race of book poets come up, who, in spite of their periwigs and petit-maîtres, talk as romantically of "the bays" as if they were priests of Delphos.'

In Chapman's translation of Homer occur the words: 'The fortresses of thorniest queaches.' A queach is a thick bushy plot, or a quickset hedge.

You will see Hunt—one of those happy souls
Which are the salt of the earth, and without whom
This world would smell like what it is—a tomb.
—Shelley, Letter *to Maria Gisborne*.

16 LAMB.

What youth was in thy years,
What wisdom in thy levity, what truth
In every utterance of that purest soul!
Few are the spirits of the glorified
I'd spring to earlier at the gate of heaven.
—W.S. Landor.
Encumbered dearly with old books,
Thou, by the pleasant chimney nooks,
Didst laugh, with merry-meaning looks,
Thy griefs away.
—Lionel Johnson.

18 BURTON. Compare the remark of the 'Hammock School' reviewers in Mr. G.K. Chesterton's *The Napoleon of Notting Hill*—'Next to authentic goodness in a book (and that, alas! we never find) we desire a rich badness.'

18 CHANNING. An address introductory to the Franklin lectures delivered at Boston, 1838. Channing's influence increased after his death, which occurred in 1842. In the seventies nearly 50,000 copies of his *Complete Works* were circulated in America and Europe.

19 LEIGH HUNT. The novel *Camilla* is Madame D'Arblay's; the entire passage relating to the Oxford scholar's books is given on page 199; Petrarch is quoted on page 1.

21 LANDOR. See 'Old-Fashioned Verse' on p. 168.

23 BURTON. Lord Byron is reported by Moore to have said: 'The book, in

my opinion, most useful to a man who wishes to acquire the reputation of being well read, with the least trouble, is Burton's *Anatomy of
Melancholy*, the most amusing and instructive medley of quotations and
classical anecdotes I ever perused. But a superficial reader must take
care, or his intricacies will bewilder him. If, however, he has patience to
go through his volumes, he will be more improved for literary conversation than by the perusal of any twenty other works with which I am
acquainted, at least in the English language.'

Dr. Johnson, while admitting that the *Anatomy* is a valuable work,
suggests that it is overloaded with quotation. But he adds, 'It is the only
book that ever took me out of bed two hours sooner than I wished to
rise.'

24 SOUTHEY. 'Southey's appearance is *Epic;* and he is the only existing
entire man of letters. All the others have some pursuit annexed to their
authorship'.—Lord Byron.

            Ye, loved books, no more
Shall Southey feed upon your precious lore,
To works that ne'er shall forfeit their renown,
Adding immortal labours of his own.—Wordsworth.
(Inscription for a monument in Crosthwaite Church).

29 MONTAIGNE. Michel Eyquem, Seigneur de Montaigne, began to write
his essays in his chateau at Montaigne in Périgord in 1572, at the age of
thirty-nine. The essays were published in 1580, and five editions had
appeared before his death in 1592.

The Essayes of Michael Lord of Montaigne translated by John Florio
were first published in 1603. The translator was born in London about
1553, and he died in 1625. It is this translation from which my excerpts
are given, and it is the only book known to have been in Shakespeare's
library; the volume contains his autograph, and is now in the British
Museum.

Emerson classes Montaigne in his *Representative Men* as the Sceptic. He
calls to mind that Gibbon reckoned, in the bigoted times of the period,
but two men of liberality in France—Henry IV and Montaigne—and
adds, 'Though a Biblical plainness, coupled with a most uncanonical
levity, may shut his pages to many sensitive readers, yet the offence is
superficial. … I know not anywhere the book that seems less written. It
is the language of conversation transferred to a book.'

30 DENHAM. Dominico Mancini wrote the *Libellus de quattuor Virtutibus*,
published in Paris, 1484.

33 JOHNSON. The excerpts from Johnson and from Boswell's *Life* are taken,
where possible, from Dr. Birkbeck Hill's Oxford edition.

40 MILTON. Milton's prose masterpiece was printed, in a modified form,
by Mirabeau, under the title *Sur la Liberté de la Presse*, imité de l'Anglais,
de Milton.

42 LEIGHTON.
Methinks in that refulgent sphere
That knows not sun or moon,
An earth-born saint might long to hear
One verse of 'Bonnie Doon'.
—O.W. Holmes.

42 HAZLITT. 'Because they both wrote essays and were fond of the Eliza-
bethans,' Mr. Augustine Birrell says, 'it became the fashion to link
Hazlitt's name with Lamb's. Hazlitt suffered by the comparison.'

43 HUNT. The poet is Wordsworth and the lines 'Oh that my name' are
found in 'Personal Talk'. See page 44.

48 MACAULAY. 'Macaulay is like a book in breeches.'—Sydney Smith.

50 FULLER. 'Fuller's language!' Coleridge writes: 'Grant me patience,
Heaven! A tithe of his beauties would be sold cheap for a whole library
of our classical writers, from Addison to Johnson and Junius inclusive.
And Bishop Nicolson!—a painstaking old charwoman of the Antiquar-
ian and Rubbish Concern! The venerable rust and dust of the whole firm
are not worth an ounce of Fuller's earth!'

 The rest of this essay will be found on page 71. The learned man
referred to in the last paragraph is Erasmus.

53 ADDISON. 'The multiplication of readers is the multiplication of loaves.
On the day when Christ created that symbol, he caught a glimpse of
printing. His miracle is this marvel. Behold a book. I will nourish with
it five thousand souls—a million souls—all humanity. In the action
of Christ bringing forth the loaves, there is Gutenberg bringing forth
books. One sower heralds the other.... Gutenberg is for ever the auxiliary of life; he is the permanent fellow-workman in the great work of
civilization. Nothing is done without him. He has marked the transition
of the man-slave to the free man. Try and deprive civilization of him,
you become Egypt.'—Victor Hugo on Shakespeare.

53 DE QUINCEY. 'The few shelves which would hold all the true classics
extant might receive as many more of the like as there is any chance that
the next two or three centuries could produce, without burthening the
select and leisurely scholar with a sense of how much he had to read.'—
C. Patmore, *Principle in Art: William Barnes.*

55 SWIFT. '"The Battle of the Books" is the fancy of a lover of libraries.'—
Leigh Hunt.

 The royal library at St. James's alluded to was one of the nine privi-
leged libraries which received copies of new books under the Copyright
Act of Anne. The privilege passed to the British Museum in 1757, when
George II made over the royal collection to the nation.

57 BACON. Sir William Temple in his *Essay on the Ancient and Modern Learning*
(pp. 52, 99) concludes 'with a Saying of Alphonsus Sirnamed the Wise,
King of Aragon: That among so many things as are by Men possessed or
pursued in the Course of their Lives, all the rest are Bawbles, Besides
Old Wood to Burn, Old Wine to Drink, Old Friends to Converse with,
and Old Books to Read.'

58 GOLDSMITH. Horace Walpole wrote to the Rev. William Cole (Letter
2337; Oxford edition): 'There is a chapter in Voltaire that would cure
anybody of being a great man even in his own eyes. It is the chapter in
which a Chinese [man] goes into a bookseller's shop, and marvels at not
finding any of his own country's classics.'

60 HAZLITT. 'William Hazlitt, I believe, has no books, except mine; but he
has Shakespeare and Rousseau by heart.'—LEIGH HUNT.

63 HAZLITT. Hazlitt wrote this essay in Florence, on his honeymoon, and
it opens with a quotation from Sterne: 'And what of this new book, that

the whole world make such a rout about?' Lord Byron had died in the previous year, 1824.

> 'Laws are not like women, the worse for being old.'
> —The Duke of Buckingham's speech in the House of Lords in Charles the Second's time (Hazlitt's note).

64 MACAULAY. Pyrgopolynices (Plautus: *Miles Gloriosus*); Thraso (Terence: *Eunuch*); Bobadil (Ben Jonson: *Every Man in his Humour*); Bessus (Beaumont and Fletcher: *A King and no King*); Pistol (*The Merry Wives of Windsor*); Parolles (*All's Well that Ends Well*); Nephelococcygia (Aristophanes: *The Birds*—the cuckoos' town in the clouds); Lilliput (Swift: *Gulliver's Travels*—the pygmies' country).

70 WITHER. Bevis of Hampton, a hero of early mediaeval romance. The story has been published by the Early English Text Society.

Compare 'The common rabble of scribblers and blur-papers which nowadays stuff stationers' shops.'—Montaigne.

71 FULLER. The other portion of this essay will be found on page 50. Arius Montanus was the court chaplain of Philip II of Spain, and he personally superintended the printing of the *Biblia Polyglotta* (8 vols., 1569–73), the most famous of the books printed by Christophe Plantin. The printing office is one of the sights of Antwerp, whose council bought the property from Plantin's descendants in 1876 for £48,000.

Compare also: 'Evil books corrupt at once both our manners and our taste.'—Fielding.

72 ADDISON. Addison 'takes off the severity of this speculation' with an anecdote of an atheistical author who was sick unto death. A curate, to comfort him, said he did not believe any besides the author's particular friends or acquaintance had ever been at the pains of reading his book, or that anybody after his death would ever inquire after it. 'The dying Man had still so much the Frailty of an Author in him, as to be cut to the Heart with these Consolations; and without answering the good Man, asked his Friends about him (with a Peevishness that is natural to a sick Person) where they had picked up such a Blockhead?' It seems that the author recovered, 'and has since written two or three other Tracts with the same Spirit, and very luckily for his poor Soul with the same success.'

73 MILTON. 'For he [Pliny the Elder] read no book which he did not make extracts from. He used to say that "no book was so bad but some good might be got out of it." '—Pliny the Younger.

75 BAXTER. 'Richard, Richard, dost thou think we will let thee poison the court? Richard, thou art an old knave. Thou hast written books enough to load a cart, and every book as full of sedition as an egg is full of meat.'—Judge Jeffreys' address at Baxter's trial.

76 COBBETT. Cobbett attacks Dr. Johnson, because in a pamphlet he urged war on the American colonies; Burke, because in another pamphlet he urged war on revolutionary France. 'The first war lost us America, the last cost us six hundred millions of money, and has loaded us with forty millions a year of taxes.'

77 MORE. Tom Hickathrift, who killed a giant at Tylney, Norfolk, with a cartwheel. He dates from the Conquest, and was made governor of Thanet.

78 AUSTEN. *Cecilia* and *Camilla*, both by Mme. D'Arblay; *Belinda*, by Miss Edgeworth.

'She [Diana] says of Romance: "The young who avoid that region escape the title of Fool at the cost of a celestial crown."'—George Meredith, *Diana of the Crossways*.

78 HERSCHEL. 'The most influential books, and the truest in their influence, are works of fiction.'—R.L. Stevenson.

80 MILTON. South said that *Eikon Basilike* was 'composed with such an unfailing majesty of diction, that it seems to have been written with a sceptre rather than a pen'.

Milton condemns the king for having 'so little care of truth in his last words, or honour to himself, or to his friends, or sense of his afflictions, or of that sad hour which was upon him, as immediately before his death to pop into the hand of that grave bishop [Juxon] who attended him, for a special relic of his saintly exercises, a prayer stolen word for word from the mouth of a heathen woman praying to a heathen god; and that in no serious book, but the vain amatorious poem of Sir Philip Sidney's *Arcadia*'.

82 DRYDEN. Hazlitt, who could not 'much relish Ben Jonson', describes him as 'a great borrower from the works of others, and a plagiarist even from nature; so little freedom is there in his imitations of her, and he appears to receive her bounty like an alms'. J.A. Symonds, stating that Jonson 'held the prose writers and poets of antiquity in solution in his spacious memory', points out that such looting on his part of classical treasuries of wit and wisdom was accounted no robbery in his age.

84 PATTISON. Matthew Arnold, in the preface to *Literature and Dogma* (1873), points out that 'To read to good purpose we must read a great deal, and be content not to use a great deal of what we read. We shall never be content not to use the whole, or nearly the whole, of what we read, unless we read a great deal.'

86 MITFORD. 'Every abridgement of a good book is a stupid abridgement.' —Montaigne.

89 TENNYSON. J. J. Jusserand, in the first annual Shakespeare lecture before the British Academy (July 5, 1911), used eloquent language which might be said to justify bibliographies:— 'Books, like their authors, have their biography. They live their own lives. Some behave like honourable citizens of the world of thought, do good, propagate sound views, strengthen heart and courage, assuage, console, improve those men to whose hearths they have been invited. Others corrupt or debase, or else turn minds towards empty frivolities. In proportion to their fame, and to the degree of their perenniality, is the good or evil that they do from century to century, eternal benefactors of mankind or deathless malefactors. Posted on the road followed by humanity, they help or destroy the passers-by; they deserve gratitude eternal, or levy the toll of some of our life's blood, leaving us weaker; highwaymen or good Samaritans. Some make themselves heard at once and continue to be listened to for ever; others fill the ears for one or two generations, and then begin an endless sleep; or, on the contrary, long silent or misunderstood, they awake from their torpor, and astonished mankind discovers with surprise long-concealed treasures like those trodden upon by the unwary visitor of unexplored ruins.'

90 HELPS. 'My desire is ... that mine adversary had written a book.'—The Author of Job, ch. 31.

'Curll, Pope's victim and accomplice ... hit on one of those epoch-making ideas which are so simple when once they are conceived, so difficult, save for the loftiest genius, in their first conception. It occurred to him that, in a world governed by the law of mortality, men might be handsomely entertained on one another's remains. He lost no time in putting his theory into action. During the years of his activity he published some forty or fifty separate *Lives*, intimate, anecdotal, scurrilous sometimes, of famous and notorious persons who had the ill-fortune to die during his lifetime.... His books commanded a large sale, and modern biography was established.'—Sir W. Raleigh. *Six Essays on Johnson*.

It is related in *The Percy Anecdotes* that 'A gentleman calling on Archbishop Tillotson observed in his library one shelf of books of various forms and sizes, all richly bound, finely gilt and lettered. He inquired what favourite authors these were that had been so remarkably distinguished by his Grace. "These," said the Archbishop, "are my own personal friends; and what is more I have made them such (for they were avowedly my enemies), by the use I have made of those hints which their maliee had suggested to me. From these I have received more profit than from the advice of my best and most cordial friends; and therefore you see I have rewarded them accordingly." '

90 DISRAELI. Compare Emerson: 'There is properly no history, only biography; and Carlyle: 'History is the essence of innumerable biographies.'

'Those that write of men's lives,' says Montaigne, forasmuch as they amuse and busy themselves more about counsels than events, more about that which cometh from within than that which appeareth outward; they are fittest for me.'

93 JONSON. This was printed in the First Folio of Shakespeare's works, 1623, on the page opposite the Droeshout portrait.

96 MILTON. These lines were printed anonymously in the Second Folio Shakespeare, 1632, and, it is believed, this was Milton's first appearance as a poet.

96 DRYDEN. This was printed under the engraving in Tonson's folio edition of *Paradise Lost* (1688). Mr. F.A. Mumby, in *The Romance of Bookselling*, recalls that in Moseley's first edition of Milton's poems there was an atrocious portrait of the poet by William Marshall. Milton wrote four lines in Greek, which the artist, innocent of that language, gravely cut into the plate, lines that Dr. Masson has thus translated:

That an unskilful hand had carved this print
You'd say at once, seeing the living face;
But, finding here no jot of me, my friends,
Laugh at the botching artist's mis-attempt.

98 CARLYLE. Abelard, born 1079, died 1142, is less known now as a famous teacher at the University of Paris than as the lover of Héloise.

102 TRAPP and BROWNE. When George I sent a present of some books, in November 1715, to the University of Cambridge, he sent at the same time a troop of horse to Oxford. This inspired Dr. Trapp and provoked the rejoinder from Sir William Browne.

103 EARLE. Mr. A.S. West, in his edition of Earle's *Micro-cosmographie; or a*

Piece of the World discovered; in Essayes and Characters, says: 'The critic supposed that *omneis* was the original form of the accusative plural of *omnis*, and that the forms *omnes* and *omnis* had taken its place. In order to adhere to the older spelling "he writes *omneis* at length". *Quicquid* is cited as an instance of pedantry because the ordinary man wrote the word as *quidquid*. and doubtless so pronounced it. The critic's gerund may be described as "inconformable" because it resists attraction—remains a gerund and does not become a gerundive. Or Earle may have had in view passages in which the gerund of transitive verbs with *est* govern an object.'

105 GOLDSMITH. 'When Dr. Johnson is free to confess that he does not admire Gray's *Elegy*, and Macaulay to avow that he sees little to praise in Dickens and Wordsworth, why should not humbler folks have the courage of their opinions?' Such is the question asked by James Payn in the *Nineteenth Century* (March 1880), his article being entitled 'Sham Admiration in Literature'. Mr. Payn noted that 'curiously enough, it is women who have the most courage in the expression of their literary opinions', instancing the authoress of *Jane Eyre*, who 'did not derive much pleasure from the perusal of the works of the other Jane [Austen]', and Harriet Martineau, who confessed to him that she could see no beauties in *Tom Jones*.

'There is no ignorance more shameful than to admit as true that which one does not understand: and there is no advantage so great as that of being set free from error.'—Xenophon. *Memorabilia*.

108 FIELDING. 'What a master of composition Fielding was! Upon my word, I think the *Oedipus Tyrannus*, *The Alchemist*, and *Tom Jones*, the three most perfect plots ever planned.... How charming, how wholesome, Fielding always is!'—S.T. Coleridge, *Table Talk*.

113 ERASMUS. The translation is the work of Nathaniel Bailey, lexicographer and schoolmaster, who died in 1742. Desiderius and Erasmus are Latin and Greek for Gerhard 'the beloved', the name of the scholar's father.

114 COLTON. Compare R.B. Sheridan's 'Easy writing's curst hard reading.'

114 BACON. Mr. A.S. Gaye, in the new Clarendon Press edition of the *Essays*, points out that on almost every page the reader will find quotations from the Bible and from the Greek and Latin classics, especially Tacitus, Plutarch, Cicero, Virgil, Seneca, and Ovid, besides frequent allusions to biblical, classical, and mediaeval history. 'It is also remarkable that the quotations are more often than not inaccurate, not only in words but in sense.... Bacon furnished in himself an exception to the rule which he laid down in his Essay "Of Studies"; for though "reading" made him "a full man", "writing" did not make him "an exact man".'

118 BOSWELL. One of Mrs. Piozzi's anecdotes of Dr. Johnson is that he asked 'Was there ever yet anything written by mere man that was wished longer by its readers excepting *Don Quixote*, *Robinson Crusoe*, and the *Pilgrim's Progress?*' Johnson declared that the work of Cervantes was the greatest in the world, 'speaking of it, I mean, as a book of entertainment.'

123 EMERSON. Shakespeare's phrase: *Taming of the Shrew*, Act I, sc. i.

124 EMERSON. O.W. Holmes applies the proverb to the Bible. 'What you bring away from the Bible depends to some extent on what you carry to it.'

128 GIBBON. F.W. Robertson's opinion is worth recording: 'It is very
surprising to find how little we retain of a book, how little we have
really made our own, when we come to interrogate ourselves as to what
account we can give of it, however we may seem to have mastered it by
understanding it. Hundreds of books read once have passed as completely from us as if we had never read them; whereas the discipline of
mind got by writing down, not copying, an abstract of a book which is
worth the trouble, fixes it on the mind for years, and, besides, enables
one to read other books with more attention and more profit.'

130 HAMILTON. 'This assumes that the book to be operated on is your own,
and perhaps is rather too elaborate a counsel of perfection for most of
us.'—Lord Morley.

135 ADDISON. Hor. *Ars Poet.* I. 319:—
> When the sentiments and manners please,
> And all the characters are wrought with ease,
> Your tale, though void of beauty, force, and art,
> More strongly shall delight and warm the heart;
> Than where a lifeless pomp of verse appears,
> And with sonorous trifles charms our ears.—Francis.

Butler, writing of 'A small poet' (*Characters*), says: 'There was one that
lined a hat-case with a paper of Benlowe's poetry: Prynne bought it by
chance, and put a new demicastor into it. The first time he wore it he
felt a singing in his head, which within two days turned to a vertigo.' A
'demicastor' is a hat.

136 SCOTT. Mr. W.J. Courthope, in his Warton Lecture on English Poetry
before the British Academy, read on October 25, 1911, observes that
'the best illustration of historic change in "romantic" temper is perhaps
to be found in a comparison of Cervantes' account of the character of
Don Quixote [see p. 143] with Walter Scott's representation of the
romanticism of the hero of *Waverley*. Don Quixote's "fancy", says Cervantes, "grew full of what he used to read about in his books, enchant-
ments, battles, challenges, wounds, wooings, loves, agonies, and all
sorts of impossible nonsense; and it so possessed his mind that the whole
fabric of invention and fancy he read of was true, that to him no history
in the world had more reality in it."... "My intention," says Scott, "is not
to follow the steps of the inimitable Cervantes in describing such total
perversion of intellect as misconstrues the objects actually presented to
the senses, but the more common aberration from sound judgement,
which apprehends occurrences indeed in their reality, but communicates to them a tincture of its own romantic colouring." ' Scott expati-
ates at length on Waverley's reading in the third chapter of his novel.

138 BOSWELL. Macaulay writes in his review of Southey's edition of *The
Pilgrim's Progress*: 'Doctor Johnson, all whose studies were desultory,
and who hated, as he said, to read books through, made an exception
in favour of *The Pilgrim's Progress*. That work was one of the two or three
works which he wished longer. It was by no common merit that the illiterate sectary extracted praise like this from the most pedantic of critics
and the most bigoted of Tories.'

Boswell relates that Dr. Johnson 'had a peculiar facility in seizing at
once what was valuable in any book, without submitting to the labour of

perusing it from beginning to end.'

139 WALLER. 'A library well chosen cannot be too extensive, but some there are who amass a great quantity of books, which they keep for show, and not for service. Of such persons, Louis XI of France aptly enough observed, that "they resembled *hunch-backed* people, who carried a great burden, which *they never saw*".'—W. Keddie, *Cyclopaedia*.

141 BOSWELL. Dr. Birkbeck Hill points out that Boswell alludes to this opinion in one of his letters, modestly adding: 'I am afraid I have not read books enough to be able to talk from them.' Johnson particularized Langton as talking from books, 'and Garrick would if he talked seriously.'

142 SMITH. Bettinelli, a scholar and a Jesuit (1718–1808), who attacked the reputation of Dante and Petrarch.

Coventry Patmore wrote: 'If you want to shine as a diner-out, the best way is to know something which others do not know, and not to know many things which everybody knows. This takes much less reading, and is doubly effective, inasmuch as it makes you a really good, that is, an interested listener, as well as a talker.'—*On Obscure Books*.

143 COLTON. 'Methinks 'tis a pitiful piece of knowledge that can be learnt from an index and a poor ambition to be rich in the inventory of another's treasure.'—J. Glanvill, *The Vanity of Dogmatizing*.

143 CERVANTES. A whole chapter is devoted to the destruction of Don Quixote's library. (Part i, chap. vi.) The books that, condemned by the priest, were passed into the housekeeper's hands and thence into the fire were:—*Adventures of Esplandian*; *Amadis of Greece*; *Don Olivante de Laura*; *Florismarte of Hyrcania*; *The Knight Platir*; *The Knight of the Cross*; *Bernardo del Carpio*; *Roncesvalles*; *Palmerin de Oliva*; *Diana*, called the Second, by Salmantino; *The Shepherd of Iberia*; *The Nymphs of Henares*; and *The Curse of Jealousy*. The priest, however, put by for further examination or determined to save: *Amadis de Gaul*; *The Mirror of Chivalry*, and 'all other books that shall be found treating of French matters'; *Palmerin of England*; *Don Belianis*; *Tirante the White*; *Diana*, of Montemayor, and its continuation by Gil Polo; *Ten Books of the Fortune of Love*; *The Shepherd of Filida*; *The Treasure of Divers Poems* (de Padilla); *Book of Songs*, by Lopez Maldonado; *Galatea*, by Cervantes; *Araucana*; *Austriada*; *Monserrate*; and the *Tears of Angelica*. The curious reader will find these volumes traced in the admirable notes in J. Fitzmaurice-Kelly's edition of *Don Quixote* in 'The World's Classics'. Cervantes, Mr. Fitzmaurice-Kelly says, devoured in his wandering youth, 'those folios of chivalrous adventures which he, and he alone, has saved from the iniquity of oblivion'. The early association of Barabbas and books will be noticed.

It is the translation by Charles Jervas, first published in 1742, which is here employed.

The Renowned Romance of Amadis of Gaul, by Vasco Lobeira, which was expressly condemned by Montaigne, was translated from the Spanish version of Garciodonez de Montalvo by Southey.

147 RUSKIN. As Mr. Frederic Harrison points out, 'Books are no more education than laws are virtue; and, just as profligacy is easy within the strict limits of law, a boundless knowledge of books may be found with a narrow education.'

147 BARRETT BROWNING. This letter was written to 'Orion' Horne three years before Mrs. Browning's marriage in 1843, when she was thirty-seven. Compare Matthew Arnold in the preface to *Literature and Dogma* (1873): 'Nothing can be truer than what Butler says, that really, in general, no part of our time is more idly spent than the time spent in reading. Still, culture is indispensably necessary, and culture is reading; but reading with a purpose to guide it, and with system.'

149 MAURICE. This is better than Sydney Smith's attitude expressed in the question, 'Who reads an American book, or goes to an American play, or looks at an American picture or statue?'

149 BLACKIE. 'Reading is seeing by proxy—is learning indirectly through another man's faculties, instead of directly through one's own facul-ties; and such is the prevailing bias, that the indirect learning is thought preferable to the direct learning, and usurps the name of cultivation.' —Herbert Spencer, *The Study of Sociology*.

150 DAVIES.

> What is the end of Fame? 'Tis but to fill
> A certain portion of uncertain paper ...
> To have, when the original is dust,
> A name, a wretched picture, and worse bust.
> —Byron, *Don Juan*.

153 WALPOLE. Mr. Augustine Birrell in *Obiter Dicta: The Office of Literature* writes that the author's office is to make the reader happy:—

> Cooks, warriors, and authors must be judged by the effects they pro-duce: toothsome dishes, glorious victories, pleasant books— these are our demands....
>
> Literature exists to please—to lighten the burden of men's lives; to make them for a short while forget their sorrows and their sins, their silenced hearths, their disappointed hopes, their grim futures—and those men of letters are the best loved who have best performed literature's truest office.

153 CHAUCER. The book referred to is Ovid's *Metamorphoses*.

154 BOSWELL. 'Who is he that is now wholly overcome with idleness, or otherwise involved in a labyrinth of worldly cares, troubles, and discon-tents, that will not be much lightened in his mind by reading of some enticing story, true or feigned, where as in a glass he shall observe what our forefathers have done, the beginnings, ruins, ends, falls of com-monwealths, private men's actions displayed to the life, &c. Plutarch therefore calls them *secundas mensas et bellaria*, the second courses and junkets, because they were usually read at noblemen's feasts.' —R. Burton, *Anatomy*.

154 RABELAIS.

> Whence is thy learning? Hath thy toil
> O'er books consumed the midnight oil?
> —J. Gay.

155 WILSON. This is often taken to be an antique. As a matter of fact, Mr. John Wilson, a London bookseller, stated to Mr. Austin Dobson that he wrote the lines as a motto for one of his second-hand catalogues. Wilson, Mr. Dobson tells us, was amused at the vogue the lines eventually obtained.

155 CHAUCER. This is the earlier version, and to be preferred to the later, in which the passage ends:

Farwel my book and my devocioun!

wel unethe = scarcely any.

162 RICHARDSON. In his preface to *Pamela* Richardson claims to give 'practical examples worthy to be followed in the most critical and affecting cases by the modest virgin, the chaste bride, and the obliging wife'. The heroine becomes Mrs. B——, and Billy is the first-born. Locke's treatise was published in 1693, or forty-seven years before Richardson's novel, and the philosopher observes 'That most Children's Constitutions are either spoiled, or at least harmed, by *Cockering and Tenderness*'. 'Mr. B.' recommended better than he knew.

162 JOHNSON. Ruskin gives the same advice. See p. 191.

165 GIBBON. The Autobiography, in Sir Archibald Alison's opinion, is 'the most perfect account of an eminent man's life, from his own hand, which exists in any language'.

168 LANDOR. See the poem to Wordsworth on p. 21.

169 LEIGH HUNT. The friend referred to was Shelley.

170 DICKENS. Of this passage, Forster says in the *Life of Dickens*, 'It is one of the many passages in *Copperfield* which are literally true.... Every word of this personal recollection had been written down as fact, some years before it found its way into *David Copperfield*; the only change in the fiction being his omission of the name of a cheap series of novelists then in course of publication, by means of which his father had become happily the owner of so large a lump of literary treasure in his small collection of books.'

    Apropos of Defoe, Macaulay, who could not 'understand the mania of some people about Defoe', admitted that 'he certainly wrote an excellent book—the first part of *Robinson Crusoe* ... my delight before I was five years old'.

171 HAZLITT. It is reported (Dibdin relates in *Bibliomania*) that a certain man, of the name of Similis, who fought under the Emperor Hadrian, became so wearied and disgusted with the number of troublesome events which he met with in that mode of life, that he retired and devoted himself wholly to leisure and reading, and to meditations upon divine and human affairs, after the manner of Pythagoras. In this retirement, Similis was wont frequently to exclaim that '*now* he began to *live*': at his death he desired the following inscription to be placed upon his tomb.

    Here lies Similis;

    In the seventieth year of his age

    But only the seventh of his life.

In a note it is stated that 'This story is related by Dion Cassius and from him told by Spizelius in his *Infelix Literarius*.'

172 DONNE. This is the title given by Donne's editors, but is nonsense. Grosart explains that Pindar's instructress was Corinna the Theban, and that Lucan's 'help' is probably his helpmeet—Argentaria Polla, his wife who survived him.

174 DANTE. This is the famous passage in Canto V referring to Paolo and Francesca. (Gary's translation.)

180 MOORE.
>   For where is any author in the world
>   Teaches such beauty as a woman's eye?
>   —Shakespeare, *Love's Labour's Lost*, Act IV. Se. iii.

181 MORE. Warton thinks it probable that Sir Thomas More—'one of
the best jokers of the age'—may have written this epigram, which he
considers the first pointed epigram in our language. But by some the
lines are credited to Henry Howard, Earl of Surrey, who is memorable,
among other things, for introducing the sonnet from Italy into England,
a distinction which he shares with Wyatt.

182 MOORE. 'Mamurra was a dogmatic philosopher, who never doubted
about anything, except who was his father; Bombastus, one of the
names of the great scholar and quaek Paracelsus. St. Jerome was scolded
by an angel for reading Cicero, as Gratia tells the story in his *Concordan-
tia discordantium Canonum*, and says, that for this reason bishops were not
allowed to read the classics.'

188 BARRETT BROWNING.
>   Here with a Loaf of Bread beneath the Bough,
>   A Flask of Wine, a Book of Verse—and Thou
>   Beside me singing in the Wilderness—
>   And Wilderness is Paradise enow.
>   —E. FitzGerald, *Omar Khayyám*.

190 MACAULAY. 'Neither we nor divinity require much learning in women;
Francis, Duke of Brittany, son to John V, when he was spoke unto for a
marriage between him and Isabel, a daughter of Scotland, and some told
him she was meanly brought up, and without any instruction of learning, answered he loved her the better for it, and that a woman was wise
enough if she could but make a difference between the shirt and doublet
of her husband's.'— Montaigne.

191 RUSKIN. Compare Johnson's advice on page 162.

192 ADDISON. Virgil, *Aeneid*, vii. 805:
>   Unused to spinning, in the loom unskilled.
>   —Dryden.

The Virgil of Ogilby, or Ogilvy, originally a dancing-master, was
published in 1649, and was the first complete English translation
(Ogilby is mentioned by Pope, see page 281); *Cassandra*, *Cleopatra*,
Astraea, *The Grand Cyrus* and *Clelia* were French romances trans-
lated into English. Sidney called his pastoral romance *The Countess of
Pembroke's Arcadia*; Sherlock's *Discourse on Death* passed through forty
editions; *The Fifteen Comforts*, a translation of a French satirical work
of the fifteenth century; Sir Richard Baker's *Chronicle of the Kings of
England from the time of the Romans' Government unto the Death of King
James* (1641); Mrs. Manley was tried for libelling the nobility in her
*Secret Memoirs and Manners of several Persons of Quality of both Sexes from
the New Atlantis* (1707); the Fielding referred to is Beau Fielding, tried
at the Old Bailey in 1706 for a bigamous marriage with the Duchess of
Cleveland.

In Addison's time, Dr. Johnson wrote, 'in the female world, any
acquaintance with books was distinguished only to be censured.'

194 ADDISON. Hor. 2 *Ep.* ii. 61:

What would you have me do,
When out of twenty I can please not two?—
One likes the pheasant's wing, and one the leg;
The vulgar boil, the learned roast an egg;
Hard task, to hit the palate of such guests.
—Pope.

The Vindication was the work of Charles Leslie, the non-juror;
Pharamond, a romance dealing with the Frankish empire, by La
Calprenède; *Cassandra* is wrong—the French work, also by La
Calprenède, was *Cassandre* (the son of Antipater); *All for Love*, Dryden's
play; *Sophonisba*, by Lee; *The Innocent Adultery*, the second name of
Sotherne's *The Fatal Marriage*; *Mithridates* was by Lee, who also wrote *The
Rival Queens, or The Death of Alexander the Great*, and *Theodosius*; *Aureng-
Zebe*, Dryden's tragedy. (T. Arnold, *Addison*).

196 SHERIDAN. The first reference to a circulating library given in the
Oxford English Dictionary is an advertisement, June 12, 1742—'Propos-
als for erecting a Public Circulating Library in London.' Joseph Knight,
in the Oxford edition of Sheridan's *Plays*, annotates this passage fully.
Dillingham, sending his Latin translation of Herbert's *Porch* to Sancroft,
says: 'I know that if these should be once published, it would be too
late then to prevent, if not to correct a fault; I therefore shall take it as
a great kindness if you will please to put on your critical naile, and to
give your impartial censure on these papers while they are yet in the
tireing roome; and I shall endeavour to amend them with one great
or more lesser blotts.' Sancroft replies: 'I greedily took your original
in one hand, and your copy in the other, of which I had suffered one
nayl (though it pretends not to be a critical one) to grow ever since you
bespoke its service.'
Compare Herrick:—
Be bold, my book, nor be abashed, or fear
The cutting thumb-nail, or the brow severe;
But by the Muses swear, all here is good,
If but, well read or ill read, understood.
Blonds = blond laces, produced from unbleached silk.
All the works mentioned have been identified. The *Innocent Adultery* is
the alternative title of Sotherne's *Fatal Marriage*; *The Whole Duty of Man*
was by Allestree, once Provost of Eton; the 'admirable Mrs. Chapone',
an admirer of Richardson, and a contributor to the *Rambler*; 'Under the
most repulsive exterior that any woman ever possessed she concealed
very superior attainments and extensive knowledge': Fordyce was
Johnson's friend, and his sermons were specially addressed to young
women.

199 CHAUCER. *holwe* = hollow; *courtepy* = short upper coat of a coarse
material; *fithele* = fiddle; *sautrye* = psaltery; *hente* = borrow: *yaf* = gave;
scoleye = to attend school; *sentence* = sentiment; *souninge in* = conducing
to.

202 BERESFORD. *Bibliosophia; or Book-wisdom*, by the Rev. J. Beresford,
was written as 'a feeling remonstrance against the *prose* work, lately
published by the Reverend T.F. Dibdin under the title of *Bibliomania; or
Book-madness*', quoted in successive pages.

203 D'ISRAELI. The verse is imitated from the Latin of 'Henry Rantzau, a Danish gentleman, the founder of the great library at Copenhagen, whose days were dissolved in the pleasures of reading', who 'discovers his taste and ardour in the following elegant effusion'.

204 D'ISRAELI. 'An allusion and pun which occasioned the French translator of the present work an unlucky blunder: puzzled no doubt by my *facetiously*, he translates "mettant comme on l'a *très judicieusement* fait observer, l'entendement humain sous la clef". The book, and the author alluded to, quite escaped him.'— I. D'Israeli, *Curiosities of Literature: The Bibliomania*, note.

205 DIBDIN. Magliabechi was born at Florence, October 29, 1633. 'He had never learned to read; and yet he was perpetually poring over the leaves of old books that were used in his master's shop. A bookseller, who lived in the neighbourhood, and who had often observed this, and knew the boy could not read, asked him one day "what he meant by staring so much on printed paper?" Magliabechi said that he did not know how it was, but that he loved it of all things. The consequence was that he was received, with tears of joy in his eyes, into the bookseller's shop; and hence rose, by a quick succession, into posts of literary honour, till he became librarian to the Grand Duke of Tuscany.'

213 BROWNING. Sibrandus Schafnaburgensis 'is apparently', Mrs. Orr says, without adding to our store of knowledge, 'the name of an old pedant who has written a tiresome book.'

217 DE BURY. J.H. Burton, in *The Book-Hunter*, tells the following story:— It was Thomson, I believe, who used to cut the leaves with his snuffers. Perhaps an event in his early career may have soured him of the proprieties. It is said that he had an uncle, a clever active mechanic, who could do many things with his hands, and contemplated James's indolent, dreamy, 'feckless' character with impatient disgust. When the first of *The Seasons—Winter* it was, I believe—had been completed at press, Jamie thought, by a presentation copy, to triumph over his uncle's scepticism, and to propitiate his good opinion he had the book handsomely bound. The old man never looked inside, or asked what the book was about, but turning it round and round with his fingers in gratified admiration, exclaimed: 'Come, is that really our Jamie's doin' now? Weel, I never thought the cratur wad hae had the handicraft to do the like!'

226 DIBDIN. 'There are shrewd books, with dangerous frontispieces set to sale; who shall prohibit them? shall twenty licensers?'—Milton, *Areopagitica*.

227 BURNS. Mr. Andrew Lang states that Burns saw a splendidly bound but sadly neglected copy of Shakespeare in the library of a nobleman in Edinburgh, and he wrote these lines on the ample margin of one of its pages, where they were found long after the poet's death.

228 D'ARBLAY. Macaulay notes that Miss Burney 'describes this conversation as delightful; and, indeed, we cannot wonder that, with her literary tastes, she should be delighted at hearing in how magnificent a manner the greatest lady in the land encouraged literature'. The conversation took place at Windsor in December, 1785.

229 LAMB. Walter Pater says of Charles Lamb: 'He was a true "collector", delighting in the personal finding of a thing, in the colour an old book

or print gets for him by the little accidents which attest previous owner-
ship. "Wither's *Emblems*, that old book and quaint," long-desired, when
he finds it at last, he values none the less because a child had coloured
the plates with his paints.'

231   MILTON. 'The call for books was not in Milton's age what it is in the
present. To read was not then a general amusement; neither traders,
nor often gentlemen, thought themselves disgraced by ignorance. The
women had not then aspired to literature nor was every house supplied
with a closet of knowledge.'—Dr. Johnson.

232   BROWNING. The statue referred to is that of Giovanni delle Bande
Nere, father of Cosimo de' Medici, in the Piazza San Lorenzo. The
imaginative Sienese is Ademollo; the 'Frail one of the Flower' will be
recognized as *La Dame aux Camélias*. Browning 'translates' the title-page
of his 'find' thus:—

> A Roman murder-case:
> Position of the entire criminal cause
> Of Guido Franceschini, nobleman,
> With certain Four the cutthroats in his pay,
> Tried, all five, and found guilty and put to death
> By heading or hanging as befitted ranks,
> At Rome on February Twenty Two,
> Since our salvation Sixteen Ninety Eight:
> Wherein it is disputed if, and when,
> Husbands may kill adulterous wives, yet 'scape
> The customary forfeit.

236   ELIOT.
> I often wonder what the Vintners buy
> One half so precious as the stuff they sell.
> —E. FitzGerald, *Rubaiyát of Omar Khayyám*.

240   LEWIS. This is a portion of an imitation of Horace, *Ep.* 20, Bk. i.

242   GAY. The authorship of this and the following poem cannot be decided
definitely, but it is presumed that they were written by Gay and Pope
respectively, and they have been so credited in the text.

248   DE BURY. 'Would it not grieve a man of a good spirit to see Hobson finde
more money in the tayles of 12 jades than a scholler in 200 bookes?'—
The Pilgrimage to Parnassus. Hobson, the carrier, celebrated by Milton, is
the hero of 'Hobson's choice'.

248   LAMB. 'The motto I proposed for the [*Edinburgh*] *Review* was: Tenui
Musam meditamur avena—"we cultivate literature upon a little oat-
meal." '—Sydney Smith.

248   RUSKIN. Mark Pattison said that nobody who respected himself could
have less than 1,000 volumes, and that this number of octavo volumes
could be stacked in a bookcase 13 feet by 10 feet and 6 inches deep.
He complained that the bookseller's bill in the ordinary middle-class
family is shamefully small, and he thought it monstrous that a man who
is earning £1,000 a year should spend less than £1 a week on books. 'A
shilling in the pound to be spent on books,' is Lord Morley's comment,
'by a clerk who earns a couple of hundred pounds a year, or by a work-
man who earns a quarter of that sum, is rather more, I think, than can
be reasonably expected.'

259 SHAKESPEARE. Also in a later scene of the same play:—'Thou hast most traitorously corrupted the youth of the realm in erecting a grammar-school; and whereas, before, our forefathers had no other books but the score and the tally, thou hast caused printing to be used; and, contrary to the king, his crown, and dignity, thou hast built a paper-mill. It will be proved to thy face that thou hast men about thee that usually talk of a noun and a verb, and such abominable words as no Christian ear can endure to hear.'

262 WESLEY. 'Next morning he was still better: ... he desired to be drawn into the library, and placed by the central window, that he might look down upon the Tweed. Here he expressed a wish that I should read to him, and when I asked from what book, he said—"Need you ask? There is but one." '—J.G. Lockhart, *Life of Sir Walter Scott*.

'It is our *duty* to live among books, especially to live by ONE BOOK, and a very old one.'—John Henry Newman, *Tracts for the Times*.

266 DE VERE. Addison speaks of Horace and Pindar as showing, when confronted with the Psalms, 'an absurdity and confusion of style,' and 'a comparative poverty of imagination'.

Coleridge has left on record his opinion that, 'after reading Isaiah or St. Paul's Epistle to the Hebrews, Homer and Virgil are disgustingly tame to me, and Milton himself scarcely tolerable.'

Milton's own words may be recalled: 'There are no songs comparable to the songs of Sion; no orations equal to those of the Prophets.'

267 SWIFT. Compare Cowper in *Hope*:—
    In her own light arrayed,
 See mercy's grand apocalypse displayed!
 The sacred book no longer suffers wrong,
 Bound in the fetters of an unknown tongue;
 But speaks with plainness, art could never mend,
 What simplest minds can soonest comprehend.

Macaulay described the Bible as 'a book which, if everything else in our language should perish, would alone suffice to show the whole extent of its beauty and power'.

267 ARNOLD. Wordsworth's opinion was that the prophetic and lyrical parts of the Bible formed 'the great storehouse of enthusiastic and meditative imagination'.

269 ELIOT. Maggie Tulliver, during the home troubles caused by her father's bankruptcy, receives a present of books, among which is the *Imitation of Christ*.

274 GASKELL. The essay by Mrs. Gaskell, first published in *Household Words* in 1854, was suggested by an article by Victor Cousin on Madame de Sablé in the *Revue des Deux Mondes*. Madame was a habitual guest at the Hôtel Rambouillet and friend of the Duchess de Longueville: her crowning accomplishment was the ability *tenir un salon*.

281 ALCUIN. Born at York in 735, Alcuin was the adviser of Charlemagne, whose court, under the Englishman's direction became a centre of culture. After fifteen years of court life at Aix-la-Chapelle Alcuin retired to Tours, where he died in 804. His English name is given as Ealwhine. The catalogue refers to the library of Egbert, Archbishop of York. The translator is D. McNicoll.

281 POPE. For the fate of the bonfire the reader is referred to the *Dunciad* itself. Pope explains that 'this library is divided into three parts: the first
consists of those authors from whom he (the hero, i.e. Colley Cibber)
stole, and whose works he mangled; the second, of such as fitted the
shelves, or were gilded for show, or adorned with pictures; the third
class our author calls solid learning, old Bodies of Divinity, old Commentaries, old English Printers, or old English Translations; all very
voluminous, and fit to erect altars to Dulness.' Tibbald, or Theobald,
wrote *Shakespear Restored*; Ogilby, poet and printer, is mentioned by
Addison on p. 193; the Duchess of Newcastle was responsible for eight
folios of poetical and philosophical works; Settle, the hero's brother
Laureate 'for the city instead of the court'; Banks, his rival in tragedy;
Broome, 'a serving man of Ben Jonson'; De Lyra or Harpsfield, whose
five volumes of commentaries in folio were printed in 1472; Philemon
Holland, 'the translator general of his age'; Cibber's Birthday Ode as
Laureate.

William Caxton (1422–91), of course, printed, at Bruges, the first
book printed in English—the *Recuyell of the Historyes of Troye*—in 1474.
His printing press in Westminster was set up two years later. Wynkyn
de Worde, his servant and successor, started business on his own
account in 1491.

282 STERNE. 'Sterne has generally concealed the sources of his curious
trains of investigation, and uncommon opinions, but in one instance he
ventured to break through his restraint by mentioning Bouchet's *Evening Conferences*, among the treasures of Mr. Shandy's library.... I have
great reason to believe that it was in the Skelton library some years ago,
where I suspect Sterne found most of the authors of this class. I entertain little doubt, that from the perusal of this work, Sterne conceived
the first precise idea of his *Tristram*, as far as anything can be called
precise, in a desultory book, apparently written with great rapidity.'

This quotation is from Ferriar's *Illustrations of Sterne*, which was published in 1798. He seemed, Sir Walter Scott wrote, 'born to trace and
detect the various mazes through which Sterne carried on his depredations upon ancient and dusty authors.' Ferriar wrote the following lines
addressed to Sterne:—

Sterne, for whose sake I plod through miry ways,
Of antique wit and quibbling mazes drear,
Let not thy shade malignant censure fear,
Though aught of borrowed mirth my search betrays.
Long slept that mirth in dust of ancient days,
(Erewhile to Guise or wanton Valois dear;)
Till waked by thee in Skelton's joyous pile,
She flung on Tristram her capricious rays;
But the quick tear that checks our wondering smile,
In sudden pause or unexpected story,
Owns thy true mastery—and Le Fever's woes,
Maria's wanderings, and the Prisoner's throes,
Fix thee conspicuous on the throne of glory.

284 SCOTT. The modern poet is Crabbe; Thalaba is the name of Southey's
hero.

286   MONTAIGNE. In another essay Montaigne tells us that his library for a country library could pass for a very fair one.

289   BALE. 'I was called to London to wait upon the Duke of Norfolk, who having at my sole request bestowed the Arundelian Library on the Royal Society, sent to me to take charge of the books and remove them.... I procured for our Society, besides printed books, near 100 MSS., some in Greek, of great concernment. The printed books being of the oldest impressions are not the less valuable; I esteem them almost equal to MSS. Amongst them are most of the Fathers printed at Basle, before the Jesuits abused them with their expurgatory Indexes; there is a noble MS. of Vitruvius. Many of these books had been presented by Popes, Cardinals, and great persons, to the Earls of Arundel and Dukes of Norfolk; and the late magnificent Earl of Arundel bought a noble library in Germany, which is in this collection. I should not, for the honour I bear the family, have persuaded the Duke to part with these, had I not seen how negligent he was of them, suffering the priests and everybody to carry away and dispose of what they pleased, so that abundance of rare things are irrecoverably gone.'— J. Evelyn, *Diary*, August 29, 1678.

297   HELPS. Pope's *Essay on Man*:

> If parts allure thee, think how Bacon shined.
> The wisest, brightest, meanest of mankind.

The other allusions are to Johnson, Byron, Shelley, and Keats.

299   SAXE. Aristophanes' The *Clouds*, ridiculing Socrates.

300   DRUMMOND. Of Sir Thomas Bodley old Anthony Wood says: 'Though no writer, worth the remembrance, yet hath he been the greatest promoter of learning that hath yet appeared in our nation.'

It may be recalled that R. de Bury had a fine idea, although it did not fructify, to wit:—'We have for a long time held a rooted purpose in the inmost recesses of our mind, looking forward to a favourable time and divine aid, to found, in perpetual alms, and enrich with the necessary gifts, a certain Hall in the revered University of Oxford, the first nurse of all the liberal Arts; and further to enrich the same, when occupied by numerous scholars, with deposits of our books, so that the books themselves and every one of them may be made common as to use and study, not only to the scholars of the said Hall, but through them to all the students of the aforesaid University for ever.'

302   COWPER. 'This ode,' Cowper states, 'is rendered without rhime, that it might more adequately represent the original, which, as Milton himself informs us, is of no certain measure. It may possibly for this reason disappoint the reader, though it cost the writer more labour than the translation of any other piece in the whole collection.'

305   COWLEY.

> Who now reads Cowley? if he pleases yet,
> His moral pleases, not his pointed wit.
> Forgot his epic, nay, Pindaric art!
> But still I love the language of his heart.
> —Pope.

314   J.M. It cannot escape observation that Bodley and his library has been a much more fruitful theme than the University of Cambridge. This is the only poem on the latter subject which could be found: it is quoted

in Edwards's *Memoirs of Libraries*. Leigh Hunt has related his experiences in the library of Trinity College when 'the keeper of it was from home'; see p. 252.

314 WHITELOCKE. The authorship of this fine testimony is attributed to Whitelocke, but it could not be traced, by J.K. Hoyt and Anna L. Ward.

Index of Authors